Japanese Naval Action in World War II

DEATH OF A NAVY

BY ANDRIEU D'ALBAS, Captain, French Navy Reserve

Translated from the French by Anthony Rippon

WITH INTRODUCTION, NOTES, AND MAPS BY

Rear Admiral ROBERT A. THEOBALD, USN, Ret.

The Devin-Adair Company   *New York*   *1957*

*First published in 1954 by Amiot-Dumont, Paris, in the
series Bibliothèque de la Mer.*
*Copyright 1957 by The Devin-Adair Company. All rights reserved.
No portion of this book may be reproduced in any form without
written permission from the publisher, The Devin-Adair Company,
New York 10, N. Y., except by a reviewer, who may quote brief
passages in connection with a review.*
Canadian agents: Thomas Nelson & Sons, Ltd., Toronto
Library of Congress Catalog card number: 56–12141
*Printed in the United States of America
by H. Wolff, New York*
Design: Marshall Lee

Concerning the Author

Captain Andrieu d'Albas is a career naval officer and is now in the French Navy Reserve. He has had several long sojourns in Japan (one of them a two-year stretch) on detached service from the French Navy for the purpose of study.

He has close connections in Japanese maritime circles, speaks the language fluently, and is married to the daughter of a celebrated Japanese admiral.

No one could be better qualified than Captain d'Albas to reveal to the general public, which under the circumstances has never been fully informed about the sea war in the Pacific, the full story of that war from the Japanese viewpoint.

Thanks to his knowledge of the language, the author has been able to consult at first hand many Japanese documents and records not hitherto available to the public. He also has gathered verbal testimony from many who participated.

Thanks also to his knowledge of the national psychology and customs, Captain d'Albas has been able to interpret Japanese attitudes accurately and to appraise impartially the views and expectations of the Japanese high command.

Concerning Admiral Theobald

"Fuzzy" Theobald, as he is known to a generation of Annapolis men, graduated from the Naval Academy in 1906. His career with the U. S. Navy has been a brilliant one, particularly in the field of naval strategy.

From Gunnery Officer of the USS *New York* in World War I, he became Executive Officer, Naval Post Graduate School, 1919–21; Destroyer Command, Asiatic Fleet, 1922–24; Commanding Officer, Naval Post Graduate School, 1924–27; Executive Officer, USS *West Virginia,* 1927–29; Naval War College, 1929–30; Secretary of War Plans, Navy Department, and Member Joint Army-Navy Planning Commission 1930–32; Chief of Staff, Destroyers, Pacific Fleet, 1932–34; Member of Advanced Class, Naval War College Seminar on Japan and Pacific War, 1934–35; In Charge, Strategy Division, Naval War College, 1935–37; Commanding Officer, USS *Nevada,* 1937–39; Chief of Staff, U. S. Fleet, 1939–40; Commanding Cruiser Division Three, 1940; Commanding Destroyers, Pacific Fleet, Dec. 1941–May 1942; Commanding Northern Pacific Force, May 1942–January 1943; Commandant First Naval District, 1943–44; Retired, Feb. 1945.

No one is better qualified to comment on this book.

Contents

Maps

Admiral Theobald's Introduction

This book by Captain d'Albas is an achievement of the first order and a joy to read. The author was in a unique position to uncover much new material in the Japanese archives and to question World War II survivors on many points. He has compassed the farflung Pacific naval war in a single volume and has written an account that is brilliant, moving, and colorful. From the beginning, one feels the atmosphere of the Samurai: the joy of victory and the growing belief in their invincibility in the opening acts of the drama; the dwelling upon the Japanese heroics in the face of their reverses to soften as much as possible the telling of their defeats. In these latter moments, we have a full description of the Emperor's picture in its silken cover being removed to a place of safety, before the ship finds its final resting place under the waters of the sea. Or we are told of an admiral who, after long argument, consents to shift to a less damaged ship, or who, after a speech of farewell, retires to his cabin to await his end.

Then, when the nation's shrinking economy commences to handicap the navy's defensive operations, we are frequently regaled with the differences which have arisen between the army and the navy. This is, of course, an old, old story where the two services are of equal importance to their nation's defenses—for troubles have a way of remaining under cover in times of victory.

The reasons advanced in the later stages to account for the Japanese navy's growing inability to cope with the allied offensive is exactly what would be expected from a warrior who had long been accustomed to nothing but victory. And it must be quickly said that, although some of this was the result of faulty war planning, the basic reason, American industrial might, was something that the descendants of the Samurai could never hope to compete with, over the long haul. Especially when that industrial potential was coupled with a knowledge of war and a courage which were the equals of their own.

The United States navy had long known that, when war came, the Japanese navy would prove itself a highly trained, effective fighting force, led by a body of officers well versed in all aspects of the naval profession. But analysis of the Japanese character had produced certain conclusions concerning the military attributes of the officer personnel. With their knowledge of naval history, it was believed that as long as situations conformed fairly closely to historical precedent, their strategy and tactics would be soundly conceived and efficiently executed, but that in the realms of the unusual or unexpected, their reactions might be less decisive and consequently less effective.

This estimate of the Japanese military character was sustained in the late war, not to any pronounced degree on the operational side, but to an unbelievable extent in the field of planning. Japan's wars with China and Russia had placed no emphasis whatever upon wartime losses in the nation's merchant marine or upon the necessity for a program of replacements to balance or minimize the losses of combatant ships. And when Japan dropped her bombs upon Pearl Harbor, her plans for the war had completely disregarded two very important features of modern naval warfare: the maintenance of a merchant marine adequate to her wartime needs; the immediate establishment of a wartime shipbuilding program to maintain the fighting strength of her fleets at the highest possible levels. The neglect of these vital, if undramatic, factors assured Japan of defeat from the start, unless she could encompass a quick victory, and her method of initiating the war made it certain that this would not happen.

It would appear that the Japanese High Naval Command

failed to appreciate how greatly the ascendancy of the aircraft carrier had accentuated the importance of wartime shipbuilding programs. In the days of the supremacy of the modern battleship, great ships were rarely laid down after the start of a war. They took so long to build that wartime construction was confined to light cruisers, destroyers, and submarines. But in this war of carriers, all that was changed. The carrier is necessarily very vulnerable, and the wartime losses must be high. And, furthermore, an *Essex*-class carrier could be built in from 16 to 18 months, so that those laid down in early 1942 could be in the operating theaters by late 1943. The war was more than a year old before Japan announced a 20-carrier building program. And yet, only one large carrier whose keel was laid down after Pearl Harbor was actually commissioned during the war.

The industry of Japan could not match that of the United States in any wartime shipbuilding race, but that was no reason for her to neglect so completely this vital feature of modern naval warfare.

The Japanese naval attitude toward the maintenance of an adequate merchant marine was equally open to criticism. This is a two-pronged problem. The losses to this very vulnerable type of ship must be high and therefore would demand a large new construction program from the start. Also, the fact that Japan had not faced problems of commerce protection in her wars with China and Russia was no excuse for the total absence of prewar planning toward this essential operation of sea warfare, or for its almost total lack during the war. How could the Japanese navy have prepared for war, with so complete a disregard of the British methods of combating the menace of the German submarine in World War I? Japan quickly conquered her "Greater East Asia Co-prosperity Sphere" and then, almost as quickly, permitted herself to be divorced from it by losing her seaborne communications. And when an island nation loses that, she loses all capacity to wage war.

The Japanese warrior, a product of the code of the Samurai, has long been recognized as a tough, tenacious fighter. That is definitely a war asset. But the code does more; it engenders a fanaticism for death which transcends all reason and in no way helps the nation's war effort. The resistance of a garrison to the last man and the refusal of the crews of sunken ships to accept rescue at the hands of their enemies are examples.

The worst feature of this fanaticism is the fact that it is reflected in the actions of responsible commanders at important moments. The first duty of a flag officer is to exercise his command, as long and as efficiently as possible. It is therefore astounding to read of the difficulties encountered frequently by staff officers in their efforts to persuade their admiral to leave a sinking or badly disabled ship.

The penchant for going down with the ship is another useless offshoot of this fanaticism. The tradition of the sea that the captain must be the last man to leave a sinking ship is sound. But to stay when all have left and there is nothing more that can possibly be done is merely a waste of good officer material. It has been said of Rear Admiral Yamaguchi, who insisted on going down in the *Hiryu,* that he was one of the finest officers in the Japanese navy and had often been spoken of as a possible successor to Admiral Yamamoto. Is it not the duty of such an officer to live for his Emperor rather than to die a self-imposed death?

Closely related to this attitude of the Japanese mind is the tendency of a leader to commit hara-kiri if he should later discover that his decision in a certain situation was not the one he would have made if all the facts had then been known to him. Acts of this kind appear to be motivated by the Asiatic's fear of "loss of face." It is really second guessing in its worst form. A wartime commander must make the best decision he can with the information available and never thereafter permit himself a questioning backward glance. No consideration of face should ever be permitted to complicate the reasoning that leads to these decisions.

In conclusion, it may be said that if Japan had planned more soundly to maintain the strength of the fleets and her merchant marine, all she could possibly have accomplished would have been a stiffer defense against the American offensive of 1944 and 1945. This might have slowed somewhat the speed of her enemy's final advances. And then, if the atomic bombs had been dropped as they were, the date of the Japanese surrender would have occurred exactly when it did.

None of which alters the fact that Japan's two great lapses in planning placed a heavy handicap upon her war effort, especially during the last two years of the war—one that could have spelled the difference between victory and defeat if she had been fighting an opponent anywhere near her equal in national strength and industrial capacity.

ROBERT A. THEOBALD
Rear Admiral
U.S. Navy, Retired

Marblehead, Mass.
August 1956

Author's Foreword

It was a quarter to eight in the morning. On the deck of the battleship *Maryland,* moored in the roadstead of Pearl Harbor, Seaman Short was writing a postcard to his family. From over Mount Tantalus, the rising sun lit up one of the most radiant and peaceful scenes in the world. It was fine, but a little chilly; a north wind rippled the green fields of sugar cane in the Valley of Aiea. As he wrote, Short heard the boatswains' pipes announcing breakfast in the ships around him, and in the distance the church bells of Honolulu called the faithful to eight o'clock services. Soon the ships would hoist their colors, and all would be joyful animation.

There, in a narrowly confined area, lay seventy naval vessels and twenty-four auxiliaries—all the Pacific Fleet then in Hawaiian waters except one heavy cruiser and four minesweepers. The ships were observing a peacetime watch routine, and many officers and men had spent the night ashore. Glancing upward, perhaps for inspiration, Short saw a group of aircraft coming out of the clouds and apparently heading for his ship.

Strange aircraft, certainly foreign! Where were they coming from? What were their intentions? Thoughts and fancies ran through the seaman's mind with extraordinary rapidity. He, alone, among the hundreds of men who were there, many of whom must have looked up when they heard the noise of approaching engines, understood immediately what was happening, what a tremendously important event was enveloping America and the world, with the arrival of these unknown planes. A few yards away, on the deck of the *Maryland,* was an anti-aircraft gun mount. Short threw himself at this machine gun when, for the first time, he saw to the eastward another flight of strange planes, skimming the surface of the water toward the battleships and in position to deliver a torpedo attack. He aimed at the first silhouette of this flight and fired.

The big two-engine bomber was hit by the first burst. It fell sideways, threw up a wall of water from the harbor, broke into fragments, and sank. But the other two-engine aircraft continued their course; together they vomited a shower of black cylinders. Suddenly the forty torpedo aircraft turned upward and passed like lightning over the masts. A few seconds later, hell broke out.

The hull of every battleship in the outside moorings was struck at the same moment as if by some giant underwater hammer. Geysers as high as houses sprang up around them; thirty-thousand-ton battleships shuddered and heaved in an agony that was quickly increased, as rain of a different sort fell on them. From high above, fifty bombers released their loads; and from the east, fifty dive bombers screamed downward. In ten minutes, the idyllic setting became a noisy and bloody nightmare, in which only Seaman Short appeared to have understood what was happening. His prompt reaction had at least prevented one Japanese torpedo from reaching its intended target in the United States battleship row.

All that could be seen in the whole harbor was ships burning, exploding, and capsizing; around them a sheet of gray and sinister water speckled by thousands of black dots—men. Gradually the American firing began, soon becoming more intense. The fleet, or what remained of it, and the garrison of the base overcame their surprise and tried to defend themselves against the nameless, faceless attacker who had suddenly broken a quarter of a century of peace. Between the explosions could be heard the wails of klaxons, calling the crews to action stations. It was war in its starkest form.

At 0758 * word was flashed from the fleet to the United States, a signal destined to stupefy a hundred and fifty million Americans: "Air raid, Pearl Harbor. This is no drill." These last words reveal what depths of instinctive disbelief, of blind confidence, the hard truth had to pierce! This was not an exercise. They were real bombs, real corpses.

The first day of the great naval war in the Pacific had dawned: the first of 1351 days. Seaman Short had opened the account for the United States that morning, and before the "cease fire" sounded, terrible battles were to be fought on land, in the air, and at sea, in the immense expanse of the Pacific Ocean—an odd name for the scene of such events. Thousands and thousands of white and yellow men were to die: drowned, burnt, shattered by shells, pierced by bullets, worn by fatigue, sapped by hunger and fever. This pitiless war was to bring into being the greatest mass of material ever accumulated by nations, but also, perhaps, on both sides the most magnificent store of courage.

It was 0830. Fires raged in the thick smoke that covered the harbor. Fresh formations of bombers appeared on the horizon, this time to be received by machine-gun and anti-aircraft-battery fire; a greeting that would have met the first wave of attacking planes if the information possessed in Washington some three hours before that attack had been known on time in Hawaii. Acting on that information at noon, Washington time, General George C. Marshall did order that a message be sent to the general commanding the American troops in Hawaii. By one of the curious coincidences of history, his name also was Short. General Marshall's message read, "Japanese are presenting at one P.M. Eastern Time today what amounts to an ultimatum. Also they are under orders to destroy their code machines immediately. Just what significance the hour set may have, we do not know, but be on the alert accordingly. Inform naval authorities of this

---

* In the description of naval operations, the United States Navy time system will be used throughout. In this system, time is reckoned from midnight to midnight, viz.: 0025 is 25 minutes past midnight; 0810, 8:10 A.M.; 1200, noon; 1945, 7:45 P.M.; 2400, midnight. For all post-meridian times, 1200 is added to all times recorded by the twelve-hour clock.

communication. Marshall." As this message, after its coding, was sent by commercial means, General Short did not receive it until 1400 Hawaiian time, long after the Japanese had completed their attacks.

The Japanese ambassadors in Washington had attempted to deliver the note, tantamount to a declaration of war, to the State Department at 1300 Eastern Time, in accordance with instructions which they had received from Tokyo. But delivery was delayed until 1420, long past the time of delivery set by the Tokyo government.

Two great empires, two first-class naval powers, two resolute and tenacious nations were about to clash.

To understand how matters had reached this pass, let us go back and review the course of events which began five months earlier, in June 1941.

PART ONE

"Scale Mount Niitaka!"

1   The Temple of Kiyomizu

Western Europe had been ablaze for a year. France had been crushed in a campaign lasting forty days. England, penned in her island, was suffering the furious assaults of the Luftwaffe. Wholly absorbed in their own fight for survival, the Western Powers were forced to ignore the Far East. China was isolated. The way to Yunnan through Indo-China, her principal supply route, had been cut by Japanese pressure, to which the French colony could offer no effective resistance.

The Empire of the Rising Sun was officially neutral, but her leaders were divided into two factions.

The naval party coveted the Netherlands East Indies, rich in oil, rubber, and minerals, which would make Japan independent of other countries, America in particular. During the one year ending March 31, 1941, it had been necessary to import from beyond the Pacific more than thirty-six million barrels of oil. The opportunity was propitious, the prey tempting. Nevertheless, the naval leaders had studied the world situation, had weighed the problems that a great war would create for them; and, in their eyes, the conquest of the rich Malayan islands remained an object that only favorable circumstances—not at that time foreseeable—would make possible.

The army party (Kodo party), whose power had been developed over many years, was less prudent; its fanaticism was shown early in 1936, when 1400 soldiers, led by their officers, had murdered the keeper of the privy seal, Admiral Saito, the minister of finance, and the inspector-general of military training.

The paramount goal of the Kodo faction was the conquest of China. She must be occupied and become an economic protectorate. The head of this group at the time was General Hideki Tojo, former commander of the police security forces in Manchuria (Manchukuo), a man of tough character, whose intrigues and authoritarian ways impressed the officers, almost all of them sons of peasants and peasants themselves.

To the army party, Hitler's Germany, noisy with the clash of arms, seemed a model and a natural ally.

General Arita, minister of foreign affairs, took a step toward such an alliance when he made a pact with the Axis Powers against Russia. But, in 1939, when Germany offered Japan an unconditional alliance, the Court and the big industrialists agreed with Navy Minister Yonai and Admiral Yamamoto, commanding the fleet, and refused it.

But the temptation to profit by the weakness of the Allies grew, in spite of the repeated warnings of the United States to stay neutral. The warning was strengthened by the maneuvers of an American fleet in the Pacific, during April 1940, and by the basing of that fleet thereafter in Hawaiian waters.

General Arita proposed the creation of a "Greater East Asia Co-prosperity Sphere" and called for the recognition of the economic interdependence of Japan and the Netherlands East Indies.

On June 22, 1940, the Yonai cabinet fell. The new government was presided over by Prince Konoye, known for his moderation, but it contained two warmongers—General Tojo, minister of war, and the minister of foreign affairs, Yosuke Matsuoka, who did not conceal his pro-German sympathies.

Events then hurried onward inexorably. A "new deal," decreed by the government, controlled the Saibatsu trust's wide economic and financial interests. Political parties were banned.

Luxuries were forbidden: no more silken clothes, no more perfumes, no more geishas in shimmering kimonos; the streets, full of the bustle of an anonymous crowd dressed in the same ersatz material, were like ant runs.

Metal goods, even kitchen utensils, were requisitioned, and the women prized out the stones and gave their country the gold mountings of their jewelry.

In August 1940, northern Indo-China was occupied.

Neither the opposition of Prince Konoye nor that of Admiral Yamamoto could prevent the signing on September 24 of the Three-power Pact.[1]

Uneasy, the British, Dutch, and Americans met at Singapore to coordinate their policy. The conference ended in April 1941, when the three Powers declared their intention of supporting one another if the Japanese attacked any of their possessions. They agreed to declare war if the Japanese moved west of Bangkok or south of the isthmus of Kra, or if they occupied Timor.

Since July 1940, a number of national defense acts signed by President Roosevelt had restricted the export to Japan of strategic materials, particularly fuel oil and aviation gasoline.

On November 8, 1940, a new ambassador was sent to Washington—Admiral Kichisaburo Nomura, known for his pacific leanings. While this gesture of appeasement was made, the Marshalls and Carolines were reinforced, and as a result of her complete occupation of French Indo-China, in July 1941, Japan gained a monopoly of rubber and rice from that rich source, and the use of the Saigon airport.

Finally, in April 1941, Matsuoka, who believed Russia to be definitely deterred by the Tripartite Treaty from participation in either the European war or that in Asia, signed with her a non-aggression pact. The German attack on June 22 was regarded in Tokyo as a betrayal, and it cast a shadow over the relations of those prospective allies of the future.

---

1. *This was the Tripartite Treaty between Japan, Germany, and Italy, signed September 27, 1940, by which Japan agreed to ally herself with Germany and Italy against any country, then neutral, which should later enter the war against those two countries. Similarly, Germany and Italy obligated themselves to declare immediate war upon any nation which should later join China in her war against Japan. Obviously, this treaty was aimed at the United States and the Soviet Union.* (ROBERT A. THEOBALD)

In the meantime, under the influence of President Roosevelt, the United States attitude toward Japan hardened steadily. On July 26, when Japan completed her occupation of Indo-China, Japanese funds in America were frozen and all commerce between the two countries was suspended. Great Britain and Holland followed suit.

"I shall drive ahead for the first six months."

The situation of Japan was crucial. She must come to a decision; the bulk of her foreign funds were in the United States, and it was no longer possible for her to procure the imports essential to her existence and also to the pursuit of her war operations in China.

On October 12, in the council of ministers, the navy minister, Admiral Oikawa, asked that the negotiations with the United States be continued. Two days later Prince Konoye, in a spirit of conciliation, asked Tojo to withdraw his troops from the Chinese continent. A passionate dispute began. The prince had read and reread the report prepared by Admiral Yamamoto the year before, the conclusion of which was clear: "If I am ordered to fight without regard for the consequences," he wrote, "I shall drive ahead for the first six months; but when it comes to the second and the third year of war, I have no confidence at all. We have concluded the Three-power Pact and it is too late to go back on it. Nevertheless, taking things as they are, I hope that you will avoid an armed conflict with America."

Konoye, duly impressed, had before him the exalted face of General Tojo, a grim, gaunt mask, through which the eyes gleamed fanatically behind thick glasses.

"What is the use," was the war minister's cry, "of so many years of war and so much bloodshed, if today, at the bidding of the worst enemies of the country, everything is to be abandoned? Japan is strong. Her virtue will triumph over the softness of those who are satisfied with their wealth and power, and who want to deprive her of her rights."

Tojo added, speaking to Konoye:

"Once in his life, sir, a man should know when to throw himself from the top of the terrace of the temple of Kiyomizu!" *

The prince, defeated, resigned on October 18 and was succeeded by Tojo.

The die was cast.

Vainly, in an attempt to make the government reflect on the precariousness of the means the country had at her disposal, the navy minister, Admiral Shimada, demanded most of the reserves of gasoline, but his mouth was stopped by giving him all he asked for. From November 1, the government prepared its plan of operations, which aimed at gaining time by the surprise destruction of the American Pacific Fleet, and by using the respite so gained to conquer the sources of oil. Japan would make landings from amphibious forces on Luzon, on Guam, on the Malayan Peninsula, on Hongkong, and at Miri and Balikpapan in Borneo. Finally, the Dutch East Indies would be occupied.

In this way, Japan would procure the wealth she lacked. Around these conquests, she would throw a protective cordon from the Kuriles, passing by Wake and the Marshalls, including the southern and western extremities of the Malayan barrier, and ending at the frontier separating India and Burma. Behind this screen, against which enemy assaults would break, prosperity would be organized, until the day when the Americans would tire and bow to the *fait accompli*.

As for Admiral Yamamoto, he had done everything to avert war; now there was nothing left but to fight. He confided to intimate friends: "We have to choose now between civil war and foreign war. Whatever happens, the latter is a thousand times preferable."

And as war was inevitable, the Imperial Navy would do its duty, down to the supreme sacrifice.

---

* The temple of Kiyomizu, at Kyoto, is built on the side of a steep hill and its terrace, supported by enormous wooden columns, dominates the ravine. To a Japanese, "to throw oneself from the top of the terrace of the temple of Kiyomizu" is to risk all to gain all.

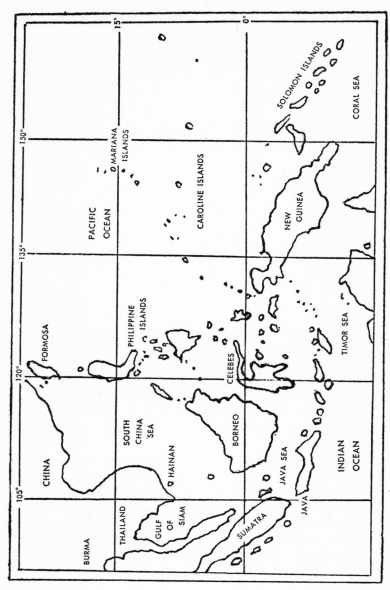

AREA OF JAPAN'S FAR-FLUNG CONQUESTS, DECEMBER 1941–MAY 1942

Pearl Harbor in miniature

In 1941, Admiral Yamamoto was fifty-seven, a year older than Tojo. Of medium height, a slight figure in his dark uniform braided with silk, he radiated intelligence and energy. An excellent bridge player, he knew how to weigh his opponent's game and how to take risks accordingly. Although he realized fully the danger which his country ran in entering, with her limited resources, a war with a power of unlimited wealth and tremendous industrial potential, that war did not take him by surprise. He had been the first Japanese naval officer to foresee the potentialities of the aircraft carrier, and since January 1941 he and his staff, in collaboration with Rear Admiral Onishi, chief of staff of the 11th Air Fleet and one of the navy's foremost aviators, had been studying an aerial attack on Pearl Harbor.

Also, the fleet had been undergoing intensive training for some time. Maneuvers, gunnery practice, attacks by aircraft, and night fighting succeeded one another without pause. Bodies were kept supple by running races, fencing with cutlasses, and by judo.

The sailors of Nippon were so trained that they could see an enemy in the darkest night at extraordinary distances; and they knew how to maneuver so that their torpedoes would reach their targets. It needed radar to deprive them of this superiority.[2]

In August 1941, an important staff exercise had for its theme the simulation of an attack on Pearl Harbor. Both forces were equipped exactly as if the operation were a deadly reality and not merely a peacetime exercise. The conclusions drawn were

---

2. *At the outbreak of the war, no Japanese ship was equipped with radar, and it was many months later before a limited number were so equipped. It was well over a year after the war's start before all their combatant ships had received their first radar installations. On the other hand, the United States navy entered the war with all its ships carrying radar, and wartime research produced remarkable advances in the various types of radar that each ship soon carried to meet its special wartime needs.* (R.A.T.)

not encouraging. Very heavy losses must be expected. Many officers, including Admiral Nagano, chief of the naval general staff, were strongly impressed by this. Also, a full-scale attack on the naval forces at Pearl Harbor would mean renouncing any thought of seizing Oahu in the same operation,[3] because the material resources required for both were not available. The troops in China and the several expeditionary forces in the process of being organized were heavy drains upon the army's strength; and, furthermore, in spite of the pact of nonaggression, the army general staff wanted to keep substantial forces in Manchuria to watch Russia, who remained an enigma to the end.

The exercise was followed in September by special training for the carrier aircraft, under the direction of Lieutenant Commander Matsuo Fuchida who, embarked in the *Akagi*, had been put in command of the First Air Fleet's air groups. On the deserted beaches of the north, teams directed by specialists reproduced on the sand a Pearl Harbor in miniature.

On this model the pilots learned to recognize the roadstead, Ford Island, along the length of which lay the berths of major units of the United States fleet, the arsenal with its quays and dry docks, and the airfields: Ewa, to the west of Pearl Harbor; Hickam Field, to the east; Wheeler Field, in the middle of Oahu; and Kaneohe Field, on the northeast corner of the island. The lessons were well learned. On the day of action, the targets were identified without hesitation.

One problem remained to be solved. The roadstead of Pearl Harbor was only some 550 yards wide and forty feet deep; this seemed to forbid the use of torpedo aircraft, because their tor-

---

3. *The question is frequently asked why, after the great success of the Japanese surprise attack, they failed to follow up with an attempt to capture Oahu. The answer is that Japan's sole aim in that attack was the weakening of the United States fleet so that it could be no threat to them during their campaigns to the south. On December 7, 1941, she had no troops nor supporting vessels required for an amphibious attack against a strongly held land base. Japan accomplished all she had hoped to achieve in her Pearl Harbor attack. (R.A.T.)*

pedoes were very likely to strike the bottom on their initial dive
and stick there. Nevertheless, it would be regrettable if this
weapon, the most efficient in a surprise attack, could not be
used. Long discussions were held on this topic by Admiral
Nagumo, commander of the Carrier Force, his chief of staff,
Rear Admiral Kusaka, Commander Genda, and Lieutenant Commander Fuchida. Finally, at the beginning of November, the
difficulty was solved. The torpedoes were to be fitted with
ailerons which would augment the action of the horizontal rud-
ders, would assure a more shallow initial dive, and would thus
allow aerially launched torpedoes to be used in waters of much
less depth than ever before.

The attack force

Training ended in mid-November. The weapon was tempered,
without a flaw; men and material were absolutely ready.

The aircraft were embarked in their respective carriers, which
weighed anchor individually for the north. During this time, the
ships which stayed at Kure intensified their radio signals, using
the call signs of the departed vessels, so that any distant ear
would be deceived and fail to notice any difference in traffic.

On the twenty-second, the Attack Force gathered in Tanran
Bay, Etorofu in the Kuriles. From this island, lost in the north of
Japan, the new armada to which the Empire had entrusted its
destiny was to set forth.

Assembled there, were the six aircraft carriers of Admiral
Nagumo: the *Kaga* and the *Akagi,* the hulls of which, originally
designed for battleships of some forty thousand tons, had been
converted after the Treaty of Washington; the *Soryu* and the
Hiryu ("Blue Dragon" and "Flying Dragon") of ten thousand
tons, recently built and speedy; and finally the *Shokaku* and the
Zuikaku ("Flying Crane" and "Lucky Stork"). These last two
ships, of about twenty-six thousand tons' displacement, had just
entered active service and had profited from the experience
gained by their predecessors. They were more powerful, and
their protection was that of a heavy cruiser.

Farther on, were anchored the vessels of the support group

under Rear Admiral Mikawa: the battleships *Hiei* and *Kiri-shima*, armed with eight 14-inch guns and twenty-one 6-inch; and the cruisers *Tone* and *Chikuma*, of ten thousand tons, which carried four gun turrets forward, each mounting three 6.1-inch guns and with two catapults at the stern.

In shallower water, grouped around their leader, Rear Admiral Omori, whose white-and-red flag flew from the mast of the light cruiser *Abukuma*, lay twelve first-class escort destroyers with evocatory names like *Wind in the Valley*, *Shore Breeze*, *Wind on the River*, *Haze*, *Summer Cloud*, *Hail*, *Summer Mist*, and *Autumn Cloud*.

Finally, near the shore were three submarines, the *I-19*, *I-21*, and *I-23*, their low silhouettes broken by the conning towers abaft the 5.5-inch guns.

Together they composed the Attack Force, the spearhead of the Japanese fleet. This Force was to rule the seas of the Far East for six months, the exact period forecast by the commander in chief.

On November 25 the following orders reached Etorofu from Admiral Yamamoto, on board the *Nagato* at Hayama:

"The Attack Force will leave Tanran Bay on the twenty-sixth and set course eastward; it will complete refueling at sea, at the point designated for meeting a group of oil tankers; it will then continue, in order to execute a raid at dawn on X-Day, the date of which will be given later. . . ."

If the negotiations with Washington, which were continuing, reached a successful conclusion, the Force was to be ready to turn back. It would also abandon its project, in the unlikely event of meeting foreign vessels which might signal its presence.[4]

---

4. *There is a large area of the northern Pacific Ocean that is often called the vacant sea, because, in this age of steam, it is usually bereft of shipping. The boundaries of this area are: at its western extremity, the shipping lanes from Honolulu to Yokohama; at its eastern extremity, the shipping lanes from Honolulu to the Strait of Juan de Fuca; on its northern extremity, the great circle route from San Francisco to Yokohama. On a sphere, the*

Night of destiny

0600, on November 26. A black night. An icy wind blew tempestuously. Waves struck dully against motionless hulls. Discreet signals blinked; decks echoed the sound of the links of the chains in the hawse pipes, as the ships weighed anchor.

The submarines had been gone some hours. They were to scout the way two hundred miles ahead. The destroyers, which were to provide a protective screen under the guidance of the *Abukuma*, sailed next. As soon as they left the shelter of land, they were shrouded in spray which slapped their bridges. The men could move about only by clutching a life line, that ran the length of the deck. The larger ships swung clear and gained the open sea to take up their stations. Finally came the group of big tankers, low in the water, with their full cargoes of oil, struck by seas which broke over their decks.

At 0800 the waves of Tanran Bay swept in, unobstructed, to crash against the shore.

The first act of the drama had begun.

---

great circle is the shortest distance between two points, and the great circle course between Yokohama and United States West Coast ports saves so much distance for ships making that voyage that these always follow those courses. This carries the Yokohama- West Coast shipping almost as far north as the Aleutian Islands. (R.A.T.)

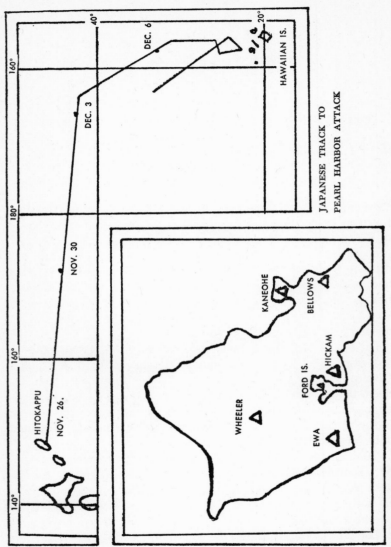

JAPANESE TRACK TO
PEARL HARBOR ATTACK

OAHU AIRFIELDS

2   The Red-and-Gold Turban

December 2, 1941. The First Attack Air Force steamed east at fourteen knots. The submarines were two hundred miles ahead of the main body. The six aircraft carriers were in two columns, preceded and surrounded by the destroyers, which were still dipping their noses into feathers of spray, although the weather had improved. The force had been able to refuel on November 30. Modern vessels are heavy consumers of oil and cannot stay away from their sources of replenishment for long. They needed fuel again on December 3.

On board the *Akagi*, flying the flag of Admiral Nagumo—a red disc on a white background—the navigator, Commander Gishiro Migura, checked the course with scrupulous care. Indeed, the success of the expedition depended on an exact knowledge of the vessels' positions; and in those regions at that season, sights of the sun and other heavenly bodies could be obtained only very intermittently.

Commander Migura had tidied himself up for the occasion. An exemplary officer in other respects, he was known for his sartorial negligence and usually appeared on the bridge in a threadbare uniform and in slippers. Today, he was dressed impeccably; his shoes gleamed with an unaccustomed luster.

The ship's commanding officer, Captain Hasegawa, never left the bridge; in this way he could keep in constant touch with the situation and aid his navigator when necessary.

On the upper bridge the heavy form of Admiral Nagumo

could be seen from time to time. He paced the hundred steps, sometimes alone, sometimes with officers of his staff.

Night fell early on that winter day. The admiral had retired to his sea cabin. An officer, almost invisible in the gloom, knocked on the door; and as it opened, the light inside switched off automatically. Then, as the door closed again, the light came on, and the officer held out a signal. The admiral took it, read it and stood up, deeply moved. He passed the signal to his chief of staff, who read, almost in a whisper, these words:

"*Niitaka Yama Nobore*" ("Scale Mount Niitaka").

It was the prearranged signal for the attack. The date was fixed for December 8 (Japanese time; December 7 east of the mid-Pacific date line).

"*Ten thousand years!*"

December 8[1] was a Sunday. Usually, the American fleet returned to Pearl Harbor for the weekend; but sometimes it sailed on Friday and returned only on Saturday of the following week. The exercise zone was near Maui; the anchorages for the vessels operating in that zone were usually at Lahaina.

If the Americans were at Lahaina, so much the better; the open and deep anchorage would facilitate the attack.

On the morning of the third, a proclamation by the admiral was read to the ships' companies assembled on deck; broadcast by loud-speakers, it reached all the men of the watch, who were unable to leave their posts of duty:

---

1. *Actually, in 1941, Sunday fell on December 7. But December 8, by the Japanese or Eastern Hemisphere calendar, was Sunday in Hawaii. The succeeding sentence shows that Japan chose that day for the attack because it was an American Sunday.*

This difference between the Japanese and American dates arises occasionally in the early chapters of the book. This happens when one or the other of the opposing forces crosses the mid-Pacific international date line in the course of an operation. The dates in the Japanese accounts are then one day later than those in the American or other Western records of the events. (R.A.T.)

"A gigantic fleet is concentrated at Pearl Harbor. This fleet must be destroyed at the start of hostilities. If our plan fails, our navy will be unable to regain the upper hand. Our surprise attack will be the Waterloo of the war which is about to start. For this, the Imperial Navy has concentrated the cream of its forces, in ships and aircraft, in order to ensure the initial success. Even if the enormous American industry turns immediately to the building of ships, aircraft, and war material, she will need many months to mobilize her power against us. If we assure our strategic position from the start, by attacking all the important points and seizing them before America is ready, we can tilt the balance in our favor. Heaven is witness to the justice of our cause."

The crews naturally had expected something important to happen, but they might well have believed themselves to be on a mere exercise, because the vessels had previously been subjected to frequent and elaborate maneuvers. The admiral's words unleashed a frenzy of enthusiasm among these pitilessly disciplined men, brimming with strength and confidence. They were carried away by their patriotism, and also by an instinctive joy in being able to turn to account at last the knowledge and skill they had acquired with so much self-denial and faith.

After noisy demonstrations and some hundred-times-repeated yells of *Banzai!* ("Ten thousand years!"), they poured out their hearts in letters to their families, which would arrive only after Fate had decided the writers' destinies.

A seaman, Kuramoto, squatting in a gun turret, wrote to his parents in a clumsy hand:

"An air attack on Hawaii! A dream come true! What will everybody say when they hear the news? How excited they will be! I can see them clapping and yelling with joy. We're going to give these Anglo-Saxon ruffians a lesson."

Lieutenant Yokoyama wrote with delicate brush strokes:

> *The tender cherry blossoms*
> *Fall from the branches*
> *Without regret*
> *At the moment of their opening.*

Like shattered pearl
My bones shall crumble
In the bay of the Pearl.
And dawn gleam bright
In exultation to find us
At the temple of Yasukuni. *

"Everyone will do his duty."

The last days passed in feverish activity. In the hangar under the flight deck, the aviation mechanics, never satisfied, checked scrupulously every bolt and piece of mechanism. Lieutenant Commander Ono, intelligence officer, listened for signals from the submarines which had been sent to the approaches to Hawaii to observe American fleet movements and to direct the attack to a favorable spot.

Some of these submarines carried, as a female whale carries her calf, a tiny craft soon to be known as a "midget submarine." These little boats, thirty-nine to forty-two feet long, were armed with two small torpedoes and carried a crew of two, who knew what little chance they had of escaping death.

December 7. The attack was due to be made on the following day. Only the last details remained to be settled. Lieutenant Commander Ono entered the admiral's cabin, where the members of his staff were gathered. Every face turned toward him as the admiral asked:

"What American forces are now at Pearl Harbor?"

Ono replied:

"Five battleships out of eight returned on the twenty-ninth. Two others left on that day and returned on the sixth. Another stayed in harbor all that time, probably for repairs. The five vessels which returned on the twenty-ninth have been there for eight days; it is time for them to sail again. They may weigh anchor today."

"That is not very likely," said Admiral Kusaka, the chief of

* Yasukuni Jinja, in Tokyo, is the temple built in memory of heroes.

staff. "Today is Saturday, December 7; they usually set out again on Tuesdays." [2]

Commander Genda, the First Air Fleet operations officer, commented, "What a pity the aircraft carriers aren't there!"

Ono continued his report: "The *Enterprise* sailed with two battleships, two heavy cruisers, and twelve destroyers. The battleships returned alone on the sixth. The *Lexington* arrived on the twenty-ninth and sailed again on the sixth with five heavy cruisers. The *Saratoga* is being repaired at San Diego and the *Wasp* is in the Atlantic. The *Yorktown* and the *Hornet* remain in the Pacific and may arrive today with the *Enterprise*." [3]

"What luck that would be!" Genda put in. "If that happened I wouldn't care if two battleships sailed."

"Easy to see that you are an airman," Lieutenant Commander Oishi replied. "For you, the most important targets are naturally the aircraft carriers. To get three of them would be very good; but I think the destruction of eight battleships more valuable."

The chief of staff interrupted:

"There is not much chance that the aircraft carriers will return on a Saturday, and even less that the battleships will weigh anchor on a Saturday or Sunday. We can be certain of this: the eight battleships will be there tomorrow. Too bad about the aircraft carriers! We can do nothing about it."

As he left the conference, Lieutenant Commander Fuchida confided to his neighbors:

"What I most regret is that we did not bring a landing force

---

2. *Here again is a problem of days and dates. Normally, the American fleet goes to sea on Monday, by its calendar, which is Tuesday in Japan. The date for that particular Saturday was December 6 throughout the world. The Japanese chief of staff, by talking Japanese date and American day of the week, succeeds in introducing much confusion into his remarks.* (R.A.T.)

3. *Discrepancies in this Japanese pre-attack intelligence report will be seen by comparing it with the table of American forces at the time of the attack, which is found at the end of Chapter 3.* (R.A.T.)

with us to take Hawaii. We would have been masters of the
Pacific."

Lifts were bringing the aircraft to the deck, where they were
grouped astern in their order of flight. Firmly moored against
the rolling, they were surrounded by a crowd of sailors in khaki
overalls, and each motor was given one more test; negligence
must not prevent a single aircraft from taking part in the operation.

At 1700 the attack force was on the meridian of Pearl Harbor,
490 miles away.

Signals were run up the *Akagi's* mast. When they fell, the
vessels turned, one after the other, to sail south at twenty knots.

The sea strengthened at nightfall. If only bad weather did not
prevent the operation!

Again a communications officer knocked on the admiral's door.
He carried a signal from Admiral Yamamoto:

"The Empire's destiny depends on this battle. Everyone will
do his duty."

Admiral Nagumo issued an order; a few minutes afterward,
bugles shrilled "attention," and loud-speakers spread the words
of the commander in chief, words heard with every head uncovered. Hearts filled with emotion as a special quartered flag
was hoisted to the masthead: the "Z" flag flown by Admiral Togo
in the *Mikasa* on the glorious morning of May 27, 1905.*

As the ceremony ended, there burst forth spontaneously, like
a prayer, the words of the national anthem:

> *May our Sovereign's reign last*
> *A thousand generations and eight thousand generations.*
> *Until the gravel of the river*
> *Becomes rocks*
> *And these rocks are covered with moss.*

A quarter past six

0500, December 8. Few men slept during the night which,
for many of them, was to be their last. The weather had not

---

* Battle of Tsushima.

worsened, but the sea was strong enough to make the vessels pitch and roll. The bow waves left pale trails on the black water, and occasional spray burst over the flight decks, where the crews strained to hold the aircraft as they were unlashed.

Already the *Chikuma* and the *Tone* had each catapulted a seaplane, to reconnoiter Pearl Harbor and give the latest information. In the *Akagi* the aircrews were in the briefing room, where Lieutenant Commander Fuchida, who was to lead the first wave, showed the objectives on a blackboard and again repeated his instructions. Then he left, climbed the ladder to the bridge, saluted Admiral Nagumo, and said, "I am ready to carry out my mission." The admiral shook his hand. "I have confidence in you," he replied simply. Both went down to the briefing room, where those who were to take part in the attack stood rigidly at attention.

At last the hour had come! The men returned to the deck and lined up facing the bridge where the commanding officer, Captain Hasegawa, flung up his hand and shouted: "Carry out the orders."

The crews ran to their aircraft. Fuchida went to take leave of the commanding officer. His old friend Genda smiled at him and in silence put a hand on his shoulder.

A new course was indicated by signal lamp. The Force altered direction northward, to port, into the wind; to take off from a flight deck, aircraft must breast the strongest possible breeze.

The ships were pitching in a heavy swell. A pilot, an officer named Matsuda, was uneasy. "What do you think of this take-off in the dark?" he asked.

"If this were peacetime," Fuchida replied, "it would be delayed until day. But now we must go on with it. If we coordinate the take-offs with the pitching, we should get away without a crash."

He saluted and went to his aircraft, its tail painted with the red and yellow stripes of a group leader.

He was putting on his helmet when one of the mechanics, a petty officer in khaki overalls, climbed to the cockpit and offered him a red-and-gold silk turban.

"Sir, may I offer you this with respect, from the mechanics?

As they can't go themselves, they ask you to take their present with you to Pearl Harbor."

Fuchida wrapped the shining silk round his head, and the ends flapped in the breeze. The engines of the first aircraft coughed and started, slowly at first as the oil warmed up, then roaring faster and louder. Fuselage and wings seemed to quiver with impatience.

Bluish lights marked the axis of the deck and the limits of the runway. Forward, the deck control officer held a green lamp. He watched the pitching. Suddenly he swung his arm in a luminous circle.

The first aircraft shot forward as the vessel's bow plunged into a trough. The watchers held their breath while with all its power unleashed it gathered speed. As it took off, seemingly hurled into the air by the ship's bows thrusting upward, a cheer burst from every throat, a cheer renewed every time the miracle repeated itself. Not one aircraft failed to leave.

After twenty minutes the deck was empty. Other aircraft came from the lifts: fighters to provide a protective umbrella, should the Americans react and attack the aircraft carriers.

Above, circling as they sorted themselves out, were 183 fighters, bombers, and torpedo aircraft. They were so well trained in formation flying that in a few minutes each group had formed on its leader's lights.

The expedition flew in a wide circle round the fleet below; then it sped toward Oahu. It was a quarter past six.

JAPANESE TASK FORCES FOR THE PEARL HARBOR ATTACK

(This and subsequent summaries of forces have been prepared by Admiral Theobald.)

Striking Force, Vice Admiral Nagumo

> *Carrier Division 1: Akagi, Kaga*
> *Carrier Division 2: Hiryu, Soryu*
> *Carrier Division 5: Shokaku, Zuikaku* (6 CV)*
> *Battleship Division 3, Section 1: Hiei, Kirishima* (2 OBB)
> *Cruiser Division 8: Chikuma, Tone* (2 CA)
> *Destroyer Squadron 1:* 1 light cruiser, 16 destroyers
> *Train:* 11 auxiliary vessels

Advance Expeditionary Force, Vice Admiral Shimizu
> 3 light cruisers, 20 I-class submarines, 5 midget submarines, 6 auxiliary vessels

> *Carrier planes in two-wave attacks:*
> *First wave:* 49 level bombers, 51 dive bombers, 40 torpedo planes, 43
> zero fighters   (183)
> *Second wave:* 54 level bombers, 80 dive bombers, 36 zero fighters   (170)

Total planes 353

* *Abbreviations:* CV, aircraft carrier; OBB, old battleship; CA, heavy cruiser.

3 Tiger

Fuchida kept his station in the first of the forty-nine high-altitude bombers. Peering out and taking for his bearings the discreet lights of the leaders, he could make out, a little below him and some 550 yards to his right, a formation of forty torpedo aircraft; 220 yards above and 550 to his left, were fifty-one dive bombers and forty-three fighters. The three groups were commanded respectively by Lieutenant Commander Murata, Lieutenant Commander Takahashi, and Lieutenant Commander Itaya.

Flying speed was 125 knots (146 miles an hour). The wind blew from the north and pushed the machines toward their goal. But cloud hid the sea and made it impossible to calculate drift by sighting the crests of the waves.

Fuchida twirled his goniometer. Oahu was transmitting and so unwittingly guided the attacker. Even better, the American transmissions reassured the Japanese about the weather: "Partly overcast by cloud, especially on the mountains. Three thousand, five hundred feet. Visibility good. Wind north, twelve knots."

The weather, then, was excellent even beyond their hopes. About 0700, the cloud cleared; long coast lines appeared. The aircraft had arrived above Kahuku Point, the northern extremity of the island. It was time to break formation and deploy.

Fuchida hesitated for a moment because two possibilities had been foreseen.

If the group leader fired a single flare, the plan to follow was that of surprise attack. The torpedo aircraft would attack first, followed by the high-level bombers, then by the dive bombers, the principal objectives of which would be the airstrips of Hickam Field, just east of the roadstead, and Ford Island, site of the naval air installations.

If Fuchida fired two flares, the plan would be different. It was then to be supposed that the enemy was on the alert. The dive bombers would dash in first to draw the adversary's fire and create disorder; and the high-altitude bombers would try to neutralize the defense, while the torpedo aircraft dropped to water level to launch their weapons.

The reconnaissance seaplanes still had given no sign of life; everything seemed to indicate that the Americans suspected nothing. Accordingly, at 0740, Fuchida fired a single flare.

The formation opened fanwise and the dive bombers turned upward to climb to 14,370 feet. The torpedo aircraft descended to sea level; the high-altitude bombers sought the cloud ceiling.

But the fighters had not seen the flare signal, and did not deploy.

Fuchida aimed his flare pistol at them and fired. This time the fighters buzzed into action, like a swarm of wasps. But the commander of the dive bombers had not understood; he had seen two rockets and believed that he should attack first. This misunderstanding threw some disarray into the smooth working of the operation.

At last the scouting aircraft were heard: "There are ten battleships, one heavy cruiser, and ten light cruisers," the *Chikuma's* seaplane announced. "The fleet is not at Lahaina," said that of the *Tone*. The last hope of finding the aircraft carriers in their nest had vanished. Beyond the land, in the pale light of early morning, could be seen the shell forming the roadstead and its pearl, Ford Island, to the south of which some dark shapes were ranged.

There, from west to east, were the *California*, then in pairs the *Oklahoma* and the *Maryland*, the *West Virginia* and the *Tennessee*, the *Arizona* and lastly the *Nevada*.

Further on in the big dry dock of the arsenal the *Pennsylvania* stretched out her twelve 14-inch guns. Many unimportant ships

were along the quays of the arsenal and in the locks opening to
the north of the Pearl.

The prey was there. With no further thought of concealment,
Fuchida's radio signaled: "Attack!" it was 0749.

The Pearl in smoke

Lieutenant Commander Takahashi, commanding the dive
bombers, still believed that he was to attack first. His group of
fifty-one bombers split in two. He led one formation toward
Ford Island, while the other, led by Lieutenant Sakamoto, made
for the aircraft of Wheeler Field in the center of Oahu.

Takahashi waggled his wings, and the machines dived earthward with piercing screams. Soon thick columns of smoke
mounted from Hickam Field, Ford Island, and Wheeler Field.

Murata was about to launch his torpedo attack along a line
from Hickam Field. The premature bombing made him fear
obstruction from the smoke. He cut short his run in, leveled out
just above sea level, and launched his torpedoes at 0755, perhaps
five minutes earlier than arranged. At that moment Seaman
Short began to fire.

Freed of their loads, the lightened machines banked right and
left, straining upward and away.

The high-altitude bombers stayed a little to the east. No
American planes were in the air; everything was peaceful, and
the radio transmissions were full of broadcast music.

Fuchida, before making his own attack, had to inform Admiral
Nagumo and Admiral Yamamato that the surprise attack had
succeeded. His signal which reached the *Nagato* at Hiroshima
was a single word: *"Tora"* ("Tiger").

The time had come: the leader's aircraft vigorously shook its
wings. The bombers divided into groups of ten and followed
him. He climbed steeply to leave first place to the guide aircraft
whose crew had received special training. As he passed, the
captain of this machine grinned broadly as he saluted.

At last the American guns reacted—five minutes after the first
bomb had fallen. Flashes came first from the ships, then from

the land. White puffs of smoke blossomed near the bombers, which were shaken by explosions. Fuchida's machine trembled suddenly and lurched. A voice said over the radio: "Holed on port side, rudder control damaged." The pilot regained control of his machine, although a second blow, less violent, again threw him off course.

Nevertheless the squadron was above the entrance to the bay; it was the moment to plunge on the *Nevada,* whose outline showed at the right extremity of the line.

The battleship was only 330 yards away, but to reach it a curtain of fire had to be crossed, and the attackers, formed in line, seemed very vulnerable.

Time passed slowly.

The guide bomber flew like a homing pigeon returning to its loft. Fuchida bent over, removed the safety bolt that held the bomb-release mechanism, worked the lever to release the straps, and seized the handle of the bomb release. All was ready.

Another shock. The bomb of the third aircraft had fallen. Fuchida shook his fist at the captain who had released it too soon, but the latter announced, "Underside of fuselage struck. A petrol tank burst. I ask permission to stay."

It was time for Fuchida to strike. At the last moment an unlucky cloud hid the target; the captain of the leading aircraft raised his arms in the air to signal that it was too late. They had to begin over again.

The bombers broke away toward Honolulu to make way for another group. As Fuchida's squadron made a wide circle before it again attacked its objective, a huge red flame rose to a thousand feet; it was as if the aircraft had been struck by an invisible hand.

The *Arizona* had blown up. The smoke that poured from her in torrents obscured the *Nevada.* Another target had to be picked, and as the *Maryland* seemed intact the formation aimed at her.

The sky which a few minutes before had been calm with first light had become an infernal battleground streaked by flashes, across which smoke rolled in fantastic shapes.

"Fire!" The guide released his bomb and the others followed him. Fuchida threw himself flat. Through the opening he could see four projectiles gradually shrink to dots and vanish.

More smoke rolled upward; two white fountains spurted at the side of the *Maryland;* of the four bombs just fallen, two then had hit the target.

The squadron had completed its task. It continued to the north toward the aircraft carriers, while the commanding officer's aircraft banked away from them to starboard and stayed to observe the results of the operations.

Fuchida ranged over the island, picking out the blazing airfields, and afterward returned toward Pearl Harbor. There was a sight to delight him.

The old battleship *Utah,* moored west of Ford Island, had sunk. The *West Virginia* and the *Oklahoma,* torpedoed, were listing in water blackened by fuel oil; the former was sinking, the latter about to capsize. The *Nevada* and the *California* slowly settled in the water. Only the *Pennsylvania* in the dock seemed not to have been attacked.

The light craft at the quays or moored north of Ford Island smoked and listed.

The first attack was over. Its results had cost altogether three fighters, one dive bomber, and five torpedo aircraft.

Silent sky

Above Kakuku Point, black spots started into view and rapidly grew bigger; they composed the second wave of 170 aircraft under Lieutenant Commander Shimazaki. It was 0840. Fourteen minutes later the attack began. Shimazaki, at the head of fifty-four high-altitude bombers, turned toward Hickam Field and the naval air station of Kaneohe; in the northeast corner of Oahu, while the dive bombers under Lieutenant Commander Egusa turned toward the port, describing a large curve to the east.

Smoke still dirtied the sky. The anti-aircraft fire was intense; every gun in the ships and on shore was firing without pause. Egusa chose for targets the ships which seemed most menacing, because he judged these to have suffered less than the others.

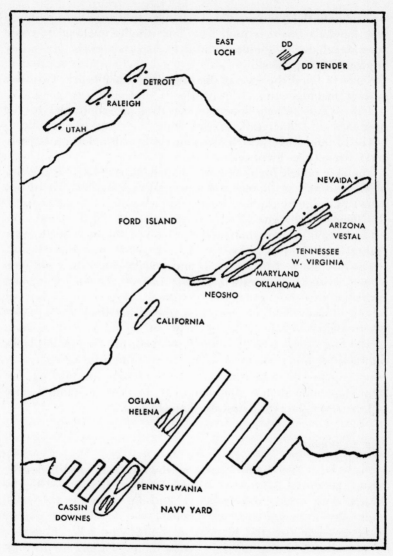

PEARL HARBOR ANCHORAGE, DECEMBER 7, 1941

One by one, the bombers dived with ear-splitting screams; then, their bombs away, they pulled out and climbed vertically, except those which, hit by gunfire, plunged, to shatter on the ground or be swallowed by the sea.

An hour later, the aircraft had dropped their loads. Then the fighters machine-gunned the airfields and gun emplacements, and the groups of the second wave disappeared northward, in their turn.

This second wave, which met more intense fire, lost six fighters and fourteen dive bombers.

The sky, which for four hours had been striped like a zebra by the passing of slender fuselages, filled with the roar of engines, and rent by explosions, had suddenly become silent—with the silence of the grave.

Columns of smoke continued to climb in the morning breeze. Over the gulf spread a cloak of black oil, iridescent in the sun.

Fuchida finished his last tour and noted that he had not seen a single American aircraft in the air. In fact, the Americans had taken no precautions against air attack. Because of a fear of sabotage, they had concentrated their machines on airfields where closer watch could be kept on them. This disposition served the Japanese plans singularly well, for their first bombs set these compact masses on fire. Some American airmen very courageously ran to their machines and managed to take off, but they were immediately dominated by an overwhelming swarm of Japanese fighters and destroyed one by one.

The flight north

Fuchida, at last, set his course northward. Some way from the island, he saw a fighter, waggling its wings. It was a straggler which, after setting out from the *Zuikaku,* had lost formation and, without navigational instruments, was unable to regain its base. It rallied to the lieutenant commander who, following orders, altered course toward a point of rendezvous fixed in advance. There he gathered in a second straggler, and the three aircraft took the road home.

An hour and a half later the Attack Force appeared. The foreparts of the aircraft carriers were encumbered by aircraft already returned; aft, all was cleared to permit the last arrivals to land. The yellow-and-red-tailed bomber rapidly lost height. The *Akagi*, which seemed like a tiny toy, swelled until it became enormous. The aircraft flattened out at deck height, came level with the ship, its wheels touched and its lowered hook caught in the arrester wire.

Fuchida climbed out to the cheers of his men and, still in his red-and-gold turban, hurried to the bridge and stood at attention in front of Admiral Nagumo, who was waiting for him, surrounded by his staff. Fuchida reported, "Four battleships sunk; one of them immediately, another capsized; the two others are at the bottom."

The admiral asked, "Then we may conclude that we have obtained the results we counted on?"

"Yes, Admiral. There is no doubt that we have inflicted heavy losses on the enemy. All the same, it would be inaccurate to suppose that we have destroyed everything; many important objectives are left. Accordingly, I would suggest a second attack."

The staff discussed the proposal. The Admiral went to his quarters with his chief of staff, who reappeared after some minutes and issued orders.

Signal flags were hoisted. The squadron increased speed toward the north. There was to be no second attack.

The aircraft, grouped forward on the flight decks, disappeared in the lifts which took them to the hangars, where mechanics dressed their wounds and made them fit for future action.

It was not till three years later, when Admiral Nagumo committed ceremonial hara-kiri at Saipan, that the reasons for his decision became known.

He judged that the first attack had given the results hoped for. Also, in a second attack, directed against an adversary on the alert, losses might well be out of proportion to the successes one might expect. And, thirdly, signals received revealed that the Americans still had fifty aircraft at their disposal, and the disposition of their aircraft carriers, cruisers, and submarines was not known.

The Japanese midget submarines were not so fortunate as the aircraft.

One of them tried to penetrate the roadstead by following a depot ship, the *Antares;* discovered by the *Condor,* then by a Catalina aircraft, she was sunk at 0654. A second profited by the prolonged delay in closing the net across the entrance; she glided through, but was seen by the destroyer *Monaghan,* which dashed down on her and cut her in two. A third struck a reef east of the canal; the destroyer *Helm,* patrolling the approaches, saw her at 0840 and opened fire. The tiny vessel struggled desperately, freed herself, and submerged, but, unable to stay long under water, she ended up beached on the west side of Oahu. The last two disappeared and were never heard of again.

Two victims of the Japanese aircraft were lost completely— the *Oklahoma* and the *Arizona.* The slightly damaged *Pennsylvania* was quickly repaired. The *Maryland* and *Tennessee* rejoined the fleet in 1942; the *Nevada* was refloated on February 12, 1942, and reentered service at the end of the following year, as did the *California* and *West Virginia.* One hundred and fifty American aircraft had been destroyed.

But the permanent installations, the workshops, the fuel tanks, and the nerve centers had not been touched. The staff of the arsenal were able to go to work immediately to repair the damage and refloat those vessels not irremediably stricken. And when new forces came to reinforce the American Pacific Fleet, they found at Pearl Harbor the indispensable resources of an almost intact base.

In Washington, the services had decoded at 0800 the secret instructions sent by Tokyo to Ambassador Nomura after the breakdown of negotiations. Paragraph 14 of these instructions advised that the conversations could not continue on the basis of the American proposals; and it expressly stated that this message must be delivered to the American authorities *at 1300.*

These facts did not particularly impress Admiral Stark. But General Marshall, returning at 1130 from a horseback ride, observed that 1300, Washington time, corresponded exactly with daybreak in Hawaii. In spite of the skepticism of his colleagues, the general prepared a warning telegram for the command at

Oahu. But this telegram, through negligence, did not reach its destination until a quarter of an hour after the attack.

American prewar action*

By the late fall of 1940, the American decrypting units in Washington had completely broken the Japanese diplomatic codes. Throughout 1941, President Roosevelt, Secretaries Hull, Stimson, and Knox, General Marshall, and Admiral Stark were reading the decodes of the dispatches between Tokyo and the various Japanese embassies and consulates, as soon as were their Japanese recipients. These American officials thus knew: early in October, that the consulate general in Honolulu was, from then on, to report the exact berthing of the individual United States ships in Pearl Harbor; by December 3, that war with Japan was imminent, as the Japanese diplomatic and consular posts in American and British territories were destroying all their codes, ciphers, and secret files; from November 28 on, that the Japanese reply to the American note of November 26 would be a declaration of war; at 3:00 P.M., Saturday, December 6, that that answer was then in the process of transmission to the Washington embassy, and that its delivery to the United States government was to be especially timed by later orders from Tokyo, obviously to synchronize with the surprise attack, known to be the characteristic technique for Japan's initiation of all her modern wars.

By 10:00 A.M., on Sunday, December 7, Zone 5 time, Washington had the 14-part declaration of war and the Tokyo order to the ambassadors to deliver it to the U.S. Government at 1:00 P.M., Washington time—7:30 A.M. in Hawaii, the time that a predawn-take-off attack would be hitting Pearl Harbor. No hint of any of this information was sent to the navy and army commanders in Hawaii, except one misleading message to Admiral Kimmel, which told him that the Japanese were destroying "some of" their codes, ciphers, and secret files. As told in the foreword, General Marshall, who arrived in his office at 11:30

* This section was written by Admiral Theobald, as his explanation of what took place in Washington immediately prior to the Pearl Harbor Attack.

A.M. that Sunday, sent the only message to Hawaii to have left
Washington on that Saturday or Sunday, concerning the decoded Japanese dispatches received on those days; and, as already stated, that word did not reach General Short until many
hours after the completion of the Japanese attacks.

It would be interesting to speculate as to: why this information was withheld from the Hawaiian commanders; what the
course of events would have been if Admiral Kimmel had been
given the information known in Washington on Saturday; what
the United States ship and plane losses might have been if the
Washington intelligence had been transmitted as early and as
quickly as possible to the Hawaiian commanders on that Sunday
morning. (R.A.T.)

"Senso!"

On the morning of December 8, the attention of passers-by in
the Nihonbashi quarter of Tokyo was caught by the bells of
newspaper boys who ran clutching their packets of papers and
shouting, "Senso! Senso!" ("War! War!") The still-damp sheets
were torn from their hands. Every stooping face registered uneasy amazement. The news spread. The silent capital seemed
gripped by deep disquiet until the Emperor's proclamation was
publicly posted:

"The revered Spirits of our Imperial Ancestors protect us from
above, and we count on the loyalty and courage of our subjects,
in our confident hope of continuing the task bequeathed us by
our fathers, to uproot evil and to reestablish in East Asia an un-
shakable peace, for the security and grandeur of our Empire."

DISPOSITION OF UNITED STATES PACIFIC FLEET, 8:00 A.M., DECEMBER 7, 1941

Commander in Chief, Admiral H. E. Kimmel

SHIPS IN PEARL HARBOR

West Virginia, Maryland, Tennessee, California, Pennsylvania, Arizona, Nevada, Oklahoma   (8 OBB)*
New Orleans, San Francisco   (2 CA)
Other Types: 6 light cruisers, 29 destroyers, 5 submarines, 9 minelayers, 10 minesweepers, 1 gunboat, 24 auxiliaries

SHIPS ABSENT FROM PEARL HARBOR

Task Force 8, Rear Admiral W. F. Halsey, 200 miles west of Oahu, returning from delivery of planes to Wake Island:
   Enterprise (CV)
   Northampton, Chester, Salt Lake City   (3 CA)
   Screen: 9 destroyers
Task Force 12, Rear Admiral J. H. Newton, 460 miles from Midway, ferrying planes to that island base:
   Lexington (CV)
   Chicago, Portland, Astoria   (3 CA)
   Screen: 5 destroyers
Task Force 3, off Johnson Island:
   Indianapolis (CA)
   Screen: 5 minesweepers
Exercise Force, 25 miles south of Oahu:
   Minneapolis (CA)
   Screen: 4 minesweepers
Convoy Escorts:
   Pensacola, in Samoan area; *Louisville* in Solomon Islands area   (2 CA)
Submarines:
   1 off Wake; 1 off Midway; 3 east of Oahu, 200 miles

* *Abbreviations:* OBB, old battleship; CV, aircraft carrier; CA, heavy cruiser.

On West Coast, under overhaul and on special service:
    Saratoga (CV)
    Colorado (OBB)
    Other Types: 3 light cruisers, 9 destroyers, 9 submarines

NAVY AND MARINE CORPS AIRCRAFT ON OAHU

Naval Air Station, Ford Island: 35 patrol bombers, 3 scout bombers, 30 utility, 4
    fighters left by carriers
Naval Air Station, Kaneohe: 36 patrol bombers, 8 utility
Marine Air Station, Ewa: 11 fighters, 32 scout bombers, 8 utility

ARMY AIRCRAFT ON OAHU

Hickam Field: 12 heavy bombers, 32 medium bombers, 12 light bombers
Wheeler Field: 4 medium bombers, 2 light bombers, 140 pursuit, 5 observation
Bellows Field: 12 pursuit, 8 observation

UNITED STATES LOSSES IN PEARL HARBOR ATTACK

SHIP LOSSES

Arizona, Oklahoma (2 OBB),* sunk and total losses
California, West Virginia (2 OBB), sunk but later restored to service
Maryland, Tennessee, Pennsylvania, Nevada (4 OBB), damaged but repaired
Helena, Raleigh (2 CL), damaged by torpedoes but restored to service
Honolulu (CL), moderately damaged by bombs but restored to service
Cassin, Downes (2 DD), total losses due to damage by bombs
Shaw (DD), damaged by bombs but restored to service
Utah (radio-controlled target ship), Oglala (minelayer), sunk and total losses
Vestal (repair ship), Curtis (seaplane tender), damaged but repaired

PLANE LOSSES

Navy and Marine Corps Losses
Naval Air Station, Ford Island: 19 patrol bombers, 4 fighters, 3
    scout bombers   **26 planes**

* *Abbreviations:* OBB, old battleship; CL, light cruiser; DD, destroyer.

Naval Air Station, Kaneohe: 27 patrol bombers, 1 observation scout   28 planes
Marine Air Station, Ewa: 9 fighters, 18 scout bombers, 6 utility   33 planes

                                                       Total   87 planes

Army Plane Losses

Hickam Field: 4 heavy bombers, 12 medium bombers, 2 light
   bombers   18 planes
Wheeler Field: 40 pursuit, 2 observation   42 planes
Bellows Field: 2 pursuit, 1 observation   3 planes

                                                      Total   63 planes

JAPANESE LOSSES IN PEARL HARBOR ATTACK

SHIP LOSSES

5 midget submarines

PLANE LOSSES

15 dive bombers, 5 torpedo bombers, 9 fighters

4 Four Days of Victory

The Japanese plan of operations was founded on the idea that the time gained by the Pearl Harbor operation would be used to conquer those territories whose possession was one of the aims of the Empire's war.

While the First Fleet sailed toward Hawaii, a Third Fleet was formed under the command of Vice Admiral Takahashi, whose flag flew in the cruiser *Hashigara*. It was composed of four heavy cruisers, three divisions of twelve destroyers, two seaplane tenders, four submarines, and sixty transports.

Part of this armada was detached at Palau, in the Marianas, from which it threatened the south of Luzon and the center of the Philippine Islands. It was charged with landing operations which were to follow one another without a break. For that purpose it had at its disposal small craft some forty-two feet long and thirteen feet in beam, and of very shallow draught. Armed with one or two machine guns and capable of eight to ten knots under the power of their Diesel engines, they could carry 129 men and land them by a bow ramp resembling a drawbridge.

On November 23—at the same time that the Attack Force was concentrating at Etorofu—Vice Admiral Kondo left the Inland Sea for the Pescadores Islands. These islands, a good base for fleets operating in the China seas, in 1884 sheltered the ships of Admiral Courbet who, on board the *Bayard*, directed the blockade of the China coast after the destruction of the arsenal of Fouchow.

From the cruiser *Takao* the admiral directed the Second Fleet, comprising the cruisers *Atago* and *Chokai,* the battleships *Haruna* and *Kongo,* and eight destroyers.

Its role was to cover the operations in Malaya. These were regarded in Tokyo as the most important, because Singapore threatened the flank of the Japanese move southward and its importance would increase as the lines of communication lengthened: its possession would be a major trump card in the conquest of the islands of the Sunda Strait.

The Japanese army was to cross the isthmus of Kra and plunge into the jungle, with landings here and there to menace the enemy's flank and to seize the airfields.

The conquest of the Philippines was to keep pace with that of Malaya. If the latter enterprise did not succeed immediately, Luzon had to be seized anyway—and at any cost—before the attack toward Singapore was renewed.

The next objectives were Borneo, the Celebes, Amboina, Timor, Bali, Sumatra, and Java.

Corregidor in its setting

On December 8, when the Attack Force neared Pearl Harbor, 192 aircraft of the Eleventh Air Fleet were assembled at Keelung, Formosa. They were to make a surprise bombing attack on the big aircraft bases in the Philippines—Clark Field and Nichols Field—which sheltered the B-17 bombers so dangerous to landing forces. In the moist heat, the crews in their flying kit grew impatient. The cloud ceiling was zero; and the wind socks hung slackly down their staffs. They were forced to wait.

Faces were turned skyward, as the noise of aircraft engines was heard dying away to the south. Hidden by low clouds, fourteen big bombers, followed by eighteen light bombers of the Army Air Force, flew to the attack: the former to bomb Baguio, north of Luzon; the latter Tugugarao airfield, in the center of the main island.

About ten o'clock the sky cleared. A siren blew; loud-speakers broadcast orders. A moment later the crews were in their machines with the engines turning over. In groups of ten they moved to the end of the cement runway. At a signal from their leader they darted forward and up, then circled the field to wait for their teammates.

Soon two groups formed, each of fifty-four bombers; thirty-four fighters for one group and thirty for the other stayed respectively 550 yards from the formations and some thousand feet above them.

A northeast wind furrowed the gray sea with whitecaps. A monotonous flight, and then a tiny island appeared in the murk—Batan.*

The north coast of Luzon was only 150 miles away. To evade detection, the groups banked west, then resumed their southward course, parallel to the coast. Suddenly, turning abruptly to port, they plunged earthward where Manila Bay opened out like a jewel case to disclose the island of Corregidor. But the attackers had no eyes for the roadstead packed with vessels, or for the town climbing the flanks of the hills.

The two formations deployed in squadrons. Fifty-four bombers sheered toward Clark Field, northwest of Manila Bay, the other fifty-four converged on Nichols Field, some miles to the south. The fighters climbed, ready to swoop on possible opponents. But they did not have to intervene.

Bombs began to fall. Thick clouds of smoke rose from the earth as gasoline bombs burst into high, bright flames.

Freed of their loads, the machines forged northward, again without any attempt at concealment. They flew over the torn soil of the island, a green carpet of luxuriant vegetation.

In their turn, the fighters dived toward the airfields. They swept over them almost at ground level, their rattling machine guns preventing the ground staff from fighting the fires, thus adding to the damage caused by the bombing. Then, increasing speed, they caught up with the bombers as they reached the sea.

When the formation landed on Formosa, not a single aircraft was missing.

* This is Batan Island, not Bataan Peninsula. The island is due north of Luzon.

On the attacked airfields, twelve Flying Fortresses and thirty Curtiss aircraft had been destroyed by fire. Many other aircraft were badly damaged and put out of action.

A second attack was made on December 10 by sixty bombers screened by a hundred fighters. The latter immediately shot down thirty-five American planes which tried to interfere.

Part of the expedition bombed the Nielson and Nichols airfields; the others circled for two hours over Cavite, at nearly thirty thousand feet, an altitude beyond the reach of anti-aircraft fire. In spite of this, the bombing was accurate. The arsenal was hit and completely burned. The changing wind fanned the flames, which spread over the town. Struck by bombs, the submarine *Sealion* and the minesweeper *Bittern* never put to sea again. A depot containing 230 torpedoes was wiped out.

Thenceforth, the American Asian Fleet, deprived of the support of land-based aircraft, could no longer interfere in those waters. The invasion fleet could hold its course safe from enemy interference. The occupation of the island of Batan, which had been planned to cover the operations, seemed unnecessary.

The "cloud on the mountain"

After the eleventh, the landing forces of the Third Fleet weighed anchor in three groups.

Only when six hundred miles from Luzon were the anti-aircraft guns manned; the lookouts scanned the sky to avoid all chance of surprise. Speed was slow, because fuel was scarce and had to be used with the utmost economy.

The light cruiser *Natori*, flying the flag of Rear Admiral Hara, led the First Surprise Attack Force, bound for Aparri, in the north of the island.

Under the protection of six escort destroyers, which bombarded the coast, the troops embarked in the special landing craft. In spite of the swell, the little craft grounded safely on the beach. Infantrymen jumped into the breakers, and the first to land dashed ahead to act as sharpshooters to cover the main landing with their light weapons. In a few hours, the supplies were ashore; and in spite of the determined resistance of some

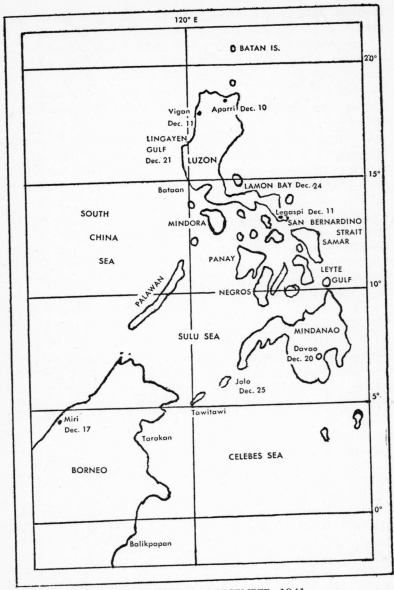

JAPANESE PHILIPPINE OPERATIONS, DECEMBER 1941

American detachments holding the area, the Aparri airfield was taken. It was unusable for the moment and had to be repaired.

Some enemy aircraft which had escaped the destruction of December 8 and 10 arrived above the flotilla. Falling bombs raised fountains of white water, which the wind dispersed; a minesweeper suffered a direct hit, broke in two, and sank, and another vessel was damaged and lost its steam through a gaping wound.

A similar scene occurred at Vigan, where the Second Surprise Attack Force landed troops from its five transports. The operation was protected by five destroyers under Rear Admiral Nishimura on board the light cruiser *Naka*.

There, too, the American airmen did their best. A small submarine chaser disappeared in spray; a transport, hit several times and ablaze, settled stern first, then abruptly reared and plunged vertically into the depths.

The force which was originally selected to attack Batan Island took station west of Vigan, ready to intervene if necessary. Between the two groups, watching the progress of the landings, was the destroyer *Yamagumo* ("Cloud on the Mountain"), upon which might be seen the slender figure of Rear Admiral Hirose.

Admiral Takahashi's covering force stayed to watch events from the south of the points attacked, ready to prevent interference from any vessels from Manila. Led by the light cruiser *Kuma* ("Bear"), the heavy cruisers *Ashigara* and *Maya* patrolled ceaselessly; seaplanes from the two tenders kept a distant watch.

A double kill

While these operations proceeded smoothly in the Philippines, a violent drama was enacted on the coasts of Malaya.

The Japanese troops, which had crossed the peninsula of Kra, multiplied their landings to reach the British airfields more quickly. Small detachments of silent men, stubborn and indomitable, thrust across jungle which had been thought impenetrable. They overran every obstacle, withstood all strain: a handful of rice sufficed to keep them alive. These men had been told to march south, and they marched. On December 8, they swarmed over Singora; on the eighth and ninth, Kota Bahru.

Meanwhile, as a Japanese aerial photograph of December 8 showed, the British battleship *Prince of Wales* and the battle cruiser *Repulse* had arrived at Singapore.

Although the *Repulse* dated from 1916, the *Prince of Wales* had been in service only since 1940 and was the last word in naval construction. She was armed with ten 14-inch guns, and in the event of air attack could use sixteen 5.25-inch, thirty-two 40-mm., and many automatic weapons of 12.7-mm. caliber.

Admiral Sir Tom Phillips, who commanded the group, wanted to attack immediately. It cannot be said that the Royal Navy had not done everything possible to dam the Japanese onrush. In spite of the absence of air cover, he weighed anchor, passed through the straits of Singapore, sighted the lighthouse of Buitan between squalls, and thrust boldly into the China Sea.

In the afternoon of December 9, a Japanese reconnaissance submarine of the Second Fleet signaled the approach of the British ships. The message was received in Saigon at 1600. Captain Sonokawa read it. He was in command of the Genzan squadron of the 22nd Air Flotilla, a unit of the 11th Air Fleet (Formosa). On the landing field a group of aircraft were loading bombs for Singapore: they were Bettys, equally capable of being used as torpedo aircraft. The heavy bombs were brought by trolley under the bellies of the machines and fitted by block and tackle into the jaws that gripped them and the straps that also held them to prevent an untimely release.

Sonokawa hurried from his office, interrupted the work, and ordered the substitution of torpedoes for bombs.

Without looking up, the men began the new task, while the captains of the aircraft ran to the hangar to check the air pressure of the torpedoes. The compressors quivered, the trolleys rolled. In spite of the zealous efforts and the haste that brought sweat streaming down faces drawn by fatigue, the squadron was not ready till 1800. Night was about to fall. But the enemy force was too dangerous: it had to be attacked at any price, no matter where or how.

The heavily laden bombers took off in the twilight. Sonokawa had warned Admiral Kondo, whose battleships *Haruna* and *Kongo* were the backbone of the surface Japanese covering forces in the Malayan area.

The aircraft crisscrossed and cast over the point where the adversary had been spotted, like hounds on the trail of a fox. But the night was dark, and the monsoon wind blew violently. The machines drew a blank and returned to their base at midnight.

The crews rested while their aircraft were being refueled. At 0315, an orderly woke Sonokawa: the British force had been sighted again, now sailing south toward Singapore.

At 0600, ten aircraft of the Genzan squadron, each carrying two sixty-kilogram bombs, set out to find them.

An hour later an attack force of twenty-seven bombers and sixty-one torpedo aircraft of the Genzan, Mihoro, and Kanoya squadrons took off. Divided into three groups, this massive air fleet followed the 105th meridian. Visibility was still bad. It was not till 1100 that the search group signaled, "Enemy in sight!"

All that was to be seen thirteen thousand feet below on the immense expanse of water, streaked by moving shadow and light, were two slim lines which merged imperceptibly into the froth of their wakes. To the Japanese airmen, these tiny sticks were much more than just two warships: they were the power of Britain herself, not long since the uncontested mistress of the seas.

Half an hour later, the kill began. The Genzan squadron attacked first. From eight thousand feet, it aimed eighteen bombs at the *Prince of Wales*. While this attack was being made, the torpedo aircraft dived toward the boiling sea to hurl their torpedoes at the two battleships, from heights between sixty and 150 feet.

The British ships were lit by flashes. Every gun fired deafeningly. But what could they do, without air cover, against these swarms of wasps arriving from all directions?

Countless fountains of white water gushed up around the two vessels; but many blows struck home. The *Prince of Wales* was able to hold her course at full speed, but the *Repulse* was forced to slow, and the attack on her was simplified.

The Genzan squadron was succeeded by the Mihoro squadron. Two groups, each of nine bombers, attacked the two ships; nine torpedo aircraft hurled themselves at the *Prince of Wales* and eight at the *Repulse*. Even if the bombs had not caused serious damage, several torpedoes struck home. The great hulls began to list tragically.

It was the turn of the Kanoya squadron. Six torpedo aircraft assailed the *Prince of Wales;* twenty others centered on the *Repulse*. The latter had already been struck by a dozen torpedoes; [1] she poured smoke and listed farther. She was five miles astern of her leader. Struck again, she received her death blow and stopped. On the captain's command, her crew threw into the water everything that would float and slithered down her side into the sea.

At 1230, the *Repulse* capsized completely, and the heavy vessel disappeared in a cyclonic upheaval.

The *Prince of Wales* fought on against death. Her guns were silent now: of all the air fleet that had attacked her so fiercely, only one, an observation aircraft, remained on the scene.

But the water rose inexorably, through the gaps torn by the torpedoes. The boilers were flooded, and the electricity was cut off. The order to abandon ship was given, and the men below decks climbed up the escape ladders to the light of day.

The battleship, no longer with way on her, heeled over slowly. Her green underwater paint came prominently into view, and over it clambered groups of men, who threw themselves into the sea. The bilge keels showed in a swirl of water and, massively, the vessel sank to the crash of underwater explosions, most probably those of the bursting boilers on contact with the inrushing cold waters.

The *Prince of Wales* became the tomb of Admiral Phillips,

---

1. *This is probably a Japanese exaggeration. The tough* Yamato *was to sink under approximately this number of torpedo hits. The underwater compartments of the* West Virginia *were unbelievably distorted by seven torpedo hits. It is highly doubtful if the hull of the* Repulse, *a battle cruiser, was anything like as strong as those of the* Yamato *and* West Virginia. (R.A.T.)

whose conduct had done honor to the traditions of the Royal Navy.

The destruction of these two proud ships, one of the principal episodes of the early days of the war at sea, had cost only one aircraft of the Genzan squadron and three of the Kanoya squadron. On the airfields of the 22nd Flotilla the day's results were cheered and future exploits were envisaged. [2]

After four days

Palau is an atoll at the southwestern end of the chain of the Marianas—the sort of island formed over thousands of years by the massing of coral in these warm seas—an atoll shaped like an irregular circlet around a lagoon of unequal depth. The size of the land area varies; in certain places it permits the establishment of airfields. In the lagoon, ships find calm water, although the channels of approach are perilously narrow and tortuous. On these narrow strips of land grow cocoa palms, whose seeds are carried by the winds; but human settlement depends on the importation of all necessities.

It was to Palau that the Third Surprise Attack Force had been sent, under the command of Rear Admiral Kubo, whose flag flew in the light cruiser *Nagara*.

This force was to carry out a landing at Legaspi, on the southernmost peninsula of Luzon, with six destroyers, two seaplane tenders, and seven transports. Rear Admiral Takagi was ordered to cover the operation. His force consisted of the heavy cruisers *Nachi, Haguro,* and *Myoko;* a small (seven-thousand-ton) carrier, *Ryujo,* and six destroyers, led by the light cruiser *Jintsu.*

The arrangements were similar to those for the preceding landings.

---

2. *The loss of the* Prince of Wales *and* Repulse *quickly confirmed the academic peacetime tactical studies. Unless powerfully screened by fighter aircraft, the losses of naval vessels when strongly attacked by enemy aircraft will always be prohibitive.* (R.A.T.)

On December 11, almost without a blow being struck, the flag of the Rising Sun floated over Legaspi.

Luzon was thus gripped between pincers of Japanese aircraft in her extreme north and south and thereby isolated. American aircraft coming from the Visayas would be intercepted by fighter aircraft from Legaspi; and minefields in San Bernardino Strait, between Luzon and Samar, and in Surigao Strait, made communication most hazardous between the Pacific Ocean and the South China and Sulu seas.

These lightning operations all took place between December 8 and 11, 1941. Never, perhaps, has a naval power started a war so brilliantly, striking simultaneously in every direction with equal success, matching audacity with competency, and speed with opportunity. At such times a nation seems borne on by destiny, and it appears that nothing can resist it. [3]

---

3. *The universal successes of the rapid Japanese early moves were as brilliant as the author claims they were. The only operation, however, in which they might have received stiffer opposition was that at Pearl Harbor. All the other attacks resulted about as might be expected, except the surprise achieved in the attacks on the main Luzon airfields. That has always been difficult to understand.* (R.A.T.)

DISPOSITION OF UNITED STATES ASIATIC FLEET, DECEMBER 8, 1941

Commander in Chief, Admiral T. C. Hart

Units in the Manila Bay-Olongapo area:
   Patrol Wing 10: Langley (OCVL)*, *Childs* (seaplane tender) (4 fighters, 28 patrol bombers)
   4 destroyers,† 26 submarines, 6 gunboats, 5 minesweepers

* *Abbreviations*: OCVL, old light carrier; CA, heavy cruiser, CL, light cruiser.
   All U.S. Asiatic Fleet destroyers were World War I vintage.

Train: 2 submarine tenders, 2 oil tankers

Houston (CA) at Iloilo, P.I., *Boise* (CL) at Cebu, P.I., 1 submarine off Lingayen, 1 submarine in Sorsogon Bay, P.I.

Units in Borneo: Marblehead (CL), 5 destroyers at Tarakan; *Black Hawk* (destroyer tender), 4 destroyers at Balikpapan

PART TWO
Toward Co-prosperity

5 Strategic Considerations*

Japan thus launched her war to conquer and annex the lands to the south, and integrate their wealth into her expanding Empire, political and economic. This was the ultimate aim and true meaning of the so-called Asiatic Co-prosperity Sphere. But, as she planned that war, she never lost sight of her most immediate and pressing wartime need, an assured supply of oil.

Her first military objective was to fence off the periphery of the area she had marked for conquest. This major operation was to be accomplished in two stages: (1) the early and simultaneous subjugation of the Malay Peninsula and the Philippine Islands; (2) the conquest of the Sunda Islands † of the Netherlands Indies, to follow as soon as war developments and the availability of the necessary forces would permit. Concurrently, secondary operations would be undertaken for the realization of two objectives: (1) control of the major oil fields in the area; (2) consolidation of her positions and the avenues of surface communication therein, by the creation of a network of securely held bases, capable of quick mutual aircraft support.

The opening overture—comprising the first four days of the war—must have caused the Japanese high commands the ut-

* This chapter was written by Admiral Theobald, for the purpose of placing the sea war in perspective at this stage.
† The Sunda Islands of the Netherlands East Indies comprise Sumatra and Java, and the lesser Sunda isles to and including Timor. They are the barrier islands that separate the Indian Ocean and the waters to their north.

most satisfaction: the *Prince of Wales* and the *Repulse,* the only enemy capital ships in Far Eastern waters, and five American battleships, all sunk; the early landings on the Kra Peninsula in Malaya easily and successfully accomplished; the American aircraft on Luzon decimated and thus effectively eliminated as a fighting force; the preliminary steps of the Luzon invasion, the occupation on that island of bases for fighter aircraft, painlessly accomplished at Aparri and Vigan in the north and Legaspi in the south.

Strong features of Japan's western Pacific position were her chains of powerful midocean bases, each within aircraft-flight radius of its neighbors. Parallel to the China coast and reaching to the South China Sea, was the Kyushu-Ryukyus-Formosa chain; extending from Honshu to the southward was the mid-Pacific chain, stretching through Ogasawara and the Marianas to the Caroline Islands, and then reaching eastward to the Marshall and Gilbert groups. The principal of these island bases were Tarawa, in the Gilberts; Wotje, Majuro, Jaluit, Kwajalein, and Eniwetok in the Marshalls; Truk and Ponape in the Carolines; and, in the Marianas, Saipan, Tinian, and Guam (after its capture by Japan), with Yap and Palau to the southwest.

With the capture of Guam and Wake, the Central Pacific was destined, for the next two years, except for three sporadic United States air raids, to enjoy the wartime calm of a Japanese lake. But, to the south, the tide of Japanese conquest, after an initial jump to New Britain and New Ireland, spread to the northeast coast of New Guinea and into the Solomon Islands. During that early wartime era of heady success, probably none of the Japanese high commands had attempted to figure out where this expansion was to end. The beginning of the end was the battle of the Coral Sea, recounted in the concluding pages of this Part Two.

The operations described in Part Two comprise Phase I of the Pacific war. The basic organization of the Japanese naval forces for the invasion of the Philippines and Malaya was as follows:

Covering Force, Vice Admiral Kondo

> *Battleship Division 3, Section 2: Kongo, Haruna* (2 OBB)*
> *Cruiser Division 4: Takao, Atago, Chokai* (3 CA)
> *Screens:* 8 destroyers

Close Covering and Support Force, Vice Admiral Takahashi

Northern Covering Force, Vice Admiral Takahashi
Cruisers: Maya, Ashigara, Kuma (2 CA, 1 CL)
Other Types: 2 converted seaplane tenders

Batan Island Surprise Attack Force, Rear Admiral Hirose †
1 destroyer, 4 torpedo boats, 2 transports, 6 assorted small craft

First Surprise Attack Force (Aparri), Rear Admiral Hara
1 light cruiser, 6 destroyers, 3 minelayers, 6 transports

Second Surprise Attack Force (Vigan), Rear Admiral Nishimura
1 light cruiser, 7 destroyers, 6 minelayers, 5 transports

Third Surprise Attack Force (Legaspi), Rear Admiral Kubo
1 light cruiser, 6 destroyers, 2 minesweepers, 7 transports, 2 seaplane carriers

Legaspi Support Force, Rear Admiral Takagi
Cruiser Division 5: Nachi, Haguro, Myoko (3 CA)
Screen: 1 light cruiser, 7 destroyers

This Japanese Third Fleet, with attached transports and troops, was the amphibious force for the Philippine, Borneo, and Celebes landing operations.

Prior to the outbreak of war, the foregoing forces had moved into position for their initial war operations. The Second Fleet first moved to Mako in the Pescadores, until it took its covering position in the South China Sea for the Kra Peninsula invasion. The forces of the Third Fleet, designated to make the preliminary attacks on Batan Island, Aparri, and Vigan, staged their attacks from Takao and Keelung in Formosa, while the Third Surprise Fleet and the Legaspi Support Force staged theirs upon Legaspi from the Palaus.

---

* *Abbreviations:* OBB, old battleship; CA, heavy cruiser; CL, light cruiser.
† Contemplated landing on Batan Island was not made.

Third Fleet support of Luzon landings

The main invasion of Luzon was initiated by two landings, one on the west coast at Lingayen Gulf, the other on the east coast at Lamon Bay. The organization of the combatant ships of the Third Fleet was the same for these landings as for the first ones of the war. The assignment of these forces was as follows:

LINGAYEN GULF
  Northern Covering Force
  First Surprise Attack Force
  Second Surprise Attack Force
  Batan Island Surprise Attack Force
LAMON BAY
  Legaspi Support Force
  Third Surprise Attack Force

The composition of the First Air Fleet, the striking force of the Pearl Harbor attack, has been set forth at the end of Chapter 2. After its return from the Hawaiian area, it was very active in the more important operations of Phase I.

The Japanese First Fleet did not appear in the active operations until the Midway campaign, which opened the second phase of the war, at the end of May 1942. During that period of almost six months, Battleship Divisions 1 and 2, with their attached destroyers, remained in the Hashirajima anchorage, near Hiroshima, in the Inland Sea. (R.A.T.)

6　The Race for Fuel

Luzon was invested on two sides. The remaining task was to strike at the heart of the island. The forces needed were assembled for landings at Lingayen in the west and Lamon in the east. Meanwhile, on December 20 a force had got a foothold at Davao in Mindanao; this operation was supported by Captain Tanaka, whose detachment consisted of the light cruiser *Jintsu* and six destroyers from the Covering Force at Palau.

On December 22 the First Surprise Attack Force from Takao in Formosa, the Second Surprise Attack Force from Mako in the Pescadores, and the Batan Island Force from Keelung in Formosa assembled before Lingayen.

Admiral Takahashi, with the Northern Covering Force, supported the operation, and Admiral Kondo, with his force, left the Malayan approaches to cover the landing.

The operation was begun in spite of bad weather. Rollers lifted the barges beached on the strand and pushed them seaward against their dragging anchors. But the soldiers of Nippon were tough and resolute. Shaken, soaked to the skin, they ran screaming at the enemy waiting in the undergrowth.

The landing took longer than was expected, but by the twenty-fifth it was all over. The American merchant ships in port at Manila had been gone since December 11. General MacArthur conducted a brilliant defense of Corregidor and Bataan Peninsula, to which the American forces were quickly compelled to retreat, in the face of overwhelming Japanese superiority. By order of President Roosevelt, General MacArthur turned the command over to General Wainwright on March 11, 1942, and departed during the ensuing night in a P.T. boat for Australia.

On April 8 Bataan Peninsula had to be evacuated. General Wainwright and the naval personnel made their way back to Corregidor, but this last position capitulated on May 6.

All the Philippines quickly thereafter fell into Japanese hands, although guerrilla action by natives continued in the mountains.

After the landing at Lingayen, the Third Fleet returned to Takao for some minor operations before making for Palau, where it found the Pearl Harbor Attack Force, minus the two aircraft carriers *Shokaku* and *Zuikaku*, which had returned to Japan.

Wake

This force did not have to wait long before it was given new objectives.

After the attack on Oahu, Vice Admiral Nagumo had turned westward at full speed to put himself beyond reach of enemy aircraft, and then, to save fuel, had slowed to cruising speed. And on December 15 a task force consisting of the carriers *Soryu* and *Hiryu* and a support group composed of the cruisers *Tone* and *Chikuma* and some destroyers were detached to cover the second attack on Wake.

This island was to be one of the links in the chain of Japanese defenses. Its position made it an excellent advanced base for long-range aircraft and for consequent support of later mid-Pacific operations projected to the eastward.

A first attack had been carried out immediately on the outbreak of war by an amphibious force assembled for that purpost at Kwajalein in the Marshalls. This force was detached from the Fourth Fleet, based on Truk; besides transports, it comprised three old light cruisers, *Yubari*, flying the flag of Rear Admiral Kajioka, *Tenryu*, and *Tatsuda*; six destroyers, and two submarines.

Since December 8 Wake had been hammered daily from the air. On the eleventh the landing force sighted the island. Full of confidence, it approached without precaution, but when near land it came under fierce fire from the defense batteries. The *Yubari* and the destroyer *Oite* were badly damaged. Captain Koyama, commanding the cruiser, turned to the admiral and suggested turning back.

"Our losses are heavy," he said. "The enemy artillery is very efficient; our preparations were inadequate." If we persist, we shall only be repulsed."

In spite of his reluctance, the admiral allowed himself to be persuaded. The little armada returned to the shelter of Kwajalein. They were obliged to start all over again, but with reinforcements.

The regular bombing attacks were resumed the following day. The attacking airmen pinpointed the gun emplacements. After the twenty-first, aircraft from the two aircraft carriers *Soryu* and *Hiryu* joined in the attacks. The island was covered by a perpetual cloud of smoke.

The second expedition had the same escort as the first, but it was also covered by a support force, the 6th Cruiser Division of Rear Admiral Goto, which had arrived from Truk. It comprised the least powerful Japanese heavy cruiser division, *Aoba, Kinugasa, Furutaka,* and *Kako,* armed with six 8-inch guns, and a few screening destroyers.

The Carrier Force was maintaining station two hundred miles to the northwest, and the Support Force was two hundred miles to the east. Thus protected, the landing troops arrived in view of the isle on December 22.

This time the defense was much weaker; most of the guns had been dismounted, and the losses in men had been heavy. On the twenty-third, after an artillery barrage, the Japanese troops landed. The same evening, the Rising Sun fluttered over the whole island.

Guam, Rabaul

Since December 8, the little island of Guam, the only American possession in the Marianas, had been subjected to fierce

bombing by aircraft from Saipan. On the tenth, Guam was occupied without difficulty by a landing force under Vice Admiral
Inouye, who came from Truk.

The outer chain of Japanese protection was completed on
January 23 by the occupation of Rabaul.

At the northeastern extremity of New Britain, Rabaul offered a magnificent, perfectly protected harbor. Its central position enabled it to dominate the coasts of New Britain, New Ireland, Papua, and the northern Solomons.

Easily conquered by the forces which had taken Wake a
month earlier, Rabaul, thanks to feverish work, was quickly
transformed into a strong base for the navy, the army, and their
supporting air forces. Hundreds of planes were installed on the
airfields, which teams of soldiers and workers laid out on the
heights that dominated the roadstead.

East of the town was the airfield of Lakunai; to the south,
fanning out, were located those of Keravat, Vukanau, Tobera,
and Rapopo.

Between New Britain and New Ireland, which could be seen
to the northeast, lay the St. George Channel, which opened at
one end on the Coral Sea and toward the Solomons; and, at the
other end, on the Bismarck Sea and toward Palau, Truk, and the
Philippines.

Throughout the war, Rabaul remained the most important
Japanese stronghold in the south; it was never subjected to surface assault.

In January, the Japanese command in the Southwest Pacific
was divided into two zones under the supreme command of Vice
Admiral Kondo, whose personal flag flew in the main covering
force of battleships, cruisers, and aircraft carriers.

Vice Admiral Takahashi, commanding the Third Fleet, was
put in charge of the eastern zone — the Philippines, Makasser
Straits, and the eastern seas.

The western zone, which comprised the China Seas and the
Malayan Peninsula and Sumatra areas, was under the control of
Vice Admiral Ozawa, commanding the First Detached Fleet.

Finally, a central force under Rear Admiral Hirose, a subordinate flag officer of the Third Fleet, was temporarily organized to seize Tarakan and the eastern part of Borneo.

The invasion would follow the prudent and tested method. It would suggest an enormous octopus stretching out some of its tentacles, strengthening them, and again stretching them out irresistibly, until the prey was completely enveloped.

Each step forward was kept carefully within the limit of air action, based on the previous conquest. When bombing had sufficiently enfeebled the defense, the transports weighed anchor under the protection of a strong escort, and with the support of a covering force. After a further softening up, by artillery, the troops were landed.

In fact, the islands were defended only by small forces which were always greatly outnumbered. Whenever a projected leap was particularly important, Vice Admiral Nagumo joined in with his aircraft carriers. That was what happened in February, during the attack on Port Darwin, and in March, during the invasion of Java and Sumatra. In March, Vice Admiral Kondo was operating around Timor and the Celebes; he bombarded the Christmas Islands and destroyed enemy commercial undertakings there.

The octopus

On its way toward Tarakan, the Eastern Force of Admiral Takahashi's command passed through Balabac Straits, circling south of Palawan, a detour to avoid the coral which barred almost all the passage and which was indicated by the lighter color of the water. The squadron entered the Sulu Sea. Here the yellowish waves bore the trunks of palm trees, torn up by tropical storms from the islands, that dot this sea. These frequent and short squalls are characteristic of the region; in a minute, the sky is completely hidden and a deluge beats down, to stop as abruptly as it started and to be replaced without transition by a resplendent sun. The covering group of Admiral Takagi comprised the heavy cruisers *Nachi, Haguro,* and *Myoko.* The convoy was escorted by ten destroyers, led by the *Jintsu* of Admiral Tanaka. The aircraft of the small carrier *Zuiho* and the seaplane

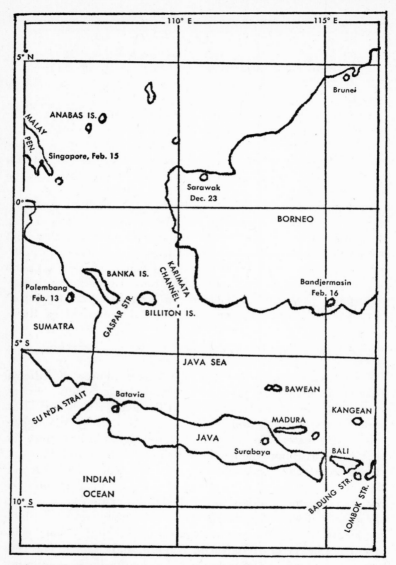

JAPANESE WESTERN THEATER OF OPERATIONS, JANUARY–MARCH 1942

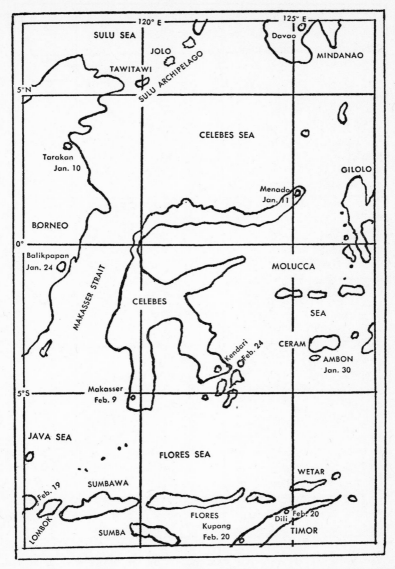

JAPANESE EASTERN THEATER OF OPERATIONS, JANUARY–MARCH 1942

tender *Chitose,* constituting the air group of Rear Admiral
Fujita, maintained the distant reconnaissance and also supported the landing. There was the Sulu Archipelago and its forests of palm trees, the barrier of atolls lining the Sulu Sea to
the south, in which is included the island of Jolo, occupied on
December 25. Straight ahead showed the heights of the Celebes.

On January 11 the peninsula of Menado, at the northeastern
end of Celebes, was occupied.

The same day, Admiral Hirose, supported by Rear Admiral
Hashimoto's group, which had turned eastward on leaving the
Sulu Sea, entered the long channel which leads across the shoals
to the roadstead of Tarakan.

The island, with its excellent sources of oil hidden in the luxuriant vegetation, fell immediately.

In British Sarawak, on the north side of the island of Borneo,
landings had started on December 17, at Miri. All Sarawak was
occupied within six days. Meanwhile, Davao in Mindanao was
taken on December 20, and with their right flank thus covered,
the Japanese were ready, after the capture of Tarakan on the
east coast of Borneo, to attack Balikpapan, the heart of the big
island, farther down the coast.

On January 22, sixteen transports weighed anchor at Tarakan. Two days later, protected by the *Naka* and the nine destroyers of Rear Admiral Tanaka's command, the Dutch oil
capital was seized—oil, which Japan so greatly needed and
which was one of the goals of the war!

Continuing its progress, Takahashi's force reached Kendari, in
southeast Celebes, on January 24. Kendari was to become an
air base to control the direct Java-Australia route. Setting out
from there, the Japanese bombed the arsenal of Surabaya.

In the naval port of Java lay an allied squadron, comprising
the Dutch cruisers *De Ruyter* and *Java,* the American cruiser
Houston, and the British cruisers H.M.A.S. *Perth* and H.M.S.
Exeter. Some old destroyers of the three nations were also at
hand.

In spite of its relative weakness, this force was a constant
menace to the Japanese, because it had the initiative and could
choose its time for a judicious attack on an isolated group, or for

a surprise attack, by night or in bad weather, on a convoy. The invaders could only have the desired freedom of movement when this danger was eliminated; in the meantime, they had to cover all their movements by groups of sufficient strength to neutralize any possible action of this whole enemy squadron.

In spite of the Japanese precautions, during the night of January 23-24, four American destroyers drove among the vessels bound for Balikpapan and sank four transports before vanishing again into the murk.

All the same, on February 2 Amboina was taken, and Makasser, at the southwest corner of Celebes, suffered a similar fate on the sixth.

On February 16, Vice Admiral Ozawa occupied Palembang, Sumatra, opposite Banka Island.

On the fifteenth the news of the capture of Singapore had set a seal on the pride and ardor of the Japanese troops. In a few months, they had seen fall into their hands, like manna from heaven, treasures they had long coveted. It seemed to them that they could do anything.

On February 17 Rear Admiral Tanaka left Amboina in the *Jintsu,* with ten destroyers and a fleet of transports. Reinforced halfway by Admiral Kondo, he arrived before Timor on the twentieth and occupied it the next day.

The vise on Java had tightened, and the preparation for the assault had been completed. But before undertaking this important operation, the Japanese navy was to strike a heavy blow at Port Darwin. This port would be the departure point for reinforcements from Australia, which could conceivably be sent to the Dutch East Indies.

At dawn on February 19 Vice Admiral Kondo's force was in the south Timor Sea. As on the morning of December 8, the decks of the four aircraft carriers *Akagi, Kaga, Hiryu,* and *Soryu* were covered with planes. That day, the sea was like silk, and there was almost no wind. But for the inevitable squalls, the expedition could expect a walk-over.

Already the black birds were turning above the squadron to take formation. The group flew off to the southward. Another squadron had already left from Kendari.

The harbor of Port Darwin was encumbered with merchant ships.

The American destroyer *Peary* had no time to act: the squadrons arrived unexpectedly over the roadstead, and the deadly waves of bombs followed one another inexorably. White fountains shot skyward, columns of smoke whirled up, and great flames spurted from stricken vessels.

Three quarters of an hour after the attack had begun, the sky had regained its absolute calm. The *Peary* had sunk. Around her masts, sticking out of the oily water, cargo ships continued to burn or settled gently in the water.

In the meantime, Rear Admiral Kubo who, on February 6, had directed the landing at Makasser from the light cruiser *Nagara*, reorganized his forces. His immediate objective was Bali. This charming island, so entirely designed for peaceful joys, was to know the clash of arms.

Kubo set out from Makasser on the eighteenth and crossed the Java Sea.

The next day the operation was over. Troops and supplies were ashore. Most of the transports departed prior to 2200 on the nineteenth, to return to base.

A few hours later came the allied naval reply: two groups of vessels successively attacked the anchorage of Sanur in Bali; the transport *Sasago Maru,* the only one left in the roadstead, burned and sank.

Soon some Japanese destroyers swung into action. In the squally night, the fight was hazardous and disjointed. Here and there searchlight beams uncovered a brilliant silhouette fringed by foam; sudden flashes lit the obscurity; sometimes a shower of sparks, a somber red glow, showed that a ship had been hit.[1] Dull explosions echoed; these were Japanese torpedoes,

---

1. *This is a condensed account of a confused night action, fought on February 19-20 in Badung Strait, the southwest arm of Lombock Strait. On the morning of the nineteenth, the Japanese had landed an occupation force at Sanur in southeast Bali, and the Allies were trying to destroy the transports from which that force had landed. However, all but one of these had departed in*

and the Japanese sailors grinned at the thought that their weapons had struck home.

The truth was quite different. The torpedoes, excellent in other ways, had a tendency to go off before striking their target.

The Japanese were soon to discover and correct this fault,[2] but for the moment they were misled.

The action ended as suddenly as it had begun. Between these ships, dashing into the night at full speed, the action could only be spasmodic; a slight alteration of course or a squall was sufficient to isolate the adversaries.

The destroyers patrolled for the rest of the night without finding anything.

No major damage was suffered by the Japanese, although the

---

time to avoid the attack. The Allies attacked in two widely separated waves, which divided the action into two phases.

After hours of maneuvering, gunfire, and torpedo attacks, little was accomplished. The Allies lost the destroyer Piet Hein, *and the light cruiser* Tromp *suffered considerable damage. The Japanese lost one transport but no cambatant ships, although the destroyer* Michishio *was severely mauled.* (R.A.T.)

2. *These Japanese torpedo failures are somewhat surprising, as this weapon, throughout the war, was the mainstay of their light-force actions. Certainly the aerial torpedoes did not fail them at Pearl Harbor.*

In the early phases of the war, the American torpedoes were most unsatisfactory, due mainly to warhead detonator failures. Also, the early recovery of an unexploded Japanese torpedo disclosed that they were using a much larger explosive charge in their warheads than were the Americans. The defects in the American torpedoes were corrected in due time, and the larger warhead, with its more devastating explosive effect, was being supplied to the destroyers and submarines soon after the start of the war's second phase.

Throughout the war, the Japanese got far greater ranges and speeds out of their torpedoes than did the Americans, through the use of oxygen instead of compressed air to provide the propulsive power. (R.A.T.)

destroyer *Michishio* needed extensive repairs; in the other camp, the destroyer *Piet Hein* was sunk and the cruiser *Tromp* had to be repaired in Australia.

JAPANESE TASK ORGANIZATION FOR THE INVASION OF JAVA

Southern Striking Force, Vice Admiral Kondo

> *Battleship Division 3:* **Kongo, Hiei, Haruna, Kirishima   (4 OBB)***
> *Carrier Division 1:* **Akagi, Kaga   (2 CV)**
> *Carrier Division 2:* **Soryu, Hiryu   (2 CV)**
> *Screens:* **1 light cruiser, 8 destroyers**

Attack Forces, Vice Admiral Takahashi

> *Fleet Flagship Group:* **Ashigara, Myoko, 2 destroyers   (2 CA)**

Eastern Attack Group, Rear Admiral Nishimura
1 light cruiser, 7 destroyers, 41 transports

Eastern Covering Group, Rear Admiral Takagi
Nachi, Haguro **(2 CA)**
Screen: **1 light cruiser, 7 destroyers**

Western Attack Group, Rear Admiral Kurita
Carrier Unit: **Ryujo (CVL), 1 seaplane carrier, 1 seaplane tender, 2 destroyers**
Supports and Screens: **3 light cruisers, 23 destroyers**
Auxiliary Vessels: **56 transports and cargo ships**

Western Covering Group: 4 heavy cruisers

* *Abbreviations:* OBB, old battleship; CV, aircraft carrier; CVL, light carrier; CA, heavy cruiser.

7   For the Honor of Batavia

Now the Japanese were ready for the conquest of Java. On February 18, Rear Admiral Kurita left Cam-Ranh Bay, Indo-China, with fifty-six transports escorted by the light cruisers *Sendai*, *Natori*, and *Yura*, twenty-five destroyers, the small aircraft carrier *Ryujo*, and two seaplane tenders. Covered by four heavy cruisers, he laid course to the south. He cruised back and forth in the vicinity of the Anambas islands while he waited for the order to proceed.

On February 19 the forty-one transports and the Escort Force of the Eastern Attack Force, commanded by Rear Admiral Nishimura, set out from Jolo. This convoy stopped at Balik-papan on the twenty-third; Rear Admiral Takagi covered it in the Makasser Straits with the heavy cruisers *Nachi* and *Haguro* and the seven destroyers, led by Tanaka in the *Jintsu*.

The Java Sea

Admiral Doorman of the Royal Netherlands Navy commanded the allied striking force in the Java Sea. Solidly built, of medium height, and with his braided cap pulled well down on his head, he was not the man to overlook the threatening Japanese prepa-rations. To forestall the impending assault, he persuaded his British and American colleagues to try a sortie.

On the evening of February 27, he weighed anchor in the *De Ruyter*, which flew his flag with its three horizontal stripes. He was followed by H.M.S. *Exeter*, the U.S.S. *Houston*, H.M.A.S. *Perth*, and H.M.N.S. *Java*, in that order.

Led by some destroyers, he laid course northeastward to pass east of Bawean. His intention was to attack the transports on their way to the Javanese coast.

The light forces of Admiral Takagi multiplied their signals as they spotted the enemy approaching at full speed. The two Japanese cruisers increased speed. At 1616 they opened fire at 28,000 yards, while the crews of the seaplanes ran toward the catapults that were to launch them skyward to observe the effects of the fire. Fierce fire ringed the British destroyer *Electra*.

The Japanese force moving west presented itself to its adversary like the cross of a T. This enabled it to bring all guns to bear, while the allied cruisers masked each other. Admiral Doorman accordingly altered course to port. He wanted to escape from a disadvantageous tactical situation, but also to get closer, because only two of his vessels were armed with 8-inch guns, and at the existing range, the twenty-five 6-inch guns were unable to fire.

Around the *De Ruyter* and the *Exeter* huge, white, ghostly shapes rose from the water and fell like rain to flood the decks. At 1629 the two lines were parallel. The two Japanese heavy cruisers fired salvos of half broadsides; their fire, directed by the aircraft buzzing overhead, was very accurate.

At 1631, a somber red glow lit the *De Ruyter;* she had been struck, but nevertheless she maintained her speed and altered course slightly to starboard to close the range.

Meanwhile the cruiser *Naka*, flagship of Rear Admiral Nishimura, led her squadron of destroyers toward the firing at high speed. This force took station at the head of the line in a flurry of spray. At what he judged to be the right moment, the admiral altered course to port; the pendant dropped on its halyard, and forty-three torpedoes whipped the water as they shot from their tubes. They failed to reach their goal, which was still too far away. The destroyers slowed and closed in on the two cruisers. Their stacks belched torrents of black smoke, and a whitish fog, produced by special apparatus, spread out behind them.

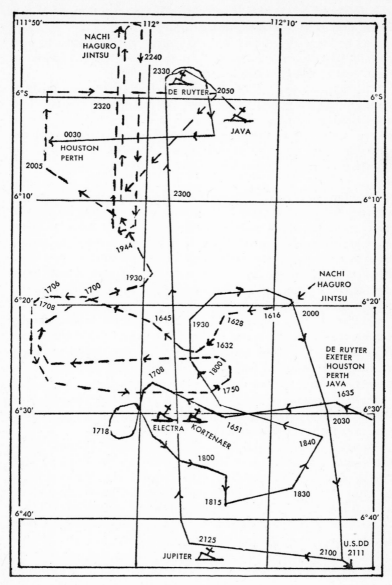

BATTLE OF JAVA SEA, FEBRUARY 27, 1942

The Allies could no longer see the results of their fire through this thick smoke screen, but the Japanese aircraft followed the Allies' movements and continued to direct the fire of their own vessels' guns.

At that point, the transports carrying the invaders of Java appeared in the northeast. Admiral Tanaka in the *Jintsu,* leading his destroyers, saw them through his glasses and cried:

"Let's finish it!"

It was 1700. Tanaka increased speed and altered course smartly to port. At his signal all his flotilla launched its torpedoes. There was an underwater onrush of formidable steel cylinders, each one capable of ripping apart the best armored vessel and drowning thousands of men. But the torpedoes had been launched in line ahead, a bad tactic, and it seemed probable that they would be wasted.

Admiral Takagi was exasperated. His two heavy warships, on a westerly course, had been firing for an hour, and although their shells had raised fountains of water all round the allied vessels, not one had been seriously hit. Nevertheless, at 1708 the *Exeter* swung sharply to port and seemed to slacken speed. It was a success due to the *Haguro,* which had chosen the English cruiser for her target. The ships following the *Exeter* also turned to port; the *De Ruyter* continued for a moment on her own. Then, when she saw herself isolated, she turned and rejoined her squadron. Near the flagship, the destroyer *Kortenaer,* probably struck by a torpedo, blew up in a great red flash.

The *Exeter*'s unexpected alteration of course had thrown disorder into the allied battle line, which tried to re-form; the vessels formed a hesitating and compact mass, an excellent target for torpedoes.

Takagi turned abruptly to port and unleashed Nishimura's destroyers to their second attack. Again a shoal of torpedoes swirled forward just beneath the surface. But the distance was again too great, and some of the torpedoes surfaced and exploded, as they had done earlier.

On their side, the allied destroyers dashed forward to avert the menace to the cruisers. H.M.S. *Electra,* aiming her eight tubes, attacked the *Jintsu;* the two other British destroyers, *Jupiter* and *Encounter*, farther away, followed suit.

Curtains of smoke still lay here and there on the scene of battle, and night had begun to fall. The *Electra* and the *Encounter* moved into one of these patches, just as three Japanese destroyers entered it from the other side; neither party knew that it had almost grazed the other.

The *Electra* came out of the smoke cloud, and as she did so, the *Jintsu* loosed on her the fire from her six 5.5-inch guns. She herself was hit but suffered only minor damage; the *Electra* had stopped and white steam billowed from her torn deck. Her boiler room had obviously been damaged. Disabled, she received a hail of shell hits, from which she was to perish.

Again the *Jintsu* and two destroyers plunged into the smoke, crossed it, and bore down on the *Exeter*, which tried to take evasive action. The big British destroyer *Jupiter*, supported by the *Encounter* and the Dutch *Witte de With*, engaged the enemy, while the *Exeter* vanished in the evening haze.

Visibility became increasingly poor; the gunfire opened brief holes of yellow light in the thickening darkness; around the big vessels, as they loosed off every gun, the destroyers continued their zigzag movements.

At 1909 the allied fleet disappeared to the northeast, covered by its destroyers.

The De Ruyter

Admiral Takagi, who saw some of the torpedoes which had been launched in earlier attacks explode at the end of their run, took them for mines and ordered the convoy, then only thirty miles away, to turn back.

The *Naka* and her escort destroyers pushed eastward to cover the southern flank of the convoy. The *Asagumo*, hit by a shell in her engine room, limped away to the northward.

The admiral, concerned for the landing force, rallied the *Jintsu* and Eastern Covering Force destroyers and sailed in a wide circle which put him twenty miles southwest of the transports, which were thus protected on both sides. Admiral Doorman had not suspected these transports to be within fifty miles of Bawean Island, which was about the same distance due north of Surabaya.

At 1927 the Japanese lookouts, straining their eyes, sighted the silhouettes of the enemy warships on a course to the northwest. These were the *De Ruyter,* the *Perth,* the *Houston,* the *Java,* and four American destroyers, with the *Jupiter* stationed one mile on the port bow of the *De Ruyter.*

The adversaries were thirteen thousand yards apart.

Star shells burst in the sky and their flares fell slowly, suspended from their parachutes. Beneath their vivid light, the surface of the sea glowed brightly and the allied ships were clearly outlined.

Fire was opened slowly at 1936. The weary men strained their will power to the utmost, but their actions were lethargic. The magazines had begun to empty, and ammunition had to be conserved.

At 1936, Admiral Doorman took evasive action against a torpedo attack, laying course to the east until 1955, when he altered course to south, thus drawing nearer to the coast. Still outlined by the flares of aircraft flying overhead, he turned west at 2100 while the American destroyers disappeared toward Surabaya.

At 2125 an explosion rent the night: the *Jupiter* had blown up on a Dutch mine. Doorman altered course at once and made off to the northward.

At 2300 the klaxons again sounded on board the *Nachi* and *Haguro,* which were on a southerly course. Fire was reopened. Takagi, to prevent the Allies from passing behind him, turned northward, parallel to his adversary.

At that moment Nishimura, determined to bring matters to a head, pressed forward at full speed. Seven hundred and fifty yards away, at point-blank range, his destroyers launched their torpedoes. The two Dutch cruisers were stopped in their tracks. The *Perth* and the *Houston* fled southward.

Flames rose from the two damaged vessels as their ammunition exploded below decks. The sea around the twisted and smoking hulls was dotted with the figures of men who had obeyed the order to jump for safety. Many of them must have sunk, exhausted, to the bottom as, one after the other, they dropped off the wreckage to which they had clung. In a few minutes, the two vessels had disappeared in the swirling water.

Admiral Doorman stood on his bridge, scorning to save himself and looking for the last time at the seas which his heroism had been unable to protect from invasion.

Point St. Nicholas

During the night, the transports of the Eastern Attack Group, a hundred miles northeast of Bawean, were ordered to resume course. Escorted by the *Naka* and her seven destroyers, this group moved toward Karanganjan, a hundred miles west of Surabaya, easily evading the submarines and aircraft.

Admiral Kurita, who had remained in Karimata Strait near Banka Island, which flanks Sumatra, laid a course on Point St. Nicholas at the northwestern end of Java.

The Javanese coast between the port of Batavia (Tanjong Priok) and Sunda Strait is fringed by hundreds of islets whose luxuriant vegetation, enriched by frequent heavy showers, shows a brilliant green against the dark water.

Banten Bay, behind the islet of Panjong, had been selected for the landing. Cape St. Nicholas is the eastern landmark of the northern entrance to Sunda Strait, the gateway to the Indian Ocean, guarded malignantly by the dark mass of Krakatau, whose double crater rises from the waves.

The landing soon started, and continued steadily. In the meantime four heavy cruisers accompanied by the aircraft carrier *Ryujo* cruised twenty miles to the north. The light cruiser *Natori* and its escort of destroyers gave close cover to the landing operations, patrolling the sectors around Banten.

During the night of February 28, at about 2330, the destroyer *Fubuki* to the east saw two vessels approaching—the *Perth* and the *Houston,* which were trying to escape through Sunda Strait.

The two cruisers saw the transports and opened fire. The *Fubuki,* turning to port, launched all her nine 21-inch torpe-

does, but these all missed their target. Already the *Sakura Maru*
was ablaze; three other transports slipped their anchors and
beached.

The two cruisers passed between Panjong Island and the
mainland, firing as they went, then turned north to double Point
St. Nicholas. But the pack of Japanese combatant ships converged on them. It was 2340 and the sea sparkled like a silver
cloak beneath the moon.

The battle which followed was fought at ranges between five
thousand and five hundred yards. As the cruisers were closing
the range, the Japanese destroyers launched attack after attack.
Four pallid sprays of water splashed the side of the *Perth*. The
Harukaze began to turn in circles, her rudder jammed by a
shell. But the damage was quickly repaired, and she joined the
Hatakaze to launch six torpedoes at the British warship.

Guns roared to the north, and the two heavy cruisers *Mogami*
and *Mikuma* were silhouetted by flashes. At 2355 the *Mikuma*,
hit by a shell from the *Houston*, ceased firing. Her electricity
supply to the guns had temporarily failed, but later she rejoined
the action.

The *Perth* was still dragging herself through the water but
made an easy target. Pierced by torpedoes and overwhelmed by
a hail of 8-inch shells, she disappeared in the waves.

Midnight passed and March had arrived.

The *Houston* continued her desperate battle, but all the Japanese fire was now concentrated on her. At 0010, steam spurted
from her torn deck as a shell burst in the engine room, cutting
the tubes and wrecking the turbines. The cruiser stopped, but
kept on firing as the men worked the guns by hand. At 0020 a
spurt of flame from the second 8-inch gun turret showed that a
shell had ignited the powder in that confined space. The American vessel rolled in her death agony, her guns smashed, her
magazines flooded, and her commander, Captain Rooks, mortally wounded.

The pack of Japanese destroyers, bounding in for the kill,
machine-gunned the superstructure of the vessel as she foun-
dered with her side torn open. At 0033, groups of men jumped
into the water, and the *Houston* too disappeared.

When the sun rose, the last act of the drama was played out in the same waters. Two Japanese warships heading north-north-east heard gunfire, and fountains of water rose round them. Binoculars disclosed the *Exeter* heading southwest toward Sunda Strait, accompanied by the destroyers *Encounter* and *Pope*.

The alarm went out by radio, and soon an aircraft arrived to circle over the cruiser like a falcon watching its prey. Admiral Takagi hurried south with the *Nachi* and the *Haguro* and discovered his adversary moving northwest. Takagi turned his gaze to starboard and gave a cry of satisfaction as his glasses disclosed the high bows of the *Ashigara* and the *Myoko*, which Admiral Takahashi, also forewarned, was leading in from the northwest.

The *Exeter*, hemmed in, was determined to sell her life dearly.

The engagement opened at 1020 at a range of seventeen thousand yards, but this was rapidly closed. The Japanese aircraft spotted the fall of shot.

About eleven o'clock, the harassed *Exeter* launched her torpedoes at the *Myoko* and the *Ashigara* to loosen their grip. The destroyers buzzed round like flies.

Half an hour later a shell hit one of the boilers in the British ship, and escaping steam shrilled from the dying vessel. She stopped, and the crew was ordered to abandon ship. One of Takahashi's destroyers gave her the *coup de grâce*.

Almost at the same time, the *Encounter* sank with a big hole in her side.

Only the *Pope* still survived. The American warship picked her way through the blankets of smoke, which lingered here and there, and hurried on to hide herself in the rain squalls. As she fled, six bombers from the *Ryujo* dived on her, one after the other, and the *Pope* slowed down, surrounded by fountains of water. A near miss had buckled her port shaft, and water entered through a hole in her side. After dropping their loads, the dive bombers moved away to the westward, but another flight replaced them, and further salvos exploded on and about the doomed ship. The old American destroyer slowly plunged into the depths.

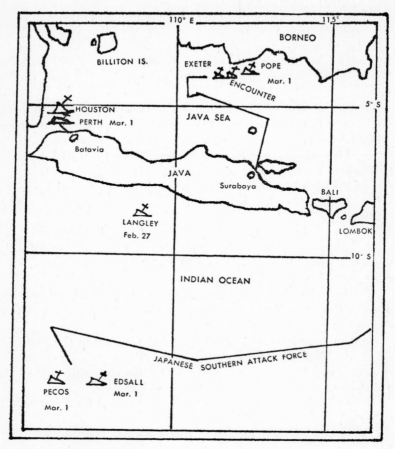

END OF ALLIED FORCES IN JAVA SEA

Through the barrier

Meanwhile, in southern Java, the Allies were relying on the port of Tjilatjap as the only place where they could still hope to land air reinforcements.

An old American aircraft carrier, the *Langley*, had been chosen to carry thirty-two aircraft to the port and had sailed in a convoy from Fremantle on February 22; but because of the immediate need for these aircraft reinforcements, she was ordered to proceed at best sustained speed without her escort.

On the morning of the twenty-seventh, at 0900, a plane passed high overhead and disappeared to the northward. A squadron of Japanese bombers of the 11th Air Fleet, which had been cooperating with Takahashi's forces after Kendari and Bandjermasin, arrived at 1140.

Nine two-engined bombers flew over the aircraft carrier at some fifteen thousand feet. As they dropped their bombs, the *Langley* turned sharply to starboard, and the bombs fell thirty-three yards to port. She escaped the second attack in the same way, but this time the bombers were strung out, and the last ones waited until the warship had completed her maneuver. In the third attack five bombs hit the ship, and she began to list. The aircraft on her deck caught fire. The ship steamed for the coast, but her engine rooms were flooded, and she lost all way. She was abandoned at 1332, and the destroyers *Edsall* and *Whipple,* which had rejoined her, sank her by gunfire and torpedo.

The survivors of the *Langley* were distributed between the two destroyers and the oil tanker *Pecos,* and the three vessels steamed southward on March 1. But Admiral Kondo was on watch; the *Hiei* and the *Kirishima* appeared and saluted the *Edsall* with their 14-inch guns. At noon, the *Pecos* was attacked by aircraft from the *Soryu,* and their work was over by 1500. Only the *Whipple,* protected by the night, was able to make her way toward Fremantle with the remaining survivors from the *Langley.*

There then remained neither naval nor air forces to participate in the defense of Java.

The land operations moved rapidly. Batavia and Bandung fell on March 5, and four days later General Ter Poorten surrendered unconditionally.

Japan's control of the Malayan and Sunda Island barriers was complete. Except for the Bataan Peninsula and Corregidor in Luzon, which held out until April 9 and May 6, respectively, all the zone north and northeast of Australia that Japan had marked for conquest in the first phase of the war was in her hands.

The Asiatic Co-prosperity Sphere rested upon solid founda-
tions, and the ultimate victory, that then seemed so certain, must
mean the realization of Japan's dream of economic preemi-
nence. [1]

---

1. *There are certain features of the Java Sea battle of February
27 that need comment. The Allies were greatly handicapped in
their attempts to operate as a tactical unit: they had no common
tactical signal code, and all orders had to be sent in plain language; this required much translation at both ends, as half the
force spoke Dutch and the other half English; they had practically no experience operating together, and were consequently
unaccustomed to each other's ways in maneuver.*

*The allied numerical superiority in cruisers meant nothing in
the long-drawn-out gun battle. The 8-inch guns of the four heavy
cruisers, two on each side, far outranged the 6-inch guns of the
three allied light cruisers. Except when the Japanese destroyers
attacked, the main batteries of those light cruisers were silent
spectators of the gun battle. Also, the Japanese had planes spotting their fall of shot, and the Allies had none, and during the
night phases of the battle, the Japanese planes kept the allied
forces illuminated with flares to supplement the star shells. The
gunnery was poor on both sides. But, with the advantages the
Japanese enjoyed, the poor quality of their marksmanship was
remarkable. Aside from the damage to the Exeter and the sinking
of the Electra, it was the torpedo and one mine that accounted
for the sinkings and main damage to the allied ships.*

*None of this is intended to becloud the very fine tactical handl-
ing of the Japanese forces throughout the battle. They deserved
their victory, but it should have been made to cost them more
than damage to one destroyer.* (R.A.T.)

OPPOSING FORCES IN JAVA SEA BATTLE, FEBRUARY 27, 1942

JAPANESE FORCES

Eastern Covering Group, **Rear Admiral Takagi**
  Nachi, Haguro   **(2 CA)***
  Destroyers, Eastern Covering Group, Rear Admiral Tanaka   (1 CL, 7 DD)
  Destroyers, Eastern Attack Group, Rear Admiral Nishimura   (1 CL, 7 DD)

UNITED STATES FORCES

Allied Striking Force, **Rear Admiral Doorman, RNN**

  H.M.S. *Exeter,* **U.S.S.** *Houston*   **(2 CA)**
  H.M.N.S. *De Ruyter,* **H.M.A.S.** *Perth,* **H.M.N.S.** *Java*   **(3 CL)**
  Netherlands destroyers: **Evertsen, Witte De With, Kortenaer**
  British destroyers: **Electra, Jupiter, Encounter**
  U.S. destroyers: **Edwards, Paul Jones, John D. Ford, Alden Pope†**

ALLIED LOSSES, FEBRUARY 27-MARCH 1, 1942

SUNK IN BATTLE OF JAVA SEA

  De Ruyter, Java, Kortenaer, Electra, Jupiter   **(2 CL, 3 DD)‡**
Sunk in Java Sea, February 28-March 1
  Houston, Exeter, Perth, Pope, Encounter, Evertsen   **(2 CA, 1 CL, 3 DD)**

* *Abbreviations:* CA, heavy cruiser; CL, light cruiser; DD, destroyer.
† Due to sinkings, heavy damage, and lack of torpedoes, the U.S. destroyers available for combat duty had been reduced to five, and the *Pope,* on detached duty on the 27th, was unable to join the forces before the battle. She is listed here because she was sunk during the Japanese mopping-up operations of the ensuing 24 hours.
‡ *Abbreviations:* CA, heavy cruiser; CL, light cruiser; DD, destroyer; OCVL, old light carrier.

Sunk in Indian Ocean, South of Java, February 27-March 1
     Langley, Edsall, Pillsbury (OCVL, 2 DD)
     Pecos (tanker)

ALLIED LOSSES IN SOUTHWEST PACIFIC CAMPAIGN, FIRST MONTHS OF 1942

UNITED STATES LOSSES

Houston (CA);* *Edsall, Stewart, Pope, Peary, Pillsbury* of 13 destroyers
Langley (OCVL); *Pecos* (tanker); *Asheville* (gunboat)
Marblehead (CL), although very badly damaged, made her way back to the United
     States.
     Boise (CL) missed the heavy late fighting of the campaign by having to retire
     for extensive repairs after striking an uncharted pinnacle rock off Timor in early
     February.

BRITISH LOSSES

Exeter (CA), *Perth* (CL), destroyers *Electra, Encounter, Jupiter*
     The only British ship to survive the campaign was the *Hobart* (CL), which was too
     low in fuel to participate in the actions at the end of February.

NETHERLANDS LOSSES

De Ruyter (CL), *Java* (CL), 7 destroyers, 1 submarine
     Tromp (CL), which had to retire to Australia for repairs after the Badung Strait
     action of February 19, was the only Netherlands vessel that survived the cam-
     paign.

* *Abbreviations:* CA, heavy cruiser; CL, light cruiser; OCVL, light carrier.

8   Spear and Armor Plate

The Japanese troops, using Siam as a base, penetrated into Burma. They took Rangoon on March 8, the eve of the surrender of Java, and then pushed onward to the Irrawaddy valley. On May 1 they occupied Mandalay, start of the Burma road and forever famed by Kipling's poem.

China was isolated, and northern India menaced.

The Andaman Islands would make a base for any allied counterattack on Burma, and the Japanese therefore occupied these on March 23. Now that the left flank against an advance upon Malaya was covered, they were reasonably secure from enemy action in those areas, with the sole exception of attacks from aircraft carriers. The two nearest allied bases were Colombo and Trincomalee on the Island of Ceylon.

Angel of death

Vice Admiral Kondo was ordered to reduce the threat represented by those bases. He left Kendari on March 26 with the battleships *Kirishima, Hiei, Haruna,* and *Kongo,* and Vice Admiral Nagumo's First Air Fleet: aircraft carriers, *Akagi, Soryu, Hiryu, Shokaku, Zuikaku;* heavy cruisers, *Tone* and *Chikuma;* light cruiser *Abukuma* and nine destroyers. This imposing squadron set course toward Colombo.

On April 5, seventy Japanese aircraft took off from the aircraft carriers and sped toward the island, whose foreshore soon appeared, fringed by high coconut palms bending their plumes above the light froth of the breakers.

To the right of Adam's Peak rose a jumble of greenery in which Lake Kandy lay like a sapphire.

Japanese fighters at once engaged the British interceptors which took off, as the bombers flew over the town, disturbing the thousands of crows which cluster there, and continued toward the port of Colombo and its dominant feature—the high building of the Grand Orient Hotel.

The roadstead was surprisingly empty.

The attacking squadrons maneuvered, heedless of the enemy fighters. The airmen, remembering Fuchida's criticisms after the bombing of Oahu, carefully picked out the workshops and all the ground installations.

The attack was costly, and twenty-four aircraft failed to return to the carriers. In the port, only a destroyer and an auxiliary cruiser had been hit. The operation had not been kept secret, and the British were expecting the attack. The ships in harbor kept a full head of steam and were able to weigh anchor at the first signal; planes on the airfields had been dispersed to prevent their being surprised and destroyed.

The afternoon of that Easter Day, however, brought compensations for the Japanese airmen. Kondo's force was on its way east, when at noon an officer hurried to the admiral with a signal from a reconnaissance aircraft: "Two big cruisers, bound eastward at twenty-seven knots, eighty miles southeast of the *Akagi.*"

Mechanics ran to the aircraft, which were still massed aft on the flight deck, and the flight leaders and captains of aircraft assembled in the briefing room.

A quarter of an hour later, following the usual routine, the formation was moving straight toward the reported position.

At 1330 the reported vessels were sighted. They were two British cruisers of ten thousand tons, trailing their long wakes in the calm sea.

The first attack was made at 1340. The dive bombers swooped on their prey, and the torpedo aircraft skimmed over the waves. Almost immediately, the *Dorsetshire,* overwhelmed, flung up her

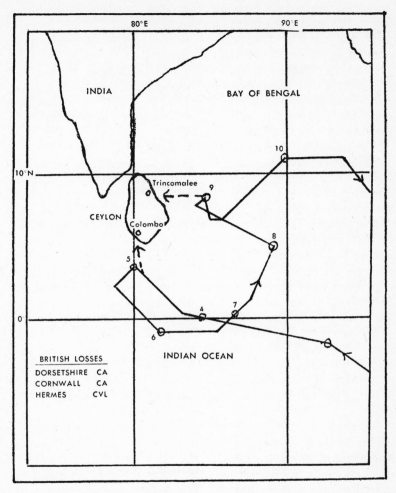

JAPANESE OPERATIONS IN THE INDIAN OCEAN, APRIL 3–10, 1942

bows and sank stern first. The storm of missiles continued to beat on the survivor, the *Cornwall,* which was struck by eight bombs. Her masts collapsed and from her burning hull shot a black pall of smoke which mingled with steam from the broken pipes. At 1359, only swirling water marked the spot where the British cruiser had last floated.

During that time, a force commanded by Admiral Kurita, comprising the small aircraft carrier *Ryuho* and six heavy cruisers, was destroying allied shipping in the Bay of Bengal. Japanese submarines were hunting off the west coast of India. Admiral Nagumo next prepared to attack Trincomalee, whose bay, the scene of one of the famed Suffren's finest pieces of seamanship, opens on the northeast corner of the island into the Bay of Bengal.

But on the afternoon of April 8 he was seen by a reconnaissance aircraft, and when, on the following day at 0725, fifty-four bombers escorted by forty fighters arrived above the harbor, they found nothing there. Eleven Hurricanes took off in time to intercept them.

It was a repetition of the attack on Colombo. The Japanese had no choice but to attack the ground installations. On their return, they found that they had again lost some twenty aircraft.

In the afternoon a reconnaissance aircraft signaled that it had sighted an aircraft carrier with an escorting destroyer. She was the old British aircraft carrier *Hermes,* which had left Trincomalee before the attack and was now returning.

The Japanese aircraft took off at once, and soon sighted the enemy off Batticaloa. Excited by the thought that at last they were able to attack an aircraft carrier, the pilots closed in for the kill and, in spite of the defenders' fire, dropped their bombs only at the last possible moment in their dives.

Twenty minutes later, hit by at least forty bombs and ablaze from stem to stern, the *Hermes* sank. The *Vampire,* her escort, was also quickly disposed of.

Fuel was now running short, and the Japanese group turned back. Admiral Nagumo again passed through Malacca Strait and brought his aircraft carriers home to Japan, to the dockyard at Kure. The admiral had every reason to be proud of his campaign. In four months he had appeared at points covering 120 degrees of longitude, one third of the earth's circumference. He had fought at Pearl Harbor, at Rabaul, at Amboina, at Port

Darwin, at Java, and at Colombo and Trincomalee. He had sunk five battleships, one aircraft carrier, two cruisers and seven destroyers, damaged several other big vessels, and sunk thousands of tons of merchant shipping. Hundreds of enemy aircraft had been destroyed, and many military installations heavily damaged.

Not one of the admiral's warships had been hit by shell, bomb, or torpedo. Like an angel of death, he had always struck from afar and remained invisible.

Lost opportunity

In February 1942, according to Japanese sources, Great Britain had made secret peace overtures to Japan.[1] It was proposed that Japan should return Malaya and Singapore to Britain, and that Britain should recognize the preponderant position of Japan in north China and should undertake to reconcile the United States and Japan to a return to their former standing. To save the faces of the Anglo-Saxon Powers, Japan was to take the initiative in proposing an armistice.

General Tojo, dazzled by the vision of the flag of the Rising Sun flying over Australia and the Indies, wanted to ignore this overture, but Seigo Nakano, leader of the *Toho kai,** who had

* The *Toho kai* was a dissident and ultranationalist group of the Democratic Party, *Minsei kai.*

---

1. *Japanese statements that Great Britain had actually made a peace proposal to Japan in the spring of 1942 seem difficult to credit. Mr. Churchill had worked long and with all his diplomatic finesse to secure the United States as an ally in the war against Hitler, and as of then, the alliance had accomplished nothing. The British Prime Minister assuredly would not have made any peace approach to Japan, no matter what the purpose behind the move, without prior consultation with President Roosevelt. And the latter would immediately have realized that, after the Pearl Harbor attack and at the nadir of the American war effort in the Pacific, the American people could not possibly have been made to understand or accept an interruption of the war against Japan.* (R.A.T.)

wind of it, felt Japanese expansionism must be stopped before
it led the country to disaster.

The struggle which developed between the two men was
ended by the death of Nakano. On October 27, 1943, he was
found face down in a pool of blood. He had committed hara-kiri
in the correct style, which demands that the body should double
up without falling on its side.

One may wonder whether, at that moment, Japan had not
missed her last opportunity to conserve something of what she
had gained. She had certainly succeeded in achieving a lightning
conquest which was even more complete and rapid than her
leaders could have hoped. But the day of reckoning fixed by
Admiral Yamamoto was near. The toughened spearhead had
pierced the adversary's armor, but the point had been blunted
in the process. The means to strengthen it was insufficient,
whereas the United States, with its matchless industrial power,
was to arm at increasing speed, to construct hundreds of vessels and thousands of aircraft, and to train with remarkable
efficiency many thousands of young airmen.

Japan's chief adversary was to have both quantity and quality,
while the air crews lost by Admiral Nagumo were never to be
replaced by men of equal combat caliber. And in May, in the
battle of the Coral Sea, the Japanese had only the two aircraft
carriers of Carrier Division 5 and one light carrier at their disposal.[2]

The Imperial Navy's traditions were the products of the Sino-
Japanese and Russo-Japanese wars in which fleet actions had
played the preponderant role and the merchant marine was
unmenaced.[3]

---

2. *That the* Shokaku *and* Zuikaku *were the only Japanese carriers
present in the Coral Sea operations between May 1 and 8, 1942,
was due to the fact that the* Akagi, Kaga, Hiryu, *and* Soryu *had
returned to Japan after their battles in the vicinity of Ceylon for
routine navy-yard overhauls and had arrived in Kure on April
22.* (R.A.T.)

3. *The tradition of immunity for vessels of the merchant marine
does not seem to be a wholly reasonable explanation. The Jap-*

Of the lessons to be drawn from 1914-1918, the Japanese historians had ignored all those which concerned submarine warfare; they grew excited only over the Coronel, Falklands, and Jutland battles, which were more spectacular and more in harmony with their romantic conception of war.

The army budget was maintained at a high level, at the expense of the navy, and as the latter was obliged to choose one policy, it decided sensibly to build and maintain a fighting fleet capable of matching that of the United States; but insufficient attention was given to the problem of the wartime protection of the nation's seaborne commerce.

On the General Staff, only one officer was concerned with the defense of internal routes, while the section for the Combined Fleet numbered ten officers. And not a single combatant unit was designated to protect maritime traffic. Troop transports were escorted by units of the Combined Fleet. The vessels engaged in providing for civilian needs were left to move on

---

anese naval officers were avid students of past naval wars. In all wars on the sea from the days of Queen Elizabeth I to and including World War I, commerce destruction and protection was always a vital and important feature of naval warfare. There can be no doubt that Japan's war plans were woefully deficient in her provisions for commerce protection, and that is one important reason why Japan's war effort weakened so noticeably after June 1944. The admirals seemed to believe that their merchant marine would be immune within the spaces of the western Pacific dominated by Japan. They overlooked, or forgot, that surface control could never prevent the infiltration of the ever-growing United States submarine force. When that force moved its base from Honolulu to the Guam-Saipan area, school was out for the practically unprotected Japanese merchant marine. Faulty planning for commerce protection in a war against the United States cannot be explained solely in terms of Japan's experiences in her wars with China and Russia. Neither country had any commerce-destruction forces of any type. Of course, in those days, the submarine had not yet become a weapon of war. (R.A.T.)

their own, so as to speed up their departures at each end of their voyages.

In December 1941 the merchant fleet was allocated as follows:—

Serving the army: 519 vessels totaling 2,160,500 tons.

Serving the navy: 482 vessels totaling 1,740,200 tons.

For civilian needs: 1582 vessels totaling 2,436,300 tons.

The civil authorities had demanded 3,000,000 tons, and the High Command had promised to return 1,100,000 tons after April, the date on which the first phase of the war was expected to end.

This phase was concluded sooner than had been expected, and without serious losses. But the American submarines were to begin hunting these vessels, which were always on the move and which fell an easy prey to them.

Meanwhile, the High Command, encouraged by its success, wanted to enlarge the occupation zone. It coveted Midway, the Aleutians, and Port Moresby, without taking into account that such operations would make additional demands on merchant shipping and also that the lines of communication would be increasingly menaced.

Replacement tonnage was not leaving the shipyards quickly enough. Because of this, Japanese seaborne communication difficulties grew, and supplies of raw material, especially oil, for the mother country dwindled. Effective organization of the conquered lands and the reinforcement of bases was to become increasingly difficult, and eventually impossible.

Most of Japan's late war troubles stemmed from this.

But in the spring of 1942, these considerations did not prevent the warriors of Japan from dreaming of victory, such a dream as has seldom fired the imagination of a race of poets and soldiers. In the four months since they had sprung upon the most fabulous wealth and splendor in the world, the Japanese had seen everything give way before them; they had only to dare, and islands and towns immediately fell into their hands, enemy fleets sank to the bottom of the sea, and generals capitulated.

It was only natural that a small, impoverished people, always bent on power and glory, should believe at such a time that their gods protected them, and that a great future was to crown their legendary "ten thousand years" of history without defeat.

9   Battle of Phantoms

The Japanese had expected to suffer between twenty and thirty percent ship losses in the conquest of the Dutch East Indies. In fact, only twenty-three warships, and all these of classes *below* that of destroyer, had been sunk (in all, 26,441 tons). This was infinitesimal from the standpoint of combat strength. Sixty-seven transports and merchant ships (314,805 tons) were sunk, or slightly less than five percent. Some hundreds of aircraft had been destroyed. The losses in men did not exceed a few thousand. Encouraged by these results, the Japanese leaders decided to speed up their strategic advances, instead of consolidating their conquests as they might have been expected to do. This meant continued enlargement of their defense perimeter through new conquests.

Operation M.O.

Three operations were envisaged: the occupation of Port Moresby in New Guinea and Tulagi in the Solomon Islands, to ensure Japanese mastery of the air over the Coral Sea; the conquest of Midway and of the western Aleutians, to enlarge the defense perimeter, to neutralize Pearl Harbor, and to draw out the American fleet, particularly its carriers, to a decisive engagement; the conquest of New Caledonia, the Fiji Islands, and the islands of Samoa, to cut the lines of communications between the United States and Australia.

These operations were planned in 1938, but the war date

of the last two operations was to be advanced in comparison with the schedule set forth in that earlier plan.

But Admiral Yamamoto saw farther into the future. He knew that, if he did not very quickly get rid of the American fleet, especially the carriers, all of which had escaped damage in the Pearl Harbor attack, he would later have to face a very powerful counterattack. For that reason, he sent his forces well beyond Far Eastern waters in search of an engagement in which Tsushima might be reenacted and the enemy naval power destroyed.

To begin with, the principal theater of the war was shifted to a part of the world which, for centuries, had seemed destined to enjoy peace.

The barrier formed by New Guinea and New Britain is extended to the southeastward by a string of islands, of which the main ones are Bougainville, Choiseul, Santa Isabel, Malaita, Guadalcanal, and San Cristobal. Upon these charming strands, forests of palm trees are reflected in the calm waters under a burning sky frequently obscured by showers. But in reality the soil of these islands is a fetid swamp, bubbling with unhealthy vapors. A few coast guards, spread over the archipelago, transmit essential information to shipping by radio and semaphore. These coast guards proved faithful to the Allies, escaping Japanese suspicion, spying on the occupation forces, and keeping the Americans informed of their movements by agreed signals.

South of New Britain lies the territory of Papua, one of the last centers of cannibalism, which comprises southeastern New Guinea and adjacent islands. Its south coast stretches to the eastward, well beyond Port Moresby. This port, with its vital airfields and facing Australia, was then in the hands of the Allies. The Japanese regarded it as a base of great value in view of the projected operations against Noumea in New Caledonia and against the southern barrier of the Coral Sea. It also made a convenient base from which to bomb Australia.

The terrain of Papua is precipitous and difficult to cross. A single track, almost impassable, climbs over the Owen Stanley mountain range. It was accordingly decided that the operation for the capture of Port Moresby would be an amphibious one.

The Japanese were unable to rely on surprise, because the enemy in Australia had some two hundred aircraft on daily patrol, and so large a movement could not escape detection by them. As to the Americans, it was presumed that they then had available only the aircraft carrier *Saratoga*.[1]

In accordance with Operation M.O., a task force organization was set up comprising the Port Moresby Invasion Group, some eleven transports, escorted by a flotilla of destroyers; the Tulagi Invasion Group, a small force whose job was to make an air base at Tulagi, in order to extend the barrier of the Solomons; a support group, comprising a seaplane tender, two light cruisers, and three gunboats, to set up an air base in the Louisiades; a covering group, under the command of Rear Admiral Goto, composed of the light aircraft carrier *Shoho,* four heavy cruisers, and a destroyer; and finally, the Carrier Striking Force, commanded by Vice Admiral Takagi and formed of the two big aircraft carriers *Shokaku* and *Zuikaku,* accompanied by two heavy cruisers and six destroyers.

The other aircraft carriers, as has been said, were not available because they needed repairs and replacement aircraft squadrons. The High Command was preparing the vital Midway expedition, so the forces destined for Operation M.O. had to be as small as possible.

Admiral Inouye, commanding the Fourth Fleet, was in supreme command of the forces selected for the action. He had his headquarters at Rabaul, where he had at his disposal six submarines and the land-based aircraft.

Inouye hoped that the Americans would react, and he banked on gripping them between the pincers formed by Goto's and Takagi's forces. The latter, coming from Truk, were to move east round San Cristobal.

---

1. *This was actually the* Lexington, *sister ship of the* Saratoga. *The latter had been torpedoed by a submarine on January 11 and was under repair at the Puget Sound Navy Yard at the time of the battle of the Coral Sea. The Japanese thought it was the* Lexington *that had been torpedoed, and they had her listed as sunk.* (R.A.T.)

The spearheads touch

At 0800 on May 3, the invasion force disembarked without difficulty at Tulagi near little Florida Island, just north of Guadalcanal, while Rear Admiral Marushige's support group cruised sixty miles to the west and Admiral Goto's powerful covering group was maintaining station south of New Georgia.

Admiral Takagi was still far to the north of Bougainville and did not enter the Coral Sea until May 4.

The American fleet, for their part, were not inactive. As previously stated, the Japanese did not keep their operations sufficiently secret. Before April 17, the American High Command knew that a Japanese force, assembling at Rabaul, was soon to enter the Coral Sea; on the twentieth, it knew that the operation would be carried out on May 3, and accordingly, the *Yorktown* group, commanded by Admiral Fletcher, and the *Lexington* group, led by Admiral Fitch, maneuvered south of Guadalcanal.

On May 4, at 0630, the harbor at Tulagi echoed to the roar of engines, and bombs sent fountains of water spouting everywhere. The crews of some small vessels, which had been there since the previous evening to cover the landing, ran to their guns; but already the silver machines had departed on their return journey to the *Yorktown*, which was waiting for them a few dozen miles away.

The destroyer *Kikuzuki* had been slightly damaged by a bomb, and a minesweeper had been holed in the side.

At 0730, came a second wave which destroyed two seaplanes. At 1400, a third attack sank four landing craft.

The results were slight; the American reaction had been too late; the transport had begun its return voyage to Rabaul, as soon as the mission was accomplished.

Blind ballet

Admiral Takagi had held his Carrier Striking Force north of Bougainville, where he had met the tankers which were to refuel his fleet. Protected by enormous fenders, the heavily laden tankers steamed alongside the big vessels, the oil hoses were quickly passed across, the pumps were soon at work, and the fuel was pouring into the tanks. At noon, as Admiral Takagi was watching the operation from the bridge, an officer hurried to him with a signal in his hand.

"Admiral, Tulagi was attacked this morning by American planes."

The admiral straightened up, entered the chart house, and was quickly measuring distances on the chart with his compasses. He was given a report of the progress of the refueling.

A few minutes later the oil tankers stood away. Signal flags were run up. The vessels of the striking force sped southeast at twenty-five knots, to gain a position one hundred miles north of Santa Isabel by midnight.

Meanwhile, the *Yorktown* after her raid again steamed to the southward, and joined the *Lexington* at 0816 on May 5. On the way, her patrol fighters shot down a scouting seaplane from Rabaul.

Admiral Inouye learned that the aircraft had not returned, and he quite rightly assumed that it had been shot down, but he did not know where. Meanwhile, the invasion fleet bound for Port Moresby had set out in accordance with the operation plan. The six destroyers of Rear Admiral Kajioka, on board the *Yubari*, escorted the five transports, carrying the special naval landing force, toward Jomard Strait in the Louisiades, and Marushige's Support Group cleared the way ahead.

At 1900 on May 5, Takagi at last cleared San Cristobal, turned west, and passed north of Rennel Island, still steaming at twenty-five knots. As for Goto, he had gone to the Shortland Islands to refuel and was to sail again at 0800 on the sixth.

That day, cloudy weather hampered air reconnaissance. The aircraft, lost in the clouds, could see the water only through occasional rifts. Takagi had been sailing south since 0930, and Admiral Fletcher after refueling had turned northwest to approach Port Moresby. The two enemy forces closed each other until they were only seventy miles apart. With only a slight change of course or an opportune strengthening of the wind to improve the visibility, the fleets might clash, and engage unexpectedly in a great naval battle. But neither side suspected that.

As this situation was developing, the low visibility had handicapped the Japanese who, with luck, might have surprised their enemy while refueling.

But it was then Takagi's turn to need fuel, because at high speeds ships consume oil very rapidly, and he therefore turned north to his waiting tankers.

Meanwhile, at 1030 the same day, while Goto's force was sixty miles south of Bougainville, four Flying Fortresses appeared in the sky. The *Shoho*'s fighters were already up. Bombs fell not far from the aircraft carrier, but her crew were avidly watching the fierce air battle. The Fortresses trailed sparks as the Japanese dived on them, climbed, and dived again. One after the other, the four big aircraft caught fire and finally whirled seaward with black smoke pouring from them, followed by the fighters waggling their wings in token of victory.

About 1200, other aircraft appeared and vanished, too far off for pursuit; an hour later, they were seen again by the Invasion Group.

Inouye was warned, and he concluded that two of his formations had been sighted by the enemy. He believed that Fletcher was five hundred miles southeast of the Japanese forces which, according to the admiral's calculations, would be attacked on the seventh. At 1520, he confirmed the plan's timetable.

The transports were to pass through Jomard Strait, just east of the foul water which extended out from the eastern point of Papua, at midnight, protected by the small aircraft carrier *Shoho*, which was attached to Goto's force and carried only twelve fighters and a dozen torpedo aircraft. She was to launch antisubmarine patrols to a radius of fifteen miles. On the evening of the sixth, about 1815, the *Shoho* accordingly recalled her aircraft and set course to the west-southwest so as to reach her launching position at the scheduled time on the following day. At midnight, she was ninety miles northeast of Deboyne, where the seaplane carrier *Kanikawa* was also standing by to start her aircraft reconnaissance.

Air surprises

On May 7, at the request of Rear Admiral Hara commanding the group of big aircraft carriers, Takagi ordered an air reconnaissance, to obviate the possibility of a threat to his rear, before sailing westward to provide closer coverage for the convoy.

At 0736, a plane signaled the presence of an aircraft carrier, accompanied by a cruiser.

Two waves of planes took off immediately from the *Zuikaku* and the *Shokaku* and flew toward the designated position, where they saw the American oil tanker *Neosho* and destroyer *Sims*. The latter was soon struck by a 500-pound bomb, and sank. The *Neosho*, hit by seven bombs, caught fire and burned until May 11, when she was scuttled. The Japanese aircraft returned —and experienced one of the most painful surprises of the naval air war. In the thin mist, they saw the enemy aircraft carriers—but they had no bombs left. Seething with rage, the airmen could only continue on their way and signal their discovery.

Admiral Fletcher had continued on his course northwest. At 0625, on the seventh, he was 115 miles from Russell Island; half an hour later he turned north and ordered Admiral Crace's Support Group, which comprised three cruisers and two destroyers, to continue northwest to attack the Port Moresby Invasion Force.

Admiral Crace pressed ahead, but at 1358 a group of aircraft from Rabaul made a furious attack on his ships, placing the small squadron in the same situation as that of the *Prince of Wales* and *Repulse* some five months earlier—under heavy air attack without any defending aircraft. On this occasion, however, the engagement turned out very differently. The attackers were greeted by an inferno of fire; the vessels spread out and zigzagged continually, so that the bombs fell in the sea and the torpedoes passed ahead or astern of the cruisers as they danced their giddy ballet. And when the aircraft had dropped every bomb and were compelled to leave, not a single vessel had been touched.

On his arrival 120 miles south of New Guinea, Crace learned

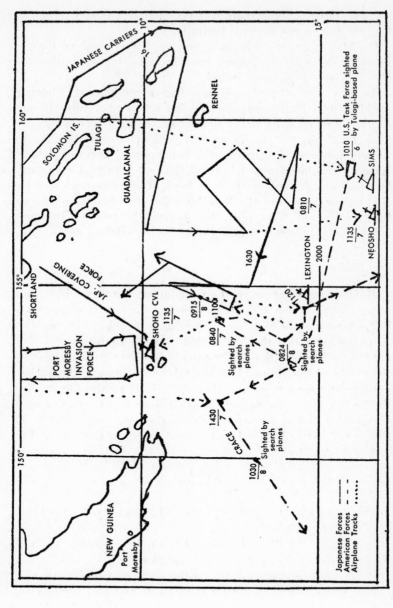

CORAL SEA ACTION, MAY 7–8, 1942

that the Japanese transports had reversed course and retired, so he held his course toward Australia.

On May 7, at 0700, Goto's forces, on a west-southwest course south of Bougainville, turned into the wind to the southeast to launch a reconnaissance patrol.

At 0830, the Covering Group had reconnoitered Fletcher's position. The *Shoho* prepared for an attack: her aircraft were in the air or on deck ready to take off, and all precautions had been taken on the carrier against fires and leaks. But the expected Japanese transports did not appear, because Admiral Inouye, who had learned in good time of Admiral Crace's raid, had ordered the convoy to turn back. The movement was carried out at 0900, and the Port Moresby Invasion Group moved back to Rabaul. That operation against the port on the south coast of New Guinea was never to be undertaken again.

The Shoho

But fleets were at sea, and an encounter was inevitable. About 1030, Goto's group saw some aircraft; they soon disappeared, but were certainly Fletcher's observation machines. Preparations were made against the forthcoming attack. Bombers and fighters took off to free the *Shoho*'s deck; the four cruisers took stations around the aircraft carrier at a good distance; the anti-aircraft guns were ready for action. At 1110 the enemy arrived.

The ten American torpedo aircraft from the *Lexington* dived seaward, and the Japanese fighters dropped from above; the *Shoho* twisted and turned and altered speed, as she watched the wakes of the torpedoes. She escaped the first wave, and the only losses were five aircraft which had been hurled into the sea from her decks. At 1125 an attack came in from the *Yorktown*.

The few fighters, some of which had been up for a long time, had not been able to regain altitude. One of the first blows struck the *Shoho* aft and rendered her rudder useless. Then the drama began. Like condors dropping on their prey, the bombers and the torpedo aircraft dived on the paralyzed carrier. In a few minutes she had been hit by thirteen bombs and seven torpe-

does and was burning everywhere. She sank at 1136. Destroyers came to save those survivors who had been able to jump
into the water, but of 1200 men, only 700 were picked up.

The Japanese aircraft in the air turned toward land or the
Zuikaku, where they refueled while waiting for further work.
Goto's Covering Group, now without an aircraft carrier, withdrew
to the northwest.

Only the aircraft carrier forces of Fletcher and Takagi now
remained on the scene.

A new form of war

For forty-eight hours these powerful squadrons struck blindly
at each other from considerable distances. Such are the new
conditions of naval warfare. They are very different from the
furious fights at close quarters of Nelson's or Surcouf's days, and
even far removed from the big artillery battles, like that of the
Falklands, where at least the ships present could see each other
as they exchanged their deadly blows. Now enemy fleets are as
phantoms to each other.

A commander receives, by radio, information which allows
him to locate his adversary, some hundreds of miles away, and
with a telephone call he lets loose against his invisible enemy
an air force carrying fire and steel.

Often the air forces pass each other halfway, so that the battle is, as it were, divided into two parts; on either side, the vessels struggle against an aerial assault like bulls attacked by
wasps. The two battlefields are separated by immense spaces
across which the air squadrons retreat after their attack; and in
this seemingly empty desert, obscure dramas are played out:
crippled machines fall, their strength exhausted; aircraft lose
their way and finish by crashing into the sea or into the undergrowth of some savage island; others are unable to rejoin their
vessels, which have been sunk in the meantime.

It is understandable that in these conditions there is, so to
speak, only one type of vessel that counts—the one which carries the only arm capable of striking the far-off, phantom force
after its discovery well beyond the horizon. In the battle of the

Coral Sea, as in almost all those which were to follow it, the former capital ships, the battleships, played an unobtrusive and decidedly minor role—that of the "star" suddenly out of date and appearing in a drama of which she no longer knows the plot. The Pacific war was to be, above all, a war of aircraft carriers. And that was seen clearly, for the first time, during the days of May 7 and 8, 1942.[2]

Wrong address

Fletcher did not know that the invasion force had changed its mind; he expected it to debouch from Jomard Strait on the morning of May 8, and he accordingly made his way to the westward.

About 1660 Admiral Takagi ordered the *Shokaku* to send a group of twelve bombers and fifteen torpedo aircraft to seek out his adversary. They made their reconnaissance on a radius of some three hundred miles.

Around the estimated position of the American force, the Japanese cast back and forth; but low clouds almost at water level limited visibility. Night fell, and they had to return; the hunt had produced no results, and the reserves of aviation fuel were running low.

---

2. *There is no question about the fact that the carrier has supplanted the battleship as the primary ship of present-day navies. But the battleship still has its wartime uses. At night or in periods of low visibility, the powerful surface ships are very comforting assets to the force commander, as the* Washington *and* South Dakota *proved on the night of November 14-15, 1942. On the night of the battle of Midway, Admiral Spruance could not hold a course to the westward because his weak surface forces, including his carriers, would be wiped out by Yamamoto's powerful fleet if the two should come into close contact during the night. If Spruance could have kept reasonably close to the Japanese fleet until daylight, his air forces could have taken a heavy toll of those enemy forces, with their own undisputed control of the air.* (R.A.T.)

After dropping their bombs into the water to lighten the aircraft, the crews turned back to their nest. In the thickening gloom, they saw the shapes of aircraft carriers sooner than they expected, and some of the planes maneuvered to land on them. They switched on their lights and flew toward the sterns of the vessels according to regulations, but something struck them as abnormal—the deck lights were not those to which Japanese pilots were accustomed. Suddenly the pilots smothered exclamations of surprise and anger. The ships were American! A few moments more and the Japanese pilots would have covered themselves with shame and ridicule by handing themselves over with their machines to the enemy it was their duty to destroy. Engines roared furiously as the pilots pulled their sticks hard back, and the squadron passed overhead almost at masthead height, climbing rapidly.

But Admiral Fletcher's crews had seen the air group, and fighters took off to open a violent battle. The Japanese defended themselves stubbornly and escaped in the darkness, but ten of them had been shot down. The others at last arrived over the *Shokaku* where, on the deck, a red and a green light marked the axis of the runway. A signaler directed the landings.

It is not easy to land on an aircraft carrier at night, and among the pilots who circled while they waited for their turn to land, were some whose hearts beat faster because it was their first experience in such a maneuver.

Acting Sublieutenant Ishikawa, who piloted a dive bomber, at last made out the signal which ordered him to land; and now that he had to act, his apprehension vanished; all his attention was absorbed in the piloting of his machine.

He turned away toward the stern of the vessel, banked and approached, while trying to keep the red and green lights in alignment. He lowered his flaps and reduced speed. The dark mass of the aircraft carrier grew larger and then became enormous; the deck appeared more clearly and seemed to approach at dizzy speed. Ishikawa cut the engine and pulled back on the stick; he felt a lurch and had just time to hear screams before a gigantic impact knocked him senseless.

Misled by the darkness, he had acted too soon, and the aircraft stalled. It lay now, a heap of scrap iron encumbering the stern with broken wings, the propeller twisted after beating the deck, and fuel trickling from the burst tanks, although luckily it did not catch fire.

A beam from an electric torch picked out what had been the cockpit and disclosed among the debris a crushed, helmeted head.

The runway had to be cleared, and a squad approached and pushed away this chaos of metal, fabric, and flesh which shortly before had been an aircraft and its crew. One last effort, and there was the noise of a splash; the broken bits of debris remaining were kicked overboard, and it was the next plane's turn to land.

When the operation was over, eleven aircraft had been destroyed as the result of bad handling, and the bridge structure bore the marks of a fire which had destroyed one of the aircraft that had crashed against it.

Inouye now knew where the Americans were, and intended to try a night attack. Goto's cruisers and the escort destroyers were to leave their convoy and swoop on the enemy.

On board the *Myoko*, Captain Yamaoka, a specialist in aviation, also advised Takagi to order a night attack to compensate for the failure of the day. The admiral approved, and gave the necessary instructions to his chief of staff, but a signal from Rabaul stated that Rear Admiral Abe, who was bringing the transports of the Port Moresby Invasion Force back to that port, feared for the safety of those vessels and asked for protection. Admiral Inouye had yielded to this request. Goto sent two heavy cruisers to reinforce Takagi's Carrier Force. This, on orders from Rabaul, was to provide air protection for the transport convoy, which the rest of Rear Admiral Goto's Covering Force was to rejoin.

On receiving these orders, Takagi leapt to his feet, dismayed at this lost opportunity. Then he resigned himself. "After all," he said to Yamaoka, "my principal mission is to protect the transports."

At 2200 the carrier landings on the *Shokaku* were completed. The Carrier Striking Force set course to the north, diverging from Fletcher, who was heading southeast.

At the limit of the "cold front"

At dawn on May 8 the Japanese were in a "cold front," where the warmer air condenses to form thick, low-lying clouds and rain squalls, both of which adversely affect the visibility conditions. The Americans, on the contrary, were in a sunny zone; their two aircraft carriers, five heavy cruisers, and seven screening destroyers could be seen from afar.

At 0600 Rear Admiral Hara, who sensed that the day would be decisive, sent a flight to scout a two-hundred-mile sector between southwest and southeast.

An hour later, he launched ninety-nine attack aircraft toward the center of the sector, and at 0825 steamed at thirty knots toward the estimated enemy position. The *Shokaku* and the *Zuikaku* were on parallel courses, eight miles apart, each protected by two cruisers and several destroyers. Additional aircraft took off from the *Shokaku* at 0915.

In the meantime, the *Lexington* too had launched eighteen search aircraft. One of these had the luck, at 0815, to sight the Japanese Carrier Force.

There were 121 Japanese aircraft in the air and 122 American, and they passed each other in their flights toward their respective adversaries.

The *Shokaku* was the first to be attacked, just as she entered the light. While altering course to avoid the American torpedo aircraft, she was hit by two bombs, in spite of the protection of her fighters. One of the bombs struck forward, and a flame of gasoline spurted in the capstan compartment, which had become a twisted mass of scrap. The other bomb fell aft on the starboard side and destroyed the engine repair shop.

The damage-control squads hurried toward the flames and used asbestos padding to block the openings through which air could enter; the extinguishers spat out their white froth and soaked the bulkheads, which were already a glowing red.

While the fight was being waged against fire, the *Shokaku* zigzagged to dodge the torpedoes. The Americans launched them from far off and their speeds were slow as they neared their target, obviously very close to their limiting range. The ship's commander and her navigator, kept informed by lookouts, followed the courses of the dangerous wakes through glasses and dodged them one after the other, sometimes turning the bow toward them, sometimes the stern.

When the *Zuikaku* in her turn emerged from the screen of bad weather, her crew was disturbed to see the burning *Shokaku*. The two vessels exchanged signals which reassured Admiral Hara that the *Shokaku* had mastered the blaze and that, save for unforeseeable events, she was in no danger. Her deck forward was torn up and no longer usable for take-off; but landings were still possible. Losses of personnel were heavy, totaling 108 killed and forty wounded.

The two carriers stayed near the edge of the cold front to escape attacks and to be ready, when the time came, to dash out and gather in their squadrons.

These tactics were judicious. The *Lexington*'s aircraft, which formed a second wave of attack, circled without seeing anything. Only some twenty torpedo aircraft found the Japanese, and they took up their positions for attack, but the Japanese fighters, circling above the vessels, dived on the attackers and shot down three. The others launched their torpedoes at too great a range, and these, consequently, were avoided without difficulty.

Death of "Lady Lex"

The parallel drama started at 1055, when the Japanese flights saw the American aircraft carriers with their decks empty. Only a few fighters took to the air, and they were immediately engaged by the Japanese, who had the advantage in both numbers and altitude.

The wind blew from the north-northeast, aiding the Japanese, who also had the sun at their backs. They were hard to make out: the gunpointers were dazzled, and their aim was poor.

At 1118 the attacking formation opened out, and two groups of torpedo aircraft dropped to water level, separated, and attacked from opposite sides of the *Lexington* to prevent her from taking evasive action. At a distance, averaging a few thousand yards, the torpedoes were launched and, driven by compressed air, made rapidly toward their target.

A fountain of water rose to port ahead of the *Lexington* and another to starboard. The pilots of the dive bombers then went into their dives, and the target grew in the bombsights until, at some two thousand feet, the pilots released their bombs and then climbed with engines screaming. At such moments, pilots "black out" for a few seconds, because of the tremendous rate of acceleration. As they turned back, they were delighted to see black smoke, streaked with flame, coiling in heavy rolls from the burning *Lexington*.

The *Yorktown* was also attacked, at 1120, by torpedo aircraft. She was threatened from one side only and altered course sharply so as to parallel the courses of the approaching torpedoes, which then passed her on both sides.

A few minutes later came the dive bombers' turn. The vessel shuddered under the shock of a 750-pound-bomb hit which penetrated as far as the fourth deck and exploded, killing sixty-six men. The fire which broke out sent smoke pouring through the hole in the flight deck.

The Japanese aircraft returned to their carriers. Four landed correctly on the *Shokaku*, but the others, seeing her still smoking, landed on the *Zuikaku*, which had room for them, because forty-three of her own aircraft failed to return.

The attack commander, as soon as he landed, hurried to Admiral Hara, waiting on the bridge, and reported:

"Admiral, the two enemy carriers are sinking."

From the deck, rose yells of triumph, as the news of the victory spread rapidly among the crews.

The admiral ordered the *Shokaku* to set course for Japan. The damaged vessel moved away to the northeast at 1300 and arrived in port after almost capsizing during the voyage.

On the American side the *Yorktown* had soon been able to extinguish the fires and was still capable of launching and receiving aircraft. The *Lexington,* after superhuman efforts, seemed saved when, at 1247, an unusual accident occurred. A running motor exploded the gases that had accumulated in a compartment which had been struck by a torpedo an hour and a half earlier. The fire broke out again with extreme violence, and the crew was forced to abandon ship. At 2000, "Lady Lex," as her crew called her, was swallowed up in a whirlpool.

At 1800 Admiral Inouye ordered Takagi to return to Truk. The attack on Port Moresby was postponed to July 3, because American land-based aircraft had become very active and were keeping a strict watch on the approaches. Also the *Shoho* was no longer there to protect the convoy, and there was only one aircraft carrier then available in the sector.

At midnight a signal from general headquarters was brought to Admiral Takagi. It was an order from Admiral Yamamoto: "Finish off the enemy."

On the ninth, at 0200, the Carrier Striking Force, minus the *Shokaku,* accordingly sailed southeast, then southwest, but without success.

At noon the following day, Goto's Covering Group, freed by the return of the convoy to Rabaul, joined Takagi who, on the eleventh, at last received the order to cease the operation.

Inouye had just learned that two new American aircraft carriers, the *Enterprise* and the *Hornet,* had been sighted 450 miles east of Tulagi. These two warships had been sent to reinforce Fletcher but had left Pearl Harbor too late to participate in the Coral Sea operations of those May days in 1942.

The warning

As mentioned earlier, the battle of the Coral Sea was the first in which fleets hundreds of miles apart made contact only by aircraft, which struck the opponent like long-range missiles.

This battle is an excellent illustration of the contrast between the tactical results and strategic consequences which so frequently characterizes these events in war.

Tactically, this was a drawn affair, as both opponents withdrew after the carrier strikes of May 8. Japan did have a distinct advantage in the ship losses sustained: the combat strength of the *Lexington* plus the *Sims* far outweighed that of the *Shoho*. But Japan's losses in aircraft and highly trained pilots marked the start of an attrition that was to become increasingly detrimental to the war efforts of her navy, from Midway on. Her enemy, from the first days of the war, had instituted tremendous programs of pilot training and aircraft and ship construction that Japan did not attempt to match. She could not have kept pace, and she did not make the effort.

Strategically, the Japanese amphibious thrust upon Port Moresby had been frustrated and was not again attempted. The advance which was designed eventually to seal off the American-Australian sea communications and establish bases for the invasion of Australia—the progressive occupation of the Solomons, the New Hebrides, New Caledonia, and finally the Fiji and Samoan Islands—had been stalled, for the time being at least.

The *Shokaku* limped home for lengthy repairs, and the *Zuikaku* returned, a little later, so weakened in aircraft and trained pilots that she was not considered available for the Midway operation, for which the fleet sailed at the end of May. What effect the presence of these two carriers would have had on the Midway battle must always remain in the realm of speculation. It cannot be disputed that six carriers against three is far greater odds than four against three, the ratio that actually existed on the day of battle.

JAPANESE FORCES IN PORT MORESBY OPERATIONS (CORAL SEA BATTLES), MAY 4-10, 1942

Task Force "M.O.," Vice Admiral Inouye (in Rabaul)

Carrier Striking Force, Vice Admiral Takagi
　　Zuikaku, Shokaku (42 fighters, 41 dive bombers, 42 torpedo bombers)　(2 CV)*
　　Myoko, Haguro　(2 CA)

* *Abbreviations:* CV, aircraft carrier; CVL, light carrier; CA, heavy cruiser; CL, light cruiser.

Screens: 6 destroyers
Invasion Force, Rear Admiral Goto

Covering Group, Rear Admiral Goto
Aoba, Kako, Kinugasa, Furutaka (4 CA)
Shoho (12 fighters, 9 torpedo bombers) (CVL)
Screen: 1 destroyer

Port Moresby Invasion Group, Rear Admiral Kajioka
Convoy: 11 transports, 1 tanker, 1 repair ship, 1 minelayer
Supports and Escorts: 1 light cruiser, 6 destroyers, 5 minesweepers
Support Unit: 2 light cruisers, 1 seaplane tender

Tulagi Invasion Group, Rear Admiral Shima
1 transport, 2 destroyers, 2 minelayers, 5 minesweepers, 2 subchasers

Land-Based Air Force (after reinforcement from Truk on May 4)
At Rabaul: 57 fighters, 86 dive bombers, 3 seaplanes
At Lae: 6 fighters
At Shortlands: 3 seaplanes
At Tulagi: 6 seaplanes

ALLIED FORCES IN PORT MORESBY OPERATIONS (CORAL SEA BATTLES), MAY 4-10, 1942

Task Force 17, Rear Admiral F. J. Fletcher

Task Group 17.1, Rear Admiral A. W. Fitch
Yorktown, Lexington (42 fighters, 25 dive bombers, 25 torpedo bombers) (2 CV)*
Screen: 4 destroyers

Attack Group, Task Group 17.2, Rear Admiral Fletcher
Minneapolis, New Orleans, Astoria, Chester, Portland (5 CA)
Screen: 5 destroyers

Support Group, Task Group 17.3, Rear Admiral J. G. Crace RN
H.M.A.S. *Australia,* U.S.S. *Chicago,* H.M.A.S. *Hobart* (2 CA, 1 CL)
Screen: 2 destroyers

* *Abbreviations:* CV, aircraft carrier; CA, heavy cruiser; CL, light cruiser.

PART THREE
The Emperor's Portrait

10 The Decisive Moment

The Japanese had lacked the means to make a landing at Pearl Harbor in December 1941. Their carefully conceived plans at that time embraced nothing beyond the surprise air attacks. The island of Midway therefore represented an advance position of great value to them. The importance of the island had been increased by the conquest of Wake, because Midway was the most westerly of the American bases, but beyond the range of attacking aircraft based on Wake.

Midway was a desolate rock, occupied only since 1903. It served as a station for the Honolulu-Guam-Manila cable and, in peacetime, as a staging point for trans-Pacific planes.

On the morning of December 8, Midway, like so many other American positions, was bombed. The seaplanes that carried out the bombing had been transported by two tenders and two destroyers. After that, the isle had also been bombarded by submarines, but without serious damage.

The conquest of Midway was part of the project to enlarge the "security perimeter" which was to be staked out by Kiska in the Aleutians, Midway, Wake, the eastern Marshalls, the Gilberts, the Solomons, New Caledonia, and Port Moresby.

On April 18, American army aircraft, launched from the *Hornet* and the *Enterprise*, 666 miles from Tokyo, bombed the Japanese capital, before going on to land in China. Japan was thus made to realize that the city in which her Emperor resided was no longer immune from such attacks, but the

General Staff wished to assure that everything possible was done to prevent a repetition.

Japanese aircraft based on Midway, operating in cooperation with those from Kiska and Wake, would be able to discover any naval force trying to pierce the northern sectors of the security perimeter.

Yamamoto was convinced that he must destroy the United States fleet in 1942 if the war were not to be lost. He believed that an attack on such an advanced position would force his enemies to undertake measures for its defense and thus enable him to crush them. His particular aim was to destroy the American carriers, all of which had escaped damage on December 7, 1941.

The Chief of the General Staff, Admiral Nagano, shared these hopes and aims. Convinced in its turn, Imperial Headquarters published the following order, dated May 5, 1942:

"The commander in chief of the Combined Fleet in cooperation with the army will invade and occupy strategic points in the Aleutians and on Midway."

Another plan was in preparation (for the third phase of the war), which envisaged the seizure of Fiji, Samoa, and New Caledonia.

Striking force versus task force

Yamamoto had a three-point plan on which he had been meditating for a long time—the occupation of the Aleutian islands; the occupation of Midway; and a decisive naval engagement.

The plan of operations was as follows:

1. The 2nd Carrier Striking Force would bomb Dutch Harbor to contain the Americans while the western Aleutians were being occupied.

2. The 1st Carrier Striking Force would bomb Midway and be prepared to attack the American fleet, should it come out. When the enemy had been thus weakened, Battleship Division 1 of the main body would hurry to the battle area to finish it off.

3. On the evening of June 5, Midway would be attacked by the five thousand troops of the Invasion Force and, as soon as it was taken, would be turned into a base for both seaplanes and land-based aircraft.

The Aleutian Screening Force would be detached from the Main Body in time to cover the northern operations and would maintain station between Midway and the Aleutians, to intercept northbound American formations.

Preliminary scouting operations were undertaken by aircraft based at Marcus, Wake, and Paramushiro.

On the strength of the battle reports, Yamamoto thought that the enemy had lost two aircraft carriers in the Coral Sea. He estimated that the Americans would be slow to react to Japanese movements when these were discovered, and that Midway would be taken without difficulty. He therefore expected that, when the decisive engagement started, the Americans would quickly find themselves in a very difficult tactical situation.

Admiral Chester Nimitz was fully warned of the Japanese intentions and made his tactical dispositions accordingly. Midway was reinforced and provided with radar.

The three aircraft carriers available at Pearl Harbor provided the backbone for two task forces. Task Force 17 was commanded by Rear Admiral Fletcher and comprised the *Yorktown*, two heavy cruisers, and five destroyers. Task Force 16, commanded by Rear Admiral Spruance, comprised the aircraft carriers *Enterprise* and *Hornet*, five heavy cruisers, one light cruiser, and nine destroyers. Nineteen American submarines set out to keep watch on the principal sectors of approach to Midway, and finally Admiral Nimitz created a North Pacific Force, commanded by Rear Admiral Robert A. Theobald and comprising two heavy cruisers, three light cruisers, and ten destroyers.

The opposing fleets thus comprised practically all the naval forces available on each side. The balance both in numbers and in fighting strength was strongly in favor of Japan, largely because of the effects of the Pearl Harbor attack and the dispersal of carrier strength to the Atlantic, but the Japanese

superiority was less than they believed it to be. The Americans
were operating near their own bases, and above all, they would
not be taken by surprise, because they knew what to expect
and had planned timely countermeasures based upon that knowledge. The attackers had a psychological advantage in that they
were full of resolution and confidence—the result of continuous
success since the start of the war.

The golden chrysanthemum

Most of the Japanese submarines were deployed to watch
Oahu; on June 3 they occupied a line running from north-
northeast to south-southwest, across the direct route from
Oahu to Midway, to intercept, report, and attack the American Pacific Fleet when it left Hawaii. But the boom went down
too late: that fleet was already well to the northward when
the watch was set.

Admiral Kakuta's Second Carrier Striking Force was the first
to weigh anchor to head for his task in the Aleutians, and on
May 26 Admiral Nagumo's Striking Force left the Inland Sea
via Bungo Strait.

Admiral Yamamoto's Main Body put to sea on May 28, the
admiral flying his flag in the magnificent, 63,000-ton battleship *Yamato*, a name recalling the original land given by the
gods to the early ancestors of the Emperor. At the battleship's
bow shone the big golden chrysanthemum which is borne on
the Imperial arms. The nine 17.9-inch guns defied any adversary.

The transports destined for Midway left Saipan on the
evening of the twenty-seventh, and Rear Admiral Kurita's Close
Support Group left Guam at the same time to maintain station
some seventy-five to a hundred miles on the flank of the Invasion
Group.

War songs echoed in all the ships.

But Admiral Nagumo was anxious. He thought the training
was insufficient, and that the situation of the opposing fleet
constituted an agonizing enigma.

The Japanese forces remained undetected longer than might
have been expected, thanks to bad weather. The daily Ameri-

can aerial reconnaissances from Midway entered a zone of cloud, three hundred miles from their base, which prevented them from seeing anything.

Nevertheless, at 0915 on June 3, an American aircraft circled the transports, which were then six hundred miles west of Midway, and in the evening at 1700, nine Fortresses attacked from heights between sixteen thousand and nineteen thousand feet. But every bomb fell into the water. About midnight, two or three torpedo aircraft dived seaward and water shot up ahead of the oil tanker *Akebono Maru*. The planes flew over the transports, machine-gunning the decks and bridges.

The *Akebono* did not sink, and the transports moved on at a modest ten knots.

The American aircraft signaled Fletcher that they had sighted the Japanese Battle Fleet to the west, but the admiral, who had left Pearl Harbor at 0900 to join Spruance on June 2, 325 miles north-northeast of Midway, knew it to be an error and that the real attack would come from the northwest.

The admiral's choice

On June 4, day broke soon after four o'clock. The wind, which had been blowing briskly from the southeast, dropped about 0800, and visibility was from thirty-five to forty miles.

The Japanese aircraft took off at 0430, when the Air Striking Force had arrived within 240 miles of Midway.

Following their usual custom, the aircraft circled over the squadron until the flights were complete, before the formation, comprising thirty-six high-level bombers (each carrying a 1764-pound bomb), thirty-six dive bombers, and thirty-six fighters, vanished to the southeast.

Then the four carriers began the exasperating wait that must endure until the attackers' return, several hours later. Admiral Nagumo paced the bridge. The *Akagi* was at the head of the starboard column, followed at four thousand-odd yards astern by the *Kaga*. Some four thousand yards to port was the high silhouette of the *Hiryu*, followed by the *Soryu*. The *Kirishima* kept station midway between the *Akagi* and the

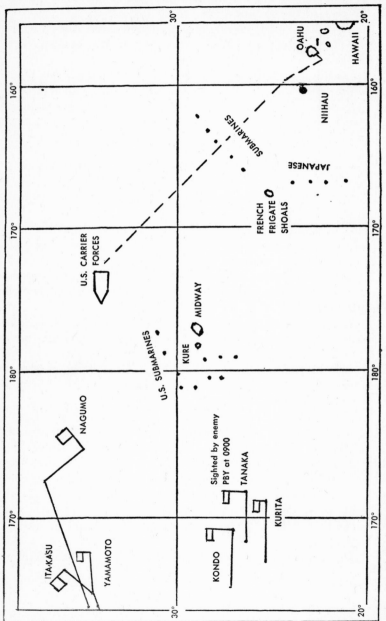

POSITION OF MIDWAY OPPOSING FORCES, 0900, JUNE 3, 1942

Hiryu and slightly ahead. The *Haruna* kept symmetrical station at the rear of the group.

All the ships were zigzagging to dodge submarines, while twenty-eight fighters, relieved every two hours, buzzed high in the sky.

Meanwhile, warned by radar which had picked up the Japanese approach, the aircraft took off from Midway to intercept the attackers. They were dominated by the Japanese fighters and scattered, and the first bomb fell at 0630. The island looked like a volcano belching enormous clouds of smoke, but the flames were from burning gasoline.

The command post was destroyed, together with the power house on Eastern Island, the fuel oil tanks on Sand Island, and the seaplane hangar. The gasoline installation was also seriously damaged.

But there had been strong resistance in the air and by anti-aircraft fire, and many of the Japanese aircraft were hit, although all but five returned to their carriers.

At 0710 the Japanese striking force saw ten American torpedo aircraft approaching without escort and maneuvering to launch their torpedoes.

Fighters swooped raucously upon them, and the audacious Americans were nearly all shot down. Those which had been able to launch their torpedoes had done so from afar, and the ships had plenty of time to dodge them. Their types of planes indicated that these attackers were land-based aircraft and could have come only from Midway.

At 0700, Admiral Nagumo received from Lieutenant Tomonaga, who led the raid on Midway, a signal which recommended that a second wave should be sent to attack the islands. The admiral thought. Three reconnaissance seaplanes had been launched between 0435 and 0442 and had made no contacts at sea; a faulty catapult had delayed the departure of the aircraft from the *Tone* for twenty minutes, and none of them had reported sighting anything. There seemed no reason to expect battle with the enemy aircraft carriers to be close at hand, and even if one should arrive, the admiral had ninety-three aircraft lined up on deck, armed with torpedoes and bombs for use against any possible sea-going adversary.

At 0715, the admiral made a decision which was to have grave consequences. He had the aircraft returned to their hangars in all the carriers, in order to clear the decks to receive the squadrons returning from Midway. During this period, the torpedoes were to be replaced by bombs, and as soon as the first wave had returned and had been taken down into the hangars, the ninety-three planes were to be brought up again to launch a new attack on the islands. But, by this procedure, the aircraft carriers would be temporarily disarmed and for some time incapable of launching either bombing or torpedo attacks on any enemy ships that might be sighted.

Bombs or torpedoes

The work of rearming the aircraft was being pushed forward feverishly, when the *Tone's* aircraft, which had been late in its take-off, at last broke silence to report, "Ten ships, apparently enemy, sighted. Bearing 010°, distant 240 miles from Midway. Course 150°, speed more than 20 knots. Time, 1728." The accident to the *Tone's* catapult was thus a stroke of destiny; the force lay precisely in the sector covered by the cruiser's seaplanes.

Admiral Nagumo now knew that the American fleet was at sea, but time was short and he considered it necessary to keep the decks cleared as the returning Midway planes would be very short of fuel. So the orders stayed unchanged.

Commander Genda, the air specialist, pleaded with the admiral to suspend the rearming operation, and at 0745, signal was made to the carriers, "Prepare to attack enemy ships. Leave those torpedoes that have not been replaced by bombs."

In answer to peremptory orders to report the composition of the enemy force, at 0809 the *Tone's* aircraft reported, "The enemy strength is five cruisers and five destroyers." Finally, eleven minutes later, it signaled, "The enemy seems to be accompanied by an aircraft carrier." It was thus 52 minutes after the American force was sighted before Admiral Nagumo knew that it contained at least one carrier. It is no easy task for a seaplane to get close enough to identify types of vessels in a force screened by fighter aircraft.

Nagumo nervously paced the admiral's bridge and stopped repeatedly to look toward Midway.

His problem had indeed become very complicated. Most of the *Akagi*'s and *Kaga*'s torpedo planes were now armed with 800-kilogram bombs. Any hit secured by these would inflict severe damage on a ship, but to accomplish this, these high-level bombers must hold a steady course during the approach to their bomb-release points. This renders them particularly vulnerable to fighter attack, and demands that they be given strong fighter protection. This consideration emphasized the second of the admiral's serious problems, because most of the fighters which were to have been used in the second-wave attacks had been sent aloft to reinforce the patrols protecting the carriers, when these were attacked by the Midway planes. There were thus no fighter aircraft available to accompany an offensive strike, until the fighters then in the air should be taken on board and refueled. At the moment, only the thirty-six dive bombers of the *Hiryu* and *Soryu* were on deck, ready to be sent on an attack mission. Without fighter protection, the aircraft losses in such an operation would be unduly high.

Rear Admiral Yamaguchi chose this moment to attempt to influence the decision of his immediate senior and signaled, "Consider it advisable to launch attack force immediately." But, after pondering all the factors, Admiral Nagumo decided that he would first recover the Midway attack planes and the second-wave fighters then on overhead patrol, to refuel and rearm, and thus restore his aircraft organizations to their full fighting strength. He also decided that, as soon as the recovery operations were sufficiently advanced, he would retire to the northward to avoid further attacks on his force. At 0855, he signaled his full decision as follows: "After completing recovery operations, force will temporarily head northward. We plan to contact and destroy enemy task force."

A few minutes earlier sixteen dive bombers had tried an attack, but the Japanese fighters leapt on them and quickly shot down eight. At 0810, fifteen Flying Fortresses, which were to have attacked the Invasion Force but were rerouted against the Carrier Striking Force, delivered a high-level attack, but the bombs all fell harmlessly into the water. At 0820, eleven dive bombers approached but, in the face of fierce opposition from the fighters, swung away from the aircraft carriers and dived on the *Haruna*, which maneuvered and dodged them easily.

A quarter of an hour later a buzz of voices rose from groups looking southeast. A voice cried, "Here they are!" They were the Japanese aircraft, at last returned from the Midway attack.

On the horizon the black dots grew rapidly. The vessels altered course to starboard to provide a head wind for the landings. Soon the first machine, its forepart riddled with holes, made a perfect landing on the deck of the *Kaga*.

At the same moment, a destroyer opened fire and hoisted the signal: "Submarine to starboard." The squadron maneuvered accordingly. The American commander of this submarine later gave an account of the striking spectacle which he then witnessed:

"The ships steamed at high speed, maneuvering to dodge us. A cruiser had just passed us and was well astern, while a battleship to port fired a broadside at our periscope. Flags ran up the masts, and every searchlight was turned on us."

Signals began arriving from everywhere, all of them identical and to the effect that American aircraft were approaching. Landings succeeded each other as fast as possible, and at 0917 all the aircraft had been taken aboard. Mechanics and armorers busied themselves as methodically as ants around the planes, refilling the tanks and fixing new bombs under the wings.

Nagumo made a ninety-degree turn to port and warned his squadron: "We are going to contact the Task Force and destroy it."

On board the *Hiryu* an officer leapt from one of the reconnaissance aircraft just landed and hurried to the bridge on which stood Rear Admiral Yamaguchi, the division's commander.

"Admiral, I have recognized three American aircraft carriers, the *Enterprise,* the *Yorktown,* and the *Hornet,*" he reported.

The admiral started. "Why didn't you signal that at once?" he asked. "This kind of information is of vital importance."

"I couldn't transmit. My R/T [radio] is out of action."

11 "The Moon Is So Bright!"

A formation of thirty-five dive bombers from the *Hornet* was on its way toward the Japanese force.

When he learned of the bombing of Midway, Admiral Spruance hurried the attack to coincide with the refueling of the aircraft which had taken part in the expedition, but Admiral Nagumo's change of course foiled this one group of would-be assailants, and after circling over the empty water for some time, they landed at Midway.

The torpedo aircraft which should have accompanied these dive bombers got lost in the clouds and formed an isolated group. Failing to find the Striking Force at the spot expected, they turned back north and luck soon favored them; at 0925 they saw the flat, massive outlines of the carriers.

The torpedo aircraft approached and dropped toward sea level. The Japanese fighters threw themselves upon them, and the escorting vessels maintained a heavy curtain of fire. For some minutes, there was a frightful melee. Some of the aircraft burst into flames, others struck the water and shattered, and in a few moments the attack was completely frustrated. Only a few torpedo aircraft, after hopelessly launching their torpedoes, slipped away to the northeast.

The torpedo aircraft from the *Enterprise* arrived immediately afterward, and the Japanese squadron maneuvered to turn their sterns toward them. The attackers, seeking to gain a more favorable position, made a wide circle to put themselves abeam of the *Kaga,* which was surrounded by fighters.

During the run-in, the American airmen came under heavy fire, and ten out of fourteen of them were shot down.

At last forty-one torpedo aircraft arrived from the *Yorktown.* They drove to the attack in waves which broke successively against the defense. But the strength of these assaults forced the fighters to descend from the heights, where they had been keeping watch, and enter the turmoil.

Only six torpedo aircraft survived the massacre.

The sky, which momentarily had been empty, suddenly became filled again as the dive bombers from the *Enterprise* and *Yorktown* began their attacks.

The Akagi

As a result of evasive action, the carrier formation had lost its good order. The *Akagi* was farthest west in line with the *Soryu,* the *Kaga* was astern and to starboard of the *Akagi,* and the *Hiryu* was far ahead.

At 1025 three bombers dived on the *Akagi.* The first bomb threw up spray thirty feet from the bridge; the second went through the deck near the after lift and exploded in the hangar, where forty loaded aircraft were waiting to be hoisted to the deck; and the third bomb burst on deck, astern and to port among the aircraft returned from Midway which were being replenished.

A gigantic fire broke out, and torpedoes exploded, throwing pieces of bodies into the air.

The damage-control squads jumped into action, and the ship turned into the wind to throw the smoke astern; but the heat was so intense that compartment after compartment caught fire, and the men were asphyxiated by the fumes.

The chief of staff ran to Admiral Nagumo and urged him to leave the ship, from which he could no longer direct his squadron. But the admiral was confident and wanted to remain. When the ship's commander, Captain Aoki, also reported that

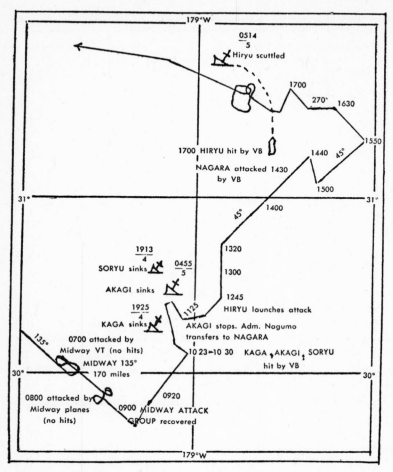

MIDWAY: TRACK OF JAPANESE STRIKING FORCE, JUNE 4, 1942

the ship was lost and must be abandoned, Nagumo became angry and bluntly refused to leave.

The scene was brief and pathetic. The three men faced one another with dignity amid the smoke and noise. Knowing the positive character of his chief, Aoki calmly remarked that the

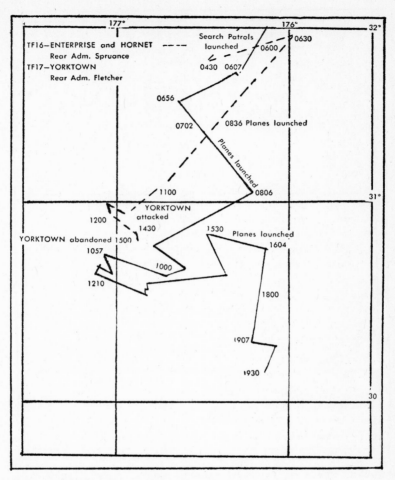

MIDWAY: TRACK OF U.S. TASK FORCES, JUNE 4, 1942

Akagi could no longer send a signal, and asked whether it was not the duty of the commander in chief, in accordance with naval custom, to transfer to a ship in sound condition in order to continue his command.

Finally the admiral saw reason and, reluctantly, his face set, allowed himself to be persuaded.

A hawser was fixed to the rail and the little procession reached the deck. The guns and machine guns were still firing, and on the blazing deck they had to step over corpses which were beginning to burn. With hands and feet injured, the admiral and his staff climbed down the hawser to a destroyer which came alongside. A few minutes later, the force commander's flag was hoisted in the cruiser *Nagara*. Captain Aoki stayed on board with his crew, who continued the fight. The *Akagi* was still under way and steered eastward, but the fire was still gaining. At 1715 it was decided to remove the portrait of the Emperor which hung in the admiral's cabin and was usually hidden behind a silken curtain; the image of the representative of the Imperial line sprung from the sun goddess must not be profaned by indifferent or nonappreciative glances. It was unveiled only for ceremonies of homage.

An officer bowed before the portrait, unhooked it with care, wrapped it, and then, choosing the least threatened passageways, returned to the deck and made his way to the place from which the admiral had climbed down.

While bo's'n's pipes rendered the honors, and the survivors stood rigidly at attention, the Imperial portrait was entrusted to a destroyer, which rapidly bore it away.

The fight against death lasted another two hours, but at 1915 the fires reached the engine rooms, and the mechanics fell one after another in appalling agonies.

Destroyers took on board 1200 survivors, a hundred of whom were wounded, and the vessel drifted until 0455 on the following morning, when she was sunk by torpedoes from Japanese destroyers.

The Kaga

Almost simultaneously with the *Akagi*, the *Kaga* was also struck by four bombs. One hit the forward elevator and exploded, killing all the personnel on the bridge including the ship's commanding officer, Captain Okada. A second went through the deck on the port side of the bridge structure, and a third pierced the deck to starboard near the rear elevator. The last bomb struck on the starboard side aft.

In the hangar were thirty aircraft, full of gasoline and loaded with explosives; the others were on deck being refueled. Six fighters were in the air.

Like the *Akagi*, the *Kaga* became a mass of flame, and smoke formed an impenetrable curtain around her. The situation was at once seen to be desperate, and destroyers came alongside and took off the Emperor's portrait and a thousand men. The others stayed on board to fight the fire.

Commander Amagi, gazing out over the waters of the sea, suddenly saw the periscope of a submarine a few thousand meters from the ship. Minutes later the wakes of three torpedoes were seen approaching. Two narrowly missed; the third hit the carrier but failed to explode. The torpedo broke into two parts; its warhead sank, but the air cylinder continued to float, spinning slowly.

Finally it stopped, empty, and a number of Japanese sailors in the water close by, waiting to be rescued, quickly clung to this excellent float, an unexpected gift from destiny.

The *Kaga* burnt fiercely until 1925, when she underwent two heavy explosions and sank, taking with her eight hundred men.

The Soryu

The *Soryu*'s crew had almost finished equipping her aircraft for an attack, and the vessel turned south into the wind, the customary maneuver for launching. Out of the sun came three waves of aircraft which, one after the other, dipped and dived. It was 1025. The ship shuddered throughout her length as three bombs hit her successively in a blinding flash. The first pierced the deck and exploded in the hangar below, where aircraft were being serviced; the second fell just ahead of the forward elevator; the third near the after elevator.

Within twenty minutes, the ship was burning so fiercely that the captain gave the order to abandon ship. The noise of torpedo and bomb explosions in the hangar added to the din and confusion. The engines were stopped, the pumps no longer drew water, and it became impossible to fight the fire. Men threw themselves into the sea and were picked up by the destroyer *Makikumo*. The crew had a deep affection for their commanding officer, Captain Yanagimoto, and when those on the destroyer saw him still standing on the bridge of the *Soryu*, some of their number persuaded the destroyer captain to help them in an attempt to rescue him.

The *Makikumo* was again taken alongside the blazing aircraft carrier, and a huge petty officer, Abe, chosen by his comrades, returned on board to persuade the captain to save himself. But it was all in vain. Captain Yanagimoto resolutely refused to leave his ship. As Abe turned sorrowfully away, he heard his captain singing "Kimigoyo," the national anthem.

At 1913, with her survivors watching from the destroyer, the *Soryu* finally sank beneath the waves. She carried with her the captain and more than seven hundred of the crew.

Voyage of no return

The *Nagara* was not equipped for use as an admiral's vessel. Admiral Nagumo, who did not have the necessary means of signaling, handed over command to Rear Admiral Abe, commanding Cruiser Division 8 in the *Tone*. The latter thought that the Americans had only one or two aircraft carriers and that they had launched most of the aircraft on the attacks.

At 1050 he had signaled Yamamoto: "Enemy sighted—one aircraft carrier, five cruisers, and ten destroyers ten degrees and 240 miles from Midway. We are sailing against them."

It was the *Yorktown* at the position indicated.

Admiral Yamaguchi, in the *Hiryu*, received the order to launch the attack, and at 1110 eighteen dive bombers set out toward the American aircraft carrier.

Among the ten torpedo aircraft and six fighters which remained on the *Hiryu's* deck and were being refueled at top speed, was Lieutenant Tomonaga's aircraft, the left tank of which had been struck during the attack on Midway. When the order came for the second wave to take off, a mechanic ran to the officer.

"Sir, the port tank has not been repaired."

"Too bad. Just fill the starboard one."

"You want the machine lined up for take-off just the same?"

"Of course, and hurry."

Those around the lieutenant were filled with emotion. One tank would permit the outward flight, but it would be impossible to return.

All Tomonaga's subordinates offered to exchange aircraft with him but, smiling, he repeated, "It's nothing, nothing."

He zipped up his flying suit, adjusted his helmet, and at 1331 took off at the head of his formation.

Meanwhile Nagumo had resumed command. Admiral Kondo, commanding the Second Fleet and the Covering Group of the Midway Invasion Force, signaled that he was hurrying forward at twenty-eight knots.

Admiral Yamamoto ordered the two auxiliary aircraft carriers *Ryuho* and *Junyo*, which were off Dutch Harbor in the Aleutians, to join the *Hiryu*. The Aleutian Covering Force was ordered to rejoin the Battle Fleet.

At noon, Nagumo received from the *Hiryu* the signal: "We are bombing the enemy aircraft carrier."

The Yorktown

The *Yorktown* had twelve fighters in the air and was refueling the patrol that had just been relieved, as well as other formations back from an attack on the Japanese. The dive bombers which had struck the *Soryu* were back, ready to land, when the radar indicated the approach of a group of enemy aircraft from the west-southwest and forty miles away.

The Japanese bombers arrived and dived to the kill. One disintegrated under anti-aircraft fire and crashed on the deck. Its bomb exploded and caused a fire which was quickly put out.

A bomb from the port side exploded in the funnel. Five of the six boilers were damaged, and speed fell to six knots. At 1220 the *Yorktown* stopped. Another bomb crashed into the vessel and exploded on the fourth deck. A store room near the gasoline tanks, containing oakum, caught fire, but carbonic acid filled the pipes and prevented an immediate catastrophe. The radar system was destroyed.

Admiral Fletcher shifted his flag to the *Astoria* and ordered the cruiser *Portland* to take the *Yorktown* in tow, but this help was not needed. For, at 1340, four of the boilers were repaired and the vessel was making twenty knots. She had again started to refuel the fighters, when a second wave of attackers was signaled. They were the torpedo aircraft from the *Hiryu,* led by Lieutenant Tomonaga's aircraft.

Exalted by their chief's heroism, the pilots handled their machines as if on exercise, in spite of terrific fire. Acting Sublieutenant Hashimoto saw Tomonaga penetrate into this hell, release his torpedo, and disappear as if he had been swallowed up by the fire.

The *Yorktown* was hit by two torpedoes at 1442. The port fuel tanks, torn apart, sent dirty black streams into the sea. The rudder no longer functioned. The few Japanese aircraft that had escaped the shells and the enemy fighters had the satisfaction of seeing, as they left, that the vessel was listing to port with increasing rapidity.

A few minutes later the *Yorktown* was abandoned.

The Hiryu

Of the imposing Japanese armada of aircraft carriers, only the *Hiryu* was still intact. About 1700 she saw new waves of silver aircraft coming toward her.

Yamaguchi ordered speed to be increased to thirty knots, and the vessel zigzagged and opened fire with all her guns. The few fighters in the air dashed at the attackers, many of which fell, leaving behind a trail of black smoke in the sky.

There were twenty-four of them, divided into four groups. The attacks of the first three waves were disjointed, and their bombs fell into the water. But, as the fourth group passed overhead, four bombs struck the *Hiryu.*

One hit the forward elevator, the platform of which was

blown away like a straw to crash against the bridge structure, sweeping away all the personnel not under cover. Another fell just abaft of the same elevator, and the two others went through the deck aft.

For the fourth time, a poignant drama was played in the last aircraft carrier, under conditions so similar as to suggest a hallucination. In spite of heroic efforts, in spite of the sacrifice of mechanics, the *Hiryu* burned rapidly and was soon unmaneuverable.

Yamaguchi warned Admiral Nagumo that he was going to transfer the crew to the destroyer *Kazakumo*, and the assembly was sounded. Of 1500 men, 800, blackened by smoke and their clothing in rags, assembled at the call of bugle and pipe. Admiral Yamaguchi addressed them from the bridge:

"I am your leader; I take responsibility for the loss of the *Soryu* and the *Hiryu*. I shall stay in this ship to the end. As for you, you must leave and continue to serve as you have done until now."

The officers surrounded him, and Commander Ito spoke for them all.

"Admiral, we understand your sacrifice. We want to share it."

The admiral shook his head.

"No. It is right that the responsible leader should share the fate of his ship. But you are indispensable to the country for the battles to come. I give you solemn orders to leave."

The officers lowered their heads. Nevertheless, before going, Ito thought it fitting to pour the traditional libations of farewell. Not far away he found a keg containing a little water, and in the hollows of their hands, those who were to survive shared the water with those who wished to die.

Before descending to the bridge of the destroyer alongside the *Hiryu*, Ito again bowed before the admiral.

"Have you no message to entrust to me?"

"No, thank you," the admiral said. Then, correcting himself, he said, "Perhaps you would be kind enough to take this to my family." And he gave him his helmet.

Noticing a strip of toweling that Ito wore hooked to his belt, Yamaguchi asked for it, so that he might tie himself to the railing to prevent his body from being parted from the ship when it capsized.

The commanding officer of the *Hiryu*, Captain Karai, who had decided to stay, still insisted that the admiral should withdraw. Yamaguchi was known for his bravery, and his death would deprive the Japanese navy of a precious leader. But the admiral smiled and only replied:

"The moon is so bright in the sky!"

This poetic response, typically Japanese in its symbolism, was at once recognized as final.

The transfer of the crew was completed. The *Hiryu* listed to port, where the *Kazakumo* lay alongside. The destroyer's captain received the order to torpedo the aircraft carrier in her death agony. The officers listened to the last instructions of Captain Karai and, before leaving, bowed before the admiral, who said:

"We shall watch the moon together."

The destroyer cast off, drew away, and at 0510 on June 5 launched four torpedoes. The *Hiryu* dipped gently but it was not until 0900 that her blackened and crackling hull turned over. The sea was covered with fuel oil and blackened debris.

Admiral Yamaguchi, like Admiral Yamamoto, was an imperturbable, well-balanced man renowned for his surety of judgment, and the whole Imperial Navy had confidence in him. His words were full of calm strength, and he welcomed death to show that "the death of the Samurai is as useful as his birth."

JAPANESE FORCES IN MIDWAY BATTLE AND
ALEUTIAN OCCUPATION, JUNE 4-5, 1942

Combined Fleet, Admiral Yamamoto

Advance Expeditionary Force: 13 I-class submarines

Carrier Striking Force, Vice Admiral Nagumo

> *Carrier Division 1:* Akagi, Kaga (42 fighters, 42 dive bombers, 51 torpedo bombers) (2 CV)*
> *Carrier Division 2:* Hiryu, Soryu (42 fighters, 42 dive bombers, 42 torpedo bombers) (2 CV)
> *Battleship Division 3, Section 2:* Haruna, Kirishima (2 OBB)
> *Cruiser Division 8:* Tone, Chikuma (2 CA)
> *Screens:* 1 light cruiser, 11 destroyers

Midway Invasion Force, Vice Admiral Kondo

> **Covering Group, Vice Admiral Kondo**
> *Battleship Division 3, Section 1:* Kongo, Hiei (2 OBB)
> *Cruiser Division 4, Section 1:* Atago, Chokai (2 CA)
> *Cruiser Division 5:* Myoko, Haguro (2 CA)
> *Carrier Unit:* Zuiho (12 fighters, 12 torpedo bombers) (CVL)
> *Screens:* 1 light cruiser, 8 destroyers

> **Close Support Group, Rear Admiral Kurita**
> *Cruiser Division 7:* Suzuya, Kumano, Mogami, Mikuma (4 CA)
> *Screen:* 2 destroyers

> **Transport Group, Rear Admiral Tanaka**
> *Transports:* 12 transports, 3 patrol boats (carrying troops)
> *Seaplane Unit:* 2 seaplane tenders (24 seaplane fighters, 4 seaplane scouts, 4 scouts)
> *Minesweeper Unit:* 4 minesweepers, 3 subchasers
> *Screens:* 1 light cruiser, 10 destroyers

Main Body, Admiral Yamamoto
> *Battleship Division 1* †: Yamato, Nagato, Mutsu (1 BB, 2 OBB)

* *Abbreviations:* CV, aircraft carrier; CVL, light carrier; OBB, old battleship; CA, heavy cruiser.
† The Midway operation was the first wartime employment of Battleship Divisions 1 and 2, which had been held at the Hashirajima anchorage in

Carrier Unit: Hosho (8 torpedo bombers) (CVL)
Screens: 1 light cruiser, 8 destroyers

Guard (Aleutian Screening Force), Vice Admiral Takasu
   Battleship Division 2: Hyuga, Ise, Fuso, Yamashiro (4 OBB)
   Screen: 2 light cruisers, 12 destroyers

Northern (Aleutian) Force, Vice Admiral Hosogoya
   Nachi, Maya, Takao (3 CA)
   Ryujo, Junyo (40 fighters, 21 dive bombers, 21 torpedo bombers)   (2 CVL)
   Screens: 6 destroyers
   Attu Invasion Unit: 1 light cruiser, 4 destroyers, 1 transport
   Kiska Invasion Unit: 2 light cruisers, 3 destroyers, 3 minesweepers, 2 transports
   Submarine Unit: 4 I-class submarines

---

the Inland Sea since the start of the war. Among these ships was the *Yamato*, one of three battleships laid down in 1936, when the Washington Naval Limitation Treaty came to an end. These three ships were by far the largest battleships ever built by any naval power. They displaced some 65,000 tons, and their main batteries consisted of nine 18-inch guns. They were high-speed vessels, of great defensive strength due to heavy armor in all vital places and tremendous compartmentation. (The author credits them with a displacement of 63,000 tons; Fuchida, in his book *Midway*, gives a figure of 68,000.)

The two other vessels of this class were the *Musashi* and *Shinano*. During her building, the latter was converted to a carrier. She was sunk inside Tokyo Bay by a United States submarine during her final trials on November 28, 1944—a short life for the world's biggest carrier, a marvelous feat by the submarine, and a horrendous indictment of Japan's coastal-defense dispositions. The *Musashi* was sunk in Kurita's force in the Leyte campaign on October 24, 1944.

UNITED STATES FORCES IN MIDWAY OPERATIONS, JUNE 1-6, 1942

Carrier Striking Force, Rear Admiral F. J. Fletcher

Task Force 17, Rear Admiral Fletcher
Yorktown (25 fighters, 37 dive bombers, 13 torpedo bombers) (CV)*
Astoria, Portland (2 CA)
Screen: 6 destroyers

Task Force 16, Rear Admiral R. A. Spruance
Enterprise, Hornet (54 fighters, 75 dive bombers, 29 torpedo bombers)
   (2 CV)
New Orleans, Minneapolis, Vincennes, Northampton, Pensacola, Atlanta (5
   CA, 1 CL)
Screens: 9 destroyers

Air force based on Midway:
Marine Fighting Squadron 221: 28 fighters
Marine Scout Bombing Squadron 240: 34 scout bombers
Navy planes: 6 torpedo bombers, 30 patrol bombers
Army Seventh Air Force: 17 heavy bombers, 4 medium bombers

* *Abbreviations:* CV, aircraft carrier; CA, heavy cruiser; CL, light cruiser.

12 Smoke and Mist

Admiral Yamamoto concluded, from the news that reached him, that the Americans had only one aircraft carrier at sea and that she had been sunk.

In the afternoon of June 4 he ordered the Aleutian Covering Force to rejoin his flag at noon the following day, and gave the same order to Kondo's Second Fleet. The Invasion Force was to retire provisionally to the northwest while awaiting further orders.

A little later the admiral was informed of the actual forces of the adversary. Nevertheless, at 1915 he sent the following signals:

"1. The enemy fleet is practically destroyed and is withdrawing eastward.

"2. The Combined Fleet is preparing to pursue the survivors and to occupy Midway.

"3. The Battle Fleet will arrive at midnight at 32.10 N., 175.43 E., course east, speed twenty knots. The Mobile Force [First Carrier Striking Force], the Occupation Force [Midway Invasion Force] less the 7th Cruiser Division, and the submarines are ordered to seek contact with the enemy and to attack him."

Nagumo replied at 2130: "The total enemy force is five aircraft carriers, six cruisers, and fifteen destroyers. It is on a westward course. We are protecting the *Hiryu* and will withdraw toward the northwest at eighteen knots."

An hour later he signaled again: "The enemy still has four

aircraft carriers, six cruisers, and fifteen destroyers. None of our aircraft carriers is seaworthy."

Yamamoto then ordered Kondo to take command of advanced operations, and Nagumo to give all his attention to the aircraft carriers and their escort.

At last, at 0255 on June 5, Yamamoto took account of the exact situation. He feared a dawn attack and ordered a general retreat.

One can visualize him on his bridge on that day of June 5. The admiral suffered from stomach trouble. With an ashen complexion and eyes burning with fever, he was plunged in profound meditation. He was an extremely brave and clear-headed man, and he undoubtedly knew the measure of the loss just inflicted on his country. To every Japanese seaman who thinks of it today, the battle of Midway was the great turning point of the Pacific war. Prior to it, Japan could still hope for victory, but after it, the will to victory was to give place to the desperate energy which can be drawn from the human soul in the last resort—the energy of despair. There can be no doubt that Admiral Yamamoto, from the tragic morning of June 5, 1942, understood this and had pictured to himself the inevitable consequences for his country.

If . . .

As already seen, at noon on June 4 Admiral Kondo had hurried toward the battle area with four heavy cruisers, one of which was the *Atago,* two battleships of the Kongo class, the light aircraft carrier *Zuiho,* and a destroyer squadron. He left the convoy almost without protection and at midnight was only 125 miles from Nagumo. Behind him Rear Admiral Tanaka was speeding with the *Jintsu* and ten destroyers.

If the *Enterprise* and the *Hornet* had continued on their westerly course, they would have fallen foul of an enormous concentration of enemy forces, from which they would have found it hard to escape. Unfortunately for the Japanese, after his attack on the *Hiryu* Admiral Spruance had withdrawn to the eastward. . . .

Two cruisers

At 2030 on the fourth, Yamamoto ordered the submarine *I-168* to shell the base at Midway until 0200, the time when Admiral Kurita's Close Support Group would arrive with the cruisers *Kumano, Suzuya, Mikuma,* and *Mogami* to complete the destruction. But at 0200 Kurita received a counterorder to rejoin the Battle Fleet.

At the start of the retreat, at 0342, the Close Support Group had to maneuver rapidly in order to evade a submarine sighted to starboard. The *Mogami* did not receive the signal in time and was slow to alter course. She struck the ship ahead, the *Mikuma*, violently on the port side, so that a shower of sparks flashed up, causing a brief fire.

The *Mogami's* bow was so twisted that, although her engines were running at turns for twenty-four knots, she was making only sixteen knots through the water. The *Mikuma*, also damaged, left a trail of fuel oil escaping from her bunkers.

The following morning, the two cruisers were lagging behind the rest of the squadron.

In the meantime, the submarine *I-168*, carrying out her orders, opened fire on Midway. The answer was so lively that she had to dive and retire.

At dawn on the sixth, all the American scout bombers left Midway to carry out a search. It extended 250 miles and located the *Mogami* and the *Mikuma*.

At 0805 the two cruisers saw six dive bombers and six high-level bombers; these had followed the shimmering track of fuel oil left by the *Mikuma*. The vessels opened violent fire. The dive bombers attacked furiously out of the sun, but their bombs fell in the water and only bomb splinters riddled the hulls and superstructures. The high-level bombers had no better luck, but one American aircraft, doubtless disabled, crashed with a horrible noise on the after turret of the *Mikuma*, and streams of blazing gasoline set fire to some of the powder in the turret. The stern of the *Mikuma* was on fire, but this was gradually brought under control by the fire-fighting squads.

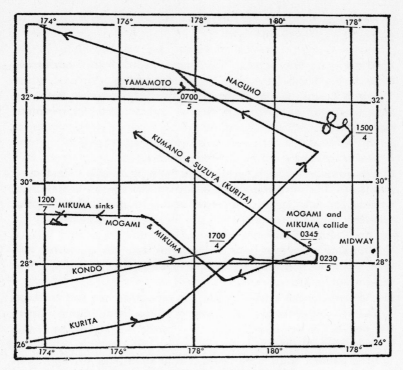

JAPANESE MOVEMENTS FOLLOWING MIDWAY BATTLE

On June 7 the two cruisers were rediscovered by reconnaissance aircraft from the *Enterprise*. A first wave of attackers reached them about 0700, consisting of twenty-six dive bombers escorted by eight fighters from the *Hornet*. The Japanese zigzagged and put up a barrage of fire, but the Americans, luckier or perhaps better trained than those of the previous evening, scored two hits on the *Mogami*.

One bomb hit the top of No. 5 turret and exploded inside, killing its entire crew. The second struck the torpedo tubes amidships and penetrated to the second deck, where fires broke out.

The *Mogami's* crew succeeded in mastering the fire, and the ship continued on her course.

At the same time, the *Mikuma* was hit by three bombs and was also set on fire. The leak forward was considerably increased.

A new attack was made at 1045 by thirty-one dive bombers, three torpedo aircraft, and twelve fighters from the *Enterprise.*

The defense fire was less intense: some gun crews had suffered heavy losses and some guns were out of action.

The *Mogami,* which was ahead, was again hit twice, once amidships and once immediately forward of the bridge, but the tireless fire-fighting squads once again went to work on the resulting fires.

The *Mikuma* suffered a worse fate. Struck by several bombs, she burned everywhere, and enormous tongues of flame shot from the rents in her side. The fire mains were cut, and she had to be abandoned.

The destroyer *Arashio* tried to run alongside but had to stand off almost immediately, so fierce was the heat. She stopped, lowered her boats into the sea, and gathered up the men who jumped from all sides.

Then came a third wave, twenty-four dive bombers and eight fighters from the *Hornet.* The *Mikuma,* disabled, was hit several more times and, still burning, with her masts collapsed and the bridge in frightful disorder, she sank during the night.

About 1445 the destroyer *Arashio* was struck aft, where the survivors from the *Mikuma* were massed. A cry of horror rose from this packed group as bloody gaps were opened in it.

The *Mogami* was pierced by a bomb which burst between decks, wiping out all the men fighting the fire. The door of one of the fuel burners was jammed and the whole compartment caught fire. Ninety men were cut to pieces or burned in a few minutes.

But the survivors gritted their teeth and carried on. The commanding officer, Captain Sogi, left the bridge as soon as he could, to go among his men to encourage them. In spite of their fatigue and suffering, they continued to fight the flames, repaired sections of the fire mains, fitted up asbestos sheets, shored the weakened bulkheads, plugged the holes, and removed inflammable material.

The fire was finally extinguished. The vessel continued to the westward and prepared for an attack by surface vessels, for reconnaissance seaplanes had been sighted in the afternoon.

A vanished dream

Admiral Yamamoto meanwhile had not lost all hope of bringing off the great naval engagement of which he had dreamed. When he learned of the attack on the *Mogami* and the *Mikuma*, he expected that Spruance would continue to pursue them and come within the radius of operation of the Japanese air forces on Wake.

The admiral sent six heavy cruisers with the *Jintsu* and destroyers to support the attacked ships. He himself set out to the southward on June 7 with the Battle and Second Fleets. On the eighth, at 0700, he turned west to refuel, while the cruisers found the *Mogami* and escorted her to Truk.

In the afternoon, when he knew the full truth, Yamamoto decided to continue the later operations he had planned and returned to Japan, worried and dispirited.

Coup de grâce

We left the *Yorktown* abandoned by her crew at 1445 on June 4, some 220 miles north-northeast of Midway. When he saw that she remained afloat, Captain Buckmaster sent a working crew back on board. They righted the list and passed a tow line to the minesweeper *Vireo*.

At dawn the following day, two Japanese reconnaissance seaplanes saw the aircraft carrier proceeding slowly to the southward; under orders from Yamamoto, the submarine *I-168*, which had shelled Midway during the night, made for the survivor. The submarine searched for her a long time because her position as given in the signal was not accurate, but finally, on the afternoon of the seventh, the *I-168* sighted the *Yorktown*. She reached her attack point carefully, moving slowly, her periscope raised only occasionally and scarcely breaking surface, and penetrated behind the protecting screen. At short range, she launched four torpedoes at 1330.

One of the torpedoes missed the target. The two following burst on the *Yorktown*'s side. The fourth cut an escort destroyer in two.

The *Vireo* cut the tow line and the salvage crew left the aircraft carrier, which gradually sank.

She was still afloat at 0600 the next morning. Then she rolled over and sank with a thunderous explosion.

In the Aleutians

The Aleutian Islands form a chain in the north Pacific, almost linking Asia and America. They are desolate lands covered by short grass, which the snow often hides. The only food is two or three species of bird, foxes, sea creatures, and a little seaweed. The weather is dreadful because the warm Japanese current, the *Kuro Shivo,* there meets the cold wind from the Bering Sea, bringing rain, snow, and fog in continuous succession.

In 1941 the islands were nearly uninhabited except for Dutch Harbor, which was the site of a small military post and airfield; Umnak Island, with substantial army air forces and a new airfield, and Atka and Attu, with their very small native populations. To the eastward were the Alaskan bases at Kodiak and Sitka, where both the army and navy had also established bases, including airfields.

The arcs of the great circles from Tokyo to Seattle and to San Francisco touch the southern shores of the Aleutian Islands. Attu is only 650 miles from Paramushiro in the Kuriles and 725 miles from Dutch Harbor, with Juneau, the capital of Alaska, 1158 miles to the east on the Alaskan mainland.

Although neither side envisaged a long occupation of these islands, because of the savage climate, each was determined to dispute the possession. Both sides were actuated by the question of prestige, but the Japanese also feared that Japanese soil might be bombed by machines based in this archipelago.

The Americans had learned that their adversaries were preparing to operate off the coast of Alaska at the same time as at
Midway. Admiral Nimitz had sent Rear Admiral Theobald north
with Task Force Eight, which comprised two heavy cruisers,
three light cruisers, nine destroyers, light vessels, and six submarines. Reconnaissance and air attack would be supplied by
land-based aircraft.

Vice Admiral Boshiro Hosogoya in the heavy cruiser *Nachi*
commanded the Japanese operations in the Aleutian area. He
had with him the Second Mobile Force (Rear Admiral
Kakuta), which comprised the two light aircraft carriers *Ryuho*
and *Junyo,* three heavy cruisers, three light cruisers, and twelve
destroyers. Rear Admiral Sentaro Omori directed the Adak-Attu
Occupation Force and Captain Takeji Ono the Kiska Occupation
Force.

The Imperial General Staff at first desired to occupy Dutch
Harbor but renounced this objective because it would have ne-
cessitated the use of too many vessels.

Accordingly the following operational plan was conceived.
The Second Mobile Force would bombard Dutch Harbor on
June 3 to deceive Nimitz and make him believe that the Japanese effort was directed against that point, and also to destroy
installations which could be used for direct or indirect attack
on Japan. Meanwhile, detachments would be landed on Kiska and
Attu.

In May, an airplane carried by the submarine *I-26* had flown
over Seattle, to make sure that the port contained no transports. The forces of the northern zone, to which Admiral
Hosogoya added everything he could obtain as reinforcements,
made ready at Ominato, north Honshu. The two amphibious
groups exercised in Mutsukikai Bay and off the coasts of Hokkaido.

In icy fog

Kakuta's group weighed anchor on May 25 bound eastward.
The Kiska Occupation Force set out two days later and put in
at Paramushiro to fuel before sailing for its destination. The

Adak-Attu Attack Force departed later and kept abreast of
the preceding force. Hosogoya himself, accompanied by supply
ships, on June 2 left Paramushiro, where he left some seaplanes and small patrol vessels. The planes took off from the two
aircraft carriers early on June 4 and disappeared almost at once
into the icy fog.

The weather, which had protected the advance of the Mobile
Force, now made things difficult for the aircraft. The *Junyo's*
group, short of fuel, had to turn back, but that from the *Ryuho*,
more fortunate, found a ceiling of nine thousand feet over Dutch
Harbor. The seaplane tender *Gillis* detected the attackers by radar
at 0540. The vessels moored in the harbor hurried to weigh anchor,
but it was too late, and at 0600 the fourteen bombers started their
attack. Fuel tanks burned, the radio station and barracks were
destroyed, the patrol bombers were pulverized or capsized at their
moorings, and some of the ships that were hit ran aground. Two
Japanese planes were shot down by the fierce anti-aircraft fire.

One aircraft signaled to Admiral Kakuta that five American
destroyers were at Makuskin Bay.

The first wave returned to the aircraft carriers, which guided
them by goniometer. A second wave set out at 0900 in search
of the signaled destroyers, but the visibility had decreased and
the aircraft circled without finding their objective. At that
moment some American fighters fell unexpectedly on the Japanese machines, shooting down two and damaging two others.

At noon the Second Mobile Force, which had gathered in its
aircraft 130 miles south of Dutch Harbor, withdrew southwest
according to plan.

Kakuta had refueled his destroyers during the night and set
course for Adak. The fog thickened, speed was reduced to nine
knots, and each vessel had to stream a "fog buoy." [1] The meteor-

---

1. *Fog buoys are small spar buoys towed astern in a fog by ships
in column formation. Each following ship keeps this buoy close
under her bow, and this, with the measured length of the towline, guarantees that she is in the wake and at the proper distance from the ship ahead.* (R.A.T.)

ological service signaled that the fog extended westward and that the sky was clear at Dutch Harbor. Kakuta turned back.

Unknown base

The *Junyo* and the *Ryuho* profited by the overcast weather to send a new wave against the American base at 1600 on June 4. Again eleven dive bombers, six high-altitude bombers, and fifteen fighters pierced the Arctic fog. The Second Mobile Force waited for them to return, making slow speed, but suddenly the noise of an aircraft was heard. It increased in volume, and a group of American reconnaissance planes passed nearby. They were swallowed immediately by the mists. Nevertheless, an attack had to be anticipated, and the anti-aircraft guns were alerted. There soon followed the roar of big four-engined aircraft; through a break in the gloom, the enemy was sighted and firing began. The bombers aimed in the supposed direction of their target. Two of them, which had come closer to take better aim, were struck by shells and dived into the sea.

In the meantime the Japanese pilots had profited by good weather to destroy four more fuel tanks at Dutch Harbor, besides damaging the base ship *Northwestern.*

Before returning to their base, the *Junyo's* aircraft pressed on over the west cape of Unalaska. This was the first time in the war that hostile armed planes had flown over the American continent.

In the middle of the deserted wastes over which they were flying, the pilots suddenly saw an odd rectangle surrounded by dumpy buildings on which antlike figures scurried about. It was crisscrossed by wide, clear strips and was plainly an airfield with its runway, an airfield hitherto unknown to the Japanese. It was on Otter Point, Umnak Island. It was guarded by fighters which dashed to the attack against the Japanese group and sent four Japanese aircraft hurtling to the ground.

The battle of Midway was developing meanwhile. On this same day at that same hour, Kakuta received an order to head south to rejoin Nagumo, and the Aleutian Screening Force was recalled to the Main Body.

Admiral Kakuta understood that the principal aircraft carrier force had been defeated, and he set out immediately at top speed, but at 1930 a counterorder sent him northward again. The two transport groups resumed their momentarily interrupted progress. Six hundred miles to the south-southwest of Kiska, Kakuta met Hosogoya, who was waiting with the *Nachi,* some battleships of the Aleutian Screening Force, and several supply ships.

Adak was only 350 miles from Otter Point and so, if occupied by the Japanese, would be exposed to heavy bombing. Accordingly, Hosogoya decided to occupy Attu instead of Adak. On the tenth, Rear Admiral Omori therefore landed 1200 men on Attu without opposition. Kiska was similarly occupied without difficulty.[2] The occupation of these latter positions was no longer of any importance, once the Japanese attack on Midway had been completely frustrated, but they were not to be evacuated until Attu was recaptured by the Americans and Kiska abandoned by the Japanese in the spring of 1943.

On June 12 Hosogoya's forces in the Aleutian area were reinforced by the *Zuikaku,* the light aircraft carrier *Zuiho,* two battleships, and four heavy cruisers, which were never of any use to him. Upon the conclusion of the Midway operations, Admiral Nimitz started the carriers *Enterprise, Hornet,* and *Saratoga,* accompanied by several heavy cruisers, to the Aleutians; but the move was countermanded on the tenth.

There was nothing for the Japanese Combined Fleet to do but to return to Japan, and this it did, after suffering its first serious defeat of the war.

---

2. *There was, of course, no possibility of opposition to the Japanese occupations of Attu and Kiska. There were no Americans on Attu. Kiska contained a party of about six weather observers.* (R.A.T.)

Conclusions *

The battle of Midway was a decisive milestone, a definite turning point in the Pacific war. The primary wartime role of the aircraft carrier had been completely substantiated by the battles of the Coral Sea and Midway. The loss of four carriers was a blow to Japan's warmaking capabilities from which she never recovered; its effects were strongly reflected in every later operation of the war.

Admiral Yamamoto had estimated, before the war, that Japan's naval offensive must be pressed to the uttermost during the first twelve months of hostilities, because the American naval strength in the Pacific would mount thereafter very rapidly. There was no comparison between the industrial capacity of the United States and that of Japan. And, despite continuing losses, often very serious, it will be seen in the later accounts how amazing was the growth of the United States naval forces during late 1943 and 1944. It far surpassed the most sanguine prewar estimates.

On the other hand, the wartime additions of ships and aircraft to the Japanese navy were surprisingly small: two battleships, the enormous *Yamato* and *Musashi,* which had been building since 1937; a few heavy cruisers, also laid down before the war, and a limited number of destroyers. The wartime carrier-building program was equally unimpressive: the *Shinano,* a converted *Yamato*-class battleship, sunk during her builder's trials in Tokyo Bay by an American submarine in November 1944, without ever seeing active service; the *Taiho,* approximately an *Essex*-class carrier, completed in 1943, one of Japan's major losses in the battle of the Philippine Sea in June 1944. Two battleships, the *Hyuga* and *Ise,* and a limited number of merchant ships, all converted to nondescript carriers of assorted sizes, completed the list. Wartime replacement programs were features of war planning that the Japanese admirals almost entirely neglected—another fact of the war that accentuated the consequences of the battle of Midway.

* This section was written by Admiral Theobald.

The Japanese unreadiness to attack the American carriers, when these were sighted on June 4, assured their defeat. These ships are extremely vulnerable, and the outcome of actions between carrier forces of approximately equal strength almost always hangs upon split-second timing. At Midway, three Japanese carriers received their death blows before one of their planes was launched against their seaborne enemy. We have seen that this unreadiness was the direct result of the decision Admiral Nagumo made at 0715, his reaction to the report from his flight commander that a second bombing attack upon Midway was necessary. This decision therefore demands careful analysis.

Admiral Yamamoto's plans for his far-flung operations envisaged two major objectives for the Midway phase of the campaign: (1) the destruction of the American fleet, especially the carriers; (2) the capture of Midway. These strategic objectives definitely established two major tactical objectives for Nagumo's forces: (1) the location and destruction of American naval forces, especially carriers; (2) the adequate softening of the Midway defenses by air attacks in preparation for the landing operations scheduled for June 5.

Duality of purpose always creates a tendency toward vacillation of execution. Yamamoto's campaign orders should have reflected this fact by assigning a clearcut priority to the first of his two major objectives, the destruction of the American naval forces. Even if the campaign orders did not contain that explicit precautionary item of instruction, Admiral Nagumo, from his first reading of those orders, should have recognized the possible conflicts of execution that his two major tasks could produce in the handling of his air forces. He must then quickly have decided that the destruction of the American naval forces was the paramount of his two tactical objectives, and that his forces must always be ready for instant action against the American carriers. The security of his own carriers, the success of the Midway operation, and the effects on the future conduct of the war all supported this inescapable conclusion.

The conflict between the two tasks required of Nagumo's Striking Force was fraught with the possibility of serious complications, because the planes had to be armed in one way for attacks against ships and in another for those against shore installations. Against ships, the planes are armed with torpedoes and thick-walled, armor-piercing bombs, whose delayed-action fuses permit them to penetrate to the bowels of the vessel before exploding. Against shore targets, thin-walled bombs with instant-acting fuses are used. The rearming of a large number of planes upon a carrier is a lengthy operation, especially when all the planes involved are sent down to the hangars as they were by the Japanese at Midway.

Admiral Nagumo's dispositions for his early morning strike on Midway were sound. He retained on his carriers 93 planes armed with bombs and torpedoes, and the necessary fighter support for attacks on American surface forces if located. But his 0715 decision to send those 93 planes to the hangars for rearming for a second attack upon Midway was fatal. His decision totally disregarded his paramount tactical task, and the *Hiryu,* which escaped the early forenoon American carrier bombing attacks, was the only one of his four carriers that launched an attack upon the American naval forces on that fateful day.

There were other important considerations that Nagumo's 0715 decision overlooked. The morning plane scout was thin and, for several reasons, could have missed the American forces if these were present. Although a second attack upon Midway was necessary, a few hours' delay would have made no particular difference in its reception or in the results it would have produced.

Prior to Midway, every Japanese operation had gone exactly according to plan, and it seems that their High Command expected that same good fortune in this campaign: the bombing of Midway would bring the American fleet out of Oahu, and the Japanese scouting line of submarines to the northward of that island would detect and report that movement. Even the early sighting of the Invasion Force by an American scouting plane does not appear to have suggested to them that all might not go as expected. They apparently gave no thought to the possibility that Admiral Nimitz might know their plans and take action accordingly; and yet, that is what happened.

What the Japanese did not appreciate in the Midway campaign was the fact that they talked too much by coded radio, and their codes could be broken. A feature article in a Midwestern newspaper by a reporter who was in the *Enterprise* at the battle of Midway attributed the American prebattle dispositions to the fact that the United States navy had broken the Japanese naval codes. Before Pearl Harbor, it was their diplomatic codes. Certainly, Admiral Nimitz's arrangements in anticipation of the Midway campaign could not have been improved. It makes a difference when full use is made of accurate knowledge.

It is axiomatic in the military art that the commander who makes the fewest mistakes will win the battle. The battle of Midway did nothing to contradict that maxim. (R.A.T.)

LOSSES IN BATTLE OF MIDWAY, JUNE 4-5, 1942

JAPANESE LOSSES

Ships sunk: Akagi, Kaga, Soryu, Hiryu (4 CV); Mikuma (CA)*
Ship heavily damaged: Mogami (CA)
Ships moderately damaged: Haruna (OBB) by near bomb miss; 3 destroyers; 1
     tanker hit by torpedo
Plane losses: 332, including those lost with 4 carriers

UNITED STATES LOSSES

Ships sunk: Yorktown (CV); Hamman (DD)
Plane losses: 109 carrier planes, 38 shore-based planes (28 Marine, 6 Navy, 4 Army)

* *Abbreviations:* CV, aircraft carrier; CA, heavy cruiser; OBB, old battleship; DD, destroyer.

PART FOUR
A Single Gun

13 Savo

Before the war, the Japanese plan *Yogekisa-kusen* prescribed a decisive battle with the American fleet to keep it out of the western Pacific. In 1941, in the course of a *Kriegspiel,* the Fourth Fleet, whose mission it was to defend the interior zone of the Southern Seas, suggested that invasions of Rabaul and of Kavieng should be followed by those of Tulagi and Deboyne. The staff of the Combined Fleet opposed this. Nevertheless, the capture of Rabaul was decided upon in order to facilitate the "decisive battle" by creating a base to cover the southern flank of Truk, the vast atoll, with its fine large harbor, whose central position made it an ideal base for the support of fleet operations, from the Marianas to the Solomon group, and from the Philippines to the Marshalls.

Rabaul was occupied on January 23, after the first successes. From the start of the war, the commander of the Fourth Fleet had strongly advocated an advance to the south as far as Lae and Salamaua in eastern New Guinea, and in the Solomons as far as Tulagi. On January 8, he had wanted to initiate these operations, but this was not authorized by higher authority, because the land-based air forces were too limited.

At the end of January, the military operations in the Malay Peninsula and the Dutch East Indies were so advanced and had proved so easy that the High Command's conservatism suddenly gave way to unlimited confidence, and on January 29 it ordered the invasion of Lae, Salamaua, Tulagi, and even Port Moresby.

But the movements on the first two were delayed until early March, and as we have seen, the second two were objectives of the Coral Sea campaign of early May.

The main difficulty was lack of transports, the need for which had made itself felt everywhere. Through lack of material, the Fourth Fleet would also be hampered in the building of fortifications and air bases on any advanced positions that might be occupied. It was only after Midway that the 11th and 13th Construction Groups, until then assigned to the occupation forces of that island, were sent south. As a consequence, the work of laying out an airstrip at Lunga was not begun until July. At that critical time, there were no airfields between Rabaul and Guadalcanal. The Eighth Fleet headquarters staff, sent to Rabaul on July 30, noted that no site in this zone had been found suitable for the establishment of new runways, and the Japanese air forces in the area were so reduced in strength that it was possible to send to Guadalcanal only a small contingent, and their service there was considered as temporary.

The Solomons, as we have seen, extend six hundred miles to the southeast of Rabaul and consist of two chains, separated by a deep channel which the Americans named the "Slot." Choiseul, Santa Isabel, and Malaita are the principal islands of the northeastern chain, as are New Georgia, Guadalcanal, and San Cristobal of the southwestern chain. Islets are dotted among the principal islands—Tulagi, Russell, Rendova, Kolombangara, Vella Lavella, Treasury, the Shortlands, and Buka, which formed the bridgehead of Bougainville. In this hot and humid region, rain falls almost continuously from November to June and the wind blows from the northeast.

The islands, and particularly Guadalcanal, are covered by jungle, the massive appearance of which provokes a feeling of disquiet and repulsion; the trees grow far apart and to a prodigious size, and their trunks are enlaced by a multitude of lianas and parasitical plants, which spread like a monstrous spider web; the mango tree and the jaquier thrive freely among the reeds and bamboo, while the taraminier bathes its leaves in the infected water of marshes. Beneath flowers of a thousand colors and heady perfume, swarm innumerable reptiles. It is extremely difficult to penetrate through these thickets into the middle of this inextricable jungle of grasses and plants. Since the end of the nineteenth century, the Solomons and the Santa Cruz group had been under British protection, with the capital at Tulagi.

Soon after the start of the war, a squadron of Catalinas had been based at Gavuta, near the capital, but on May 1, 1942, the region was abandoned as the Japanese approached. Nevertheless, the Americans decided to regain a footing there as soon as possible, because the Solomons would be a solid bastion for them on the line from America to Australia. Also they would provide an effective base from which to arrest the Japanese invasion and prepare for the allied offensive of a later phase of the war.

When they learned in July that the Japanese were building an airfield near Lunga Point on Guadalcanal, the American chiefs of staff decided to act immediately. A powerful force composed of the aircraft carriers *Saratoga, Wasp,* and *Enterprise,* the battleship *North Carolina,* five heavy cruisers, a light cruiser and fifteen destroyers, led a fleet of transports to Lunga Cape. The surprise landing began immediately on August 7, and the air camp at Guadalcanal was occupied the same day.

There were only a few hundred Japanese infantrymen there, and similarly at Tulagi which, energetically defended, was conquered only on the night of the eighth.[1]

Malady of victory

At 0800 on August 7, the news of the attack reached Rabaul. Admiral Mikawa, commanding the Eighth Fleet and the Advanced Forces of the south, received this last message from Tulagi: "We pray for the strength to support the misfortunes of war. We will resist to the last man."

---

1. *Thus was instituted the third phase of the Pacific war—the one that was definitely to end Japan's advance in the Southwest Pacific. Thereafter, the Allies were to wrest the war's strategic offensive from Japan and hold it until the surrender.* (R.A.T.)

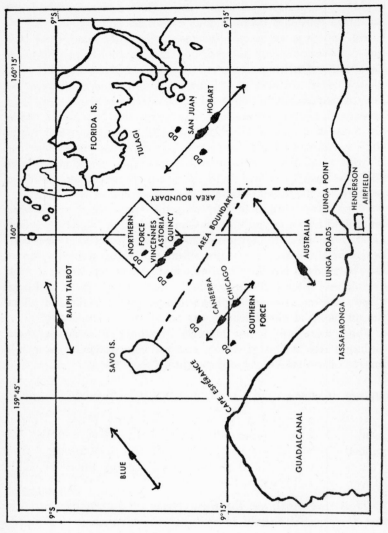

ALLIED SAVO ISLAND DISPOSITIONS, AUGUST 8, 1942

This vow was not an empty one. The Americans could not boast that they had taken a single prisoner.

The Japanese air forces reacted swiftly. At 0900 Rear Admiral Yamada, commanding the 25th Air Flotilla at Simpson Harbor, New Britain, gave the necessary orders, and at 1315, twenty-seven bombers with fighter cover arrived above the island of Savo, which guards the passage between Tulagi and Guadalcanal. The formation flew over the roadstead, from which great sprays of white water were soon rising. But not a single vessel was hit.

Two hours later, groups of dive bombers went into action and were attacked by American fighters which had taken off from the aircraft carriers operating to the southwest of Guadalcanal. Only the destroyer *Mugford* was struck by a bomb, and this did not cause any major damage.

The following day, a formation of torpedo aircraft arrived. The Americans had been given warning by one of the coast guards on Bougainville. The transports weighed anchor, took stations in cruising disposition and then, covered by a group of cruisers and destroyers, began to maneuver in unison. A wall of fire surrounded them and seventeen of the thirty-two torpedo aircraft were shot down. The destroyer *Jarvis** was the only victim of the attack. A few minutes afterward, a group of dive bombers had no more success. Exasperated, two of the pilots deliberately failed to pull out of their dives and attempted to crash upon their enemy. One of them disintegrated under the anti-aircraft fire, but the other hit thunderously on the transport *George Eliot,* which began to burn as the gasoline sent long streams of fire along her deck.

While the air forces were attacking in this way, Admiral Mikawa assembled six transports, embarked in them all the troops under his control, and sent them toward Guadalcanal under the escort of a single destroyer. At midnight on August 8, while the convoy was passing fourteen miles west of St. George Cape, the *Meiyo Maru* was sunk by a torpedo from a

---

* The badly damaged *Jarvis* departed Tulagi after dark, was fired on with torpedoes by Mikawa's force at the start of the Savo Island fight, but continued westward and was sunk by planes at 1300 on August 9.

submarine. This happening was sufficient to cause the recall to Rabaul of the remainder of the imprudent expedition.

During the evening, five heavy cruisers had left Kavieng, New Ireland—three for the Admiralty Islands and two for Rabaul—in response to an urgent call from Mikawa. At 1628, the admiral's white-and-red flag was hoisted in the cruiser *Chokai* and the five vessels set course east-northeast, to pass north of Buka. The squadron was to try to destroy, or put to flight, the naval forces supporting the American landing, and was obliged to hasten the operation in order to attack before the enemy could refit the airfield and install land-based air forces.

The American landing at Guadalcanal marked the beginning of a long, bitter struggle, in which the Japanese were ceaselessly forced to intensify their efforts.

First, they underestimated the enemy military forces; suffering from the "disease of victory," they believed that they would be able to retake this important position with 450 men. Through overconfidence, and also through lack of more adequate means, they acted in little groups. The available merchant tonnage was too limited, the aircraft carrier force was greatly reduced, and the land-based planes of the navy were the only Japanese aircraft to appear in the sky over the Solomons. The army reclaimed from its rival a certain amount of merchant tonnage and obstinately kept its air arm on the mainland and in the occupied regions of the Southern zones. Indeed, the intention of the military was to bring back to Japan and to Manchuria all the troops available at the end of the first phase of the war, in order to be prepared to counter a possible attack by Russia. The navy, regarding this as folly, used all its effort to draw the army toward the Pacific and to turn it away from the Asiatic continent. It would surely have been better to unify the national war effort as much as possible, but until the end of 1942, the Imperial Navy was left almost unsupported in its fight against the gigantic American effort.

"Every ship: attack!"

Mikawa's squadron had arrived south of New Ireland. An American aircraft which it sighted to the south-southwest, and which was one of MacArthur's planes from an Australian base, turned back almost immediately. The following day, August 8, at 1026, an aircraft recognized as Australian came nearer, until fire from the squadron put it to flight. Another Australian aircraft arrived half an hour later and prowled above the Japanese cruisers, but unfortunately there were no fighters to chase away these scouts.

Early in the morning, five Japanese seaplanes had been catapulted to carry out reconnaissance within 250 miles of the squadron. At noon two of them returned; thanks to the good weather, they were able to land on the sea and approach the cruisers, which slowed to steerage way. Crane hooks were lowered, and the aircraft were hoisted clear of the water. The admiral himself interrogated one of the pilots, who reported:

"We were greeted by very violent fire, and were only able to escape the fighters by entering the clouds. Between Tulagi and Guadalcanal, there are six cruisers, nineteen destroyers, and eighteen transports."

The Japanese were well trained in night fighting, and Mikawa decided to profit by this advantage. A surprise attack would be made in the early hours of August 9.

The operation would begin by firing torpedoes into the transport anchorage at Guadalcanal. The vessels would then turn north, bombard Tulagi, and depart through the passage opening north of Savo Island. Mikawa issued the following proclamation to the crews:

"We are going to attack victoriously by night according to the tradition of the Imperial Navy. Let each man calmly carry out his duty."

In the meantime, the Americans had disposed their forces in three patrol sectors. Admiral Crutchley held the southern sector between Savo and Cape Espérance with the cruisers

Australia, Canberra, and *Chicago* and the destroyers *Patterson*
and *Bagley.* The northern sector between Savo and Florida was
occupied by the *Vincennes,* the *Astoria,* and the *Quincy,* covered by the destroyers *Helm* and *Wilson.* The destroyers *Blue*
and *Ralph Talbot* guarded the two western entrances to the
strait.[2]

The Southern Force patrolled at twelve knots on a line northwest to southeast, turning round every half hour. The Northern Force in line ahead covered the four sides of a square, turning ninety degrees every half hour. The crews were weary, because the operations of the preceding days had been severe.

At 2315, in spite of the rain and bad visibility which had
existed for more than an hour, two Japanese seaplanes were sent
out on a last reconnaissance. One of them was reported by the
Ralph Talbot, although the *Blue* failed to pick them up on its
radar. Ordinarily, nothing can escape this magic eye, which
laughs at night and fog. It electronically calculates the time of the
two-way passage of the wave which it sends out and which is
"echoed" by an obstacle, giving the exact distance to the object
and its exact bearing. But the use of this apparatus was still not

---

2. *Despite the fact that Savo Island divided the northern entrance
into two avenues of approach, this division of forces into two
groups for night operations in such close proximity to each other
was a fatally defective tactical disposition. When either of the
separated allied groups was engaged in close action, it was impossible for the other group to distinguish friend from foe or to
have any necessary understanding as to the true situation.*

*Another important feature was the absence of Rear Admiral
Crutchley, R.N., with his flagship H.M.A.S. Australia, when the
Japanese attacked. This officer was in tactical command of the
northern groups. The British admiral had been summoned to
Lunga Point for a conference with Rear Admiral Turner, who
commanded the Amphibious Forces. The temporary absence of
Rear Admiral Crutchley made Captain Reifkohl of the U.S.S.
Vincennes the officer in temporary command of the northern
groups, but through some oversight he was never informed of this
fact.* (R.A.T.)

foolproof; the American transmissions were badly adjusted, and the two seaplanes were not troubled.[3]

The pilots gave their reports. A blazing American transport near Tulagi—the *George Eliot*—served as a beacon to show up Cape Espérance and the vessels of the southern patrol, which stood out like the figures of a shadow pantomime show on a screen.

The hour for action had arrived.

The *Chokai* took the lead, followed by the *Aoba*, the *Kako*, the *Kinugasa*, and the *Furutaka*. After them came the light cruisers *Tenryu* and *Yubari* and finally the destroyer *Yunagi*.

Thirty-four 8-inch guns, ten of 5.5-inch, twenty-seven 5-inch and 4.7-inch, and sixty-two torpedo tubes were ready to vomit fire and flame. In the dim silence, disturbed only by the drone of the fireroom blowers in the intake ventilators, the Japanese sailors peered into the night. At 0025, the lookouts signaled three cruisers south of Savo, and the alert was given. Action alerts to the gunnery organizations were sounded, gun dials were illuminated, turrets were trained, and guns were brought to bear.

At 0054, the *Chokai* sighted the destroyer *Blue* on a south-westerly course. The American destroyer saw nothing.

Mikawa turned to port to pass north of Savo, but to the

---

3. *The destroyer* Blue's *radar not only failed to pick up the two seaplanes, it also failed to detect the approach of Rear Admiral Mikawa's cruisers and destroyers. As the* Blue's *radar was searching the northern hemisphere from east through north to west, she was cruising with high hills just to the south of her. It was said at the time that this case in radar operation had never arisen previously. It seems that a high hill in this position would under certain conditions deflect or dissipate the returning, reflected radar wave so that the reflection would not record on the radar screen. Technically, the hill was said to have cast a shadow upon the radar field. With the tremendous wartime advance in radar, it is probable that this defect was eliminated in the later radar installations, if later tests proved this explanation to be the real cause of the radar failure.* (R.A.T.)

northwest a darker silhouette showed up, and the column turned back to starboard.

At 0115, the course was 150 degrees, the speed twenty-six knots. At 0132, the course was altered to ninety degrees. At 0133 the order came: "Every ship: Attack!"

The lookouts signaled two units ahead; they were the destroyers *Patterson* and *Bagley,* extended like antennae ahead of the line of cruisers which were about to reach the northwestern extremity of their beat. The *Canberra* and the *Chicago* were still more than ten thousand yards away.

In spite of the bad weather, the Japanese had discovered the enemy while remaining invisible themselves.

"Fire torpedoes!"

Salvos of torpedoes sped toward the *Bagley* and the American cruisers.[4]

---

4. The tremendous results attained by the Japanese torpedo in this close-range night action is most arresting. Every one of these torpedoes was fired by a Japanese heavy cruiser. And not one heavy cruiser in the United States navy in World War II carried torpedoes. This advantage alone was enough to assure a Japanese victory in this battle, without the many other factors which reacted so strongly in their favor.

After the London Naval Conference of 1930, which limited the displacement of heavy cruisers to 10,000 tons, the problem of avoiding unnecessary weights in future designs of these vessels became very important. Almost at once, arguments were advanced to support the elimination of torpedoes and torpedo equipment from their offensive armaments; mainly, according to the proponents of this proposal, because the heavy cruisers would always have destroyers in company to take care of the torpedo attacks, when opportunity arose.

Those who favored the retention of torpedoes in the new heavy cruisers contended that this was entirely too narrow a view of the possible tactical eventualities in the wartime life of this type. There were many reasons why their destroyers would not always be in attendance. For example, there were always numerous possibilities in cruiser operations for close-range actions, especially at

Thunder in the night

In spite of this, it was only at 0143 that the action klaxons sounded in the enemy's ships and the *Patterson* radioed the alarm. It was then useless for the attackers to remain masked.

Japanese aircraft launched flares which descended slowly above the transports moored near Lunga Point. The dark silhouettes of the *Chicago* and the *Canberra* stood out clearly against the pale light silvering the area.

The guns of the *Chokai* roared, followed almost immediately by those of the *Aoba* and the *Furutaka*. At four thousand yards, the *Canberra* was struck by two torpedoes and a storm of shells burst on her, as attested by the somber red glows of the resulting explosions. The cruiser replied with a few salvos, then fell silent, disabled.

The *Patterson* opened fire, but a shell exploded on one of her two after guns, killing all the members of the two gun crews. This did not deter the brave little ship from continuing her fire with the forward guns, as long as the Japanese were still in sight.

At 0147, the *Chicago* was hit by a torpedo which carried away part of her bow, and a shell burst against her forward mast. Mikawa had ordered the destroyer *Yunagi* to turn back to protect the rear and guard the southwestern entry to the strait. At 0144, the admiral altered course thirty degrees to the left, to sixty-nine degrees. The *Furutaka*, fifth in the line, had been somewhat confused by the alterations of course by the ships ahead, and to avoid collision with the *Kinugasa* she swung slightly to starboard and then sharply to port to course eleven degrees, followed by the *Tenryu* and the *Yubari*.

---

night or in periods of low visibility. And so, with or without destroyers in company, the heavy cruiser would be a far more powerful antagonist if she were prepared to use her own torpedoes on the enemy.

The decision was against the torpedo for the heavy cruiser. It is to be hoped that those who had their way in these arguments never read a detailed account of the Savo Island battle. (R.A.T.)

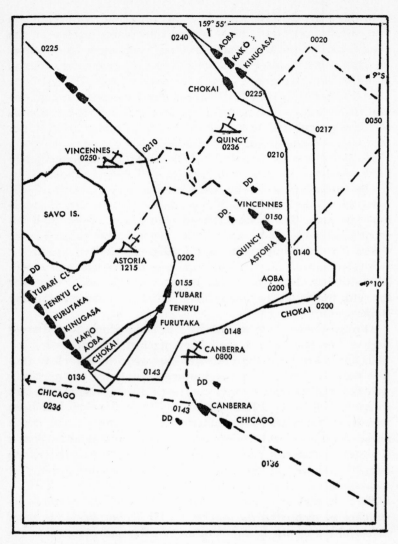

BATTLE OF SAVO ISLAND, AUGUST 9, 1942

In this way, the Japanese force was split into two groups—in the eastern formation, four cruisers in column astern of the *Chokai*, and to the west, three cruisers, temporarily in a quarter line of bearing on the *Yubari*, which was soon changed to column with that ship as guide.

At 0146, the *Tenryu* had sighted the *Vincennes* group, distant seven miles and bearing sixty degrees true. It is remarkable that this group had not seen the three Japanese cruisers nor received any warning of their approach. Two minutes later, the *Chokai* also saw the American Northern Force and immediately fired four torpedoes, one of which hit the *Astoria*.

The *Chokai's* searchlights were turned on and clearly illuminated the American cruiser, and the muzzles of the Japanese guns at once flashed. Great brilliant columns of fire shot up around the *Astoria* as a salvo struck her full amidships. Flames licked her deck, but her guns continued to fire stubbornly.

At 0202, a shell burst on her bridge, causing many casualties. At the twelfth salvo from the *Astoria*, an explosion rocked the forward turret of the *Chokai* but failed to interrupt the fire from her guns.

The searchlight beams then left the *Astoria* and were turned on the *Quincy* which, to the astonishment of the Japanese, lay with her guns still trained fore and aft and did not seem even to have her crew at action stations.

A deluge of fire rained upon her. Her seaplane caught fire on its catapult. Those on the bridge were all killed. A fountain of water rose along her side, indicating that a torpedo had struck home. A boiler room was flooded; the ready ammunition near a 5-inch gun exploded and riddled the deck with splinters. At 0235 hours, the *Quincy* capsized to port, leaving groups of men struggling on the surface of the sea.

The *Vincennes*, lit momentarily by one of the searchlights which had picked out the *Astoria*, thought that this beam came from a cruiser of the Southern Group and signaled her to extinguish her searchlight.

A salvo from the *Kako* was the reply she received, but it fell short, whereupon the *Vincennes*, undeceived, reacted with a salvo which secured a hit on the *Kinugasa*. In return, a salvo struck her full amidships, and set on fire the aircraft on their catapults, which burned like enormous funeral torches. Under the blows she received from all sides, the vessel gradually disintegrated.

She tried to escape and turned hard to starboard, but at 0155 two or three torpedoes burst in one boiler room, and at 0203 a torpedo from the *Yubari* hit another boiler room. The American cruiser could no longer fire and continued to suffer a terrible hammering from the Japanese guns.

She sank at 0250.

Mikawa ordered a cease fire and the extinguishing of all searchlights. The *Chokai* found herself astern of the *Kinugasa* as the result of a poor maneuver, but when at 0220 the Japanese admiral signaled the order of withdrawal, the *Chokai* increased speed and regained her station at the head of the column.

The *Furutaka*, the *Tenryu*, and the *Yubari* had opened fire at 0215 on the destroyer *Ralph Talbot*, which was patrolling the approaches to the northern channel. At the seventh salvo, the torpedo tubes of the American destroyer were struck and her upper-deck structure was severely damaged by the shock of the explosions. Believing it was a mistake—an odd assumption amidst the roar of battle—the *Ralph Talbot* repeatedly sent out identification signals.

The Japanese, themselves surprised, ceased fire momentarily, and the *Yubari* switched on her searchlight. Fire was resumed almost immediately, and three salvos struck home. The *Ralph Talbot*, ablaze and with a thirty-degree list to starboard, was saved from complete destruction by a sudden rain squall, under cover of which she made good her escape.

Mikawa wanted to re-form his squadron by rallying the *Furutaka*'s group, which was still separated from him, but above all, he wanted to put himself out of reach of American aircraft before daylight.

At 0240 every vessel was making thirty knots to get clear of the "Slot." At dawn they spread out; light hatches were carefully closed and anti-aircraft guns made ready to open fire, but nothing appeared in the sky.

Before reaching Bougainville Strait the admiral sent the *Aoba,* the *Kako,* the *Kinugasa,* and the *Furutaka* to Kavieng in New Ireland, while he with the other ships held course for Rabaul.

On August 10, south of Simbari, the *Kako* was struck simultaneously by four torpedoes from a submarine and sank in five minutes.

As soon as Admiral Yamamoto heard of the previous night's operation, he sent his congratulations to Mikawa: "We appreciate the courage and determination of all your crews," he said. "I count on you to continue your exploits and to do everything you find possible to support the forces of the Imperial Army, engaged in a desperate struggle."

Victory of the lookouts

The battle of Savo was a brilliant tactical success for the Japanese. At the cost of fifty-eight killed and fifty-three wounded, they had inflicted heavy losses on the enemy—four heavy cruisers sunk and one damaged. This success of the Imperial Navy was due to the extraordinarily keen sight of the Japanese lookouts and to the care with which the Combined Fleet had been trained in night fighting. But insufficient means made it impossible to exploit this victory.

It could have been different if Mikawa, hurling the adversary's naval forces out of his way, had been followed by an armada of transports protected by aircraft carriers, but there was nothing of that kind. Transports and troops were not available, and the aircraft carriers had vanished in the battle of Midway.

The American landing at Guadalcanal in spite of this brilliant riposte remained an accomplished fact.[5]

---

5. *But the Americans were fortunate in that Admiral Mikawa did not follow up his victory over their cruisers with a destructive attack upon the transports. Instead, he used the remaining dark hours to move as far to the northward as he could, in order to minimize the chances of air attacks upon his force during the*

FORCES IN BATTLE OF SAVO ISLAND, AUGUST 9, 1942

Japanese Forces, Rear Admiral Mikawa

Chokai, Aoba, Kako, Kinugasa, Furutaka   (5 CA),* Tenryu, Yubari   (2 CL); destroyer, Yunagi

Allied Forces, Rear Admiral R. K. Turner
    Northern Group: Vincennes, Astoria, Quincy   (3 CA); Helm, Wilson   (2 DD)
    Southern Group: Canberra, Chicago   (2 CA); Patterson, Bagley   (2 DD)
    Outside Patrols: Blue, Talbot   (2 DD)

NOTES:
1. No flag officer was present in the tactical area in which the battle was fought. Admiral Turner was exercising command from his flagship in Lunga Roads, Guadalcanal. Rear Admiral Crutchley R.N., in H.M.A.S. Australia, was the designated officer in tactical command of the forces in the vicinity of Savo Island, with his flagship attached to the Southern Group. At 2032, August 8, he was summoned to Lunga Roads for a conference, and he and his flagship were in that vicinity when the battle was fought.
2. Rear Admiral N. Scott with two light cruisers, operating south of Tulagi, was covering the eastern approaches to Lunga Roads. This unit took no part in the battle.

* *Abbreviations:* CA, heavy cruiser; CL, light cruiser; DD, destroyer.

---

coming daylight hours. Admiral Yamamoto was later captious about this failure.

Serious mistakes contributed to the American defeat. The premature withdrawal of the carriers from their covering position south of Guadalcanal, on the afternoon of August 8, was most unfortunate. A late-afternoon air scout, covering the northern avenues of approach, would have disclosed the advancing Japanese force: this routine precaution was overlooked. The division of the Savo Island forces into two groups for night operations in such close proximity violated the dictates of sound tactical dispositions for night operations and caused much confusion in the American forces. And, finally, the battle demonstrated the serious handicap which the lack of torpedoes must always impose upon the American heavy cruisers in a close-range night action. (R.A.T.)

Japanese officer aboard carrier giving last-minute instructions to pilots. (Official US Navy film release of excerpt from Japanese film sequence.)

left, top to bottom: Japanese air crews prepare for Pearl Harbor attack. (Wide World photos from Japanese film sequence.)

Receiving instructions aboard aircraft carrier.

Going to their planes.

A plane takes off.

Over Hawaii.

below: Pearl Harbor. Destroyers USS *Downes*, left, and USS *Cassin* battered by bomb hits December 7, 1941. The 33,100-ton battleship USS *Pennsylvania*, background, flagship of the Pacific fleet, suffered minor damage. (Official US Navy photo.)

opposite: Admiral Isoroku Yamamoto, head of the Japanese navy, who had opposed the attack on Pearl Harbor. (Wide World photo.)

above left: Admiral Osami Nagano, chief of the Japanese Naval General Staff, whose vote decided in favor of the attack. (Wide World photo.)

above right: Admiral Oikawa Koshiro, commanding Japan's China Seas fleet. (Wide World photo.)

right: Hideki Tojo, premier of Japan at the time of Pearl Harbor. (Wide World photo.)

top: Japanese Jill torpedo bomber flying safely through antiaircraft fire to attack the carrier USS *Yorktown.* (Official US Navy photo.)

bottom: A Japanese bomb scores a hit on the flight deck of an American carrier. (Official US Navy photo.)

The carrier USS *Saint Lo* burns after being struck by Japanese planes during the second battle of the Philippine Sea, October 1944. (Wide World photo.)

Small Japanese craft scamper away from larger vessels under the light of flares during an American bomber attack on Tonolei Harbor in Bougainville. A Japanese zero plane is also revealed. (Official US Navy photo.)

A Japanese carrier maneuvers in a complete circle to evade B-17s during the battle of Midway, June 1942. (Official US Navy photo.)

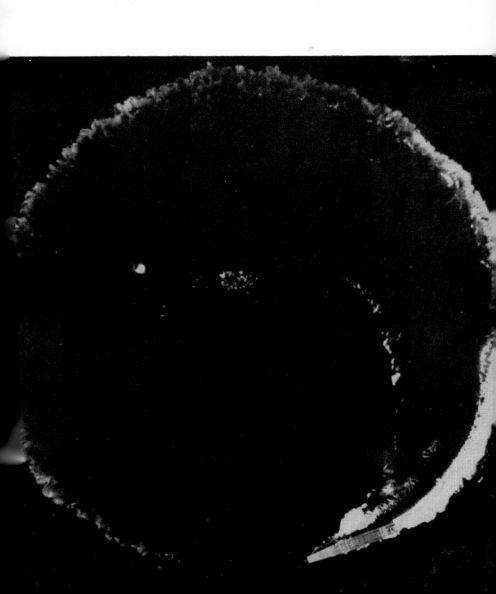

top: Damaged *Zuiho*-class carrier maneuvers at top speed to escape further strikes from US Navy planes. (Official US Navy photo.)

bottom: A small Japanese oiler sinks after being struck by Avenger torpedo bomber near Saipan. (Official US Navy photo.)

top: Japanese troopship *Kyusyu Maru* sunk off Guadalcanal. (Official US Navy photo.)

bottom: An American PT boat picks up Japanese survivors. (Wide World photo.)

top left: US Pacific Fleet landing craft launches attack against Japanese-held Peleliu Island. (Wide World photo.)

bottom left: US Sixth Fleet during the invasion of Iwo Jima. Mount Suribachi is in the background. (Official US Navy photo.)

below: US Marines camp on Tarawa beach after pre-landing bombardment. (Official US Navy photo.)

top left: Japanese suicide plane barely misses in a crash attempt on an American ship. (Wide World photo.)

center left: The carrier USS *Enterprise* struck by a Japanese suicide plane off Okinawa, May 14, 1945. The ship's huge elevator, blown out of its well some 400 feet into the air, can be seen at the tip of the smoke column. (Official US Navy photo.)

bottom left: The giant Japanese battleship *Yamato* struck by bombs as it steams at full speed. (Wide World photo.)

below: The surrender is signed, September 2, 1945, on the battleship USS *Missouri*. The Japanese delegation stands at attention as General Douglas MacArthur speaks over the radio. The guns are aimed over Tokyo Bay toward Tokyo. (Wide World photo.)

top: Death of a navy (1). Japanese prisoners of war at Guam hear the announcement of unconditional surrender. (Official US Navy photo.)

bottom: Death of a navy (2). The Japanese battleship *Ise* rests on the bottom of Kure Harbor, Japan. (Wide World photo.)

14   The Eastern Solomons

Meanwhile, at Guadalcanal, a few hundred Japanese soldiers had taken refuge in the jungle. Living in the middle of frightful swamps, with infinitely precarious food supplies and with small arms only, they fought on for months, waiting for the uncertain reinforcements which were brought to them, in spite of a thousand dangers and with considerable losses, by the navy at Rabaul.

Indeed, if the loss of Guadalcanal were to prove permanent, it would represent a serious weakening of the Japanese position in the Southern Seas. Already the Americans were building an important airfield there, Henderson Field, which would give them a strong base from which to harass the nearest enemy positions, and later to seize them. That is what Admiral Yamamoto foresaw in writing to Mikawa:

"The situation at Guadalcanal is very serious, more serious than that which faced our fathers when they understood that they must occupy Port Arthur before the arrival of the Baltic Fleet. If we do not act at once with three more divisions we can expect very grave consequences."

An entire fleet for one battalion

At Rabaul, the commanders of the Eighth Fleet, the 17th Army, and the 11th Air Fleet prepared a plan of operations to be put into effect before the end of August. Finally, after an

abortive attempt at a surprise landing on August 18, it was decided to send a reinforcement of 1500 men who, protected by
the Combined Fleet, would be landed on the twenty-fourth
("Operation K.A.").

Aircraft of the 11th Air Fleet were daily to bomb Henderson
Field, while the light vessels of the Eighth Fleet were to carry
out harassing night-bombardment raids. Indeed, the destroyers
which undertook these expeditions always arranged to be out of
reach of the American aircraft by daybreak; they traversed the
Solomons "canal" without much trouble.

Admiral Yamamoto, as mentioned earlier, had hoisted his flag
in the battleship *Yamato* at Truk. On August 21 he gave his
orders to the Covering Force which had assembled in the harbor.

The same day, at 0355, the destroyer *Kawakaze* sighted a
small vessel approaching her, and as the only possible encounters
in the approaches to Guadalcanal were with enemy ships, the
captain did not hesitate. An explosion showed that one of his
torpedoes had hit home, and the *Blue*, which was about to open
fire, was stopped dead, her stern a shapeless mass of steel plate.
The American destroyer had to be scuttled.

Again Admiral Fletcher was warned of the Japanese preparations. He covered the routes leading to the Solomons with his
three aircraft carriers—the *Enterprise*, the *Saratoga* and the
Wasp. On August 17, a fourth aircraft carrier left Pearl Harbor
with her escort and, in addition, two 35,000-ton battleships—
the *Washington* and the *South Dakota*—as well as the anti-aircraft light cruiser *Juneau*, which received orders to proceed
through Panama Canal to reinforce the Pacific Fleet.

At dawn on August 23, the Nagumo Striking Force, comprising the two big aircraft carriers *Shokaku* and *Zuikaku*, repaired after the Coral Sea "battle of phantoms," weighed anchor
at Truk. The Vanguard Group, under the command of Rear
Admiral Abe, was composed of two battleships, the *Hiei* and
the *Kirishima*, and the heavy cruisers *Suzuya*, *Kumano*, and
Chikuma.

Another squadron, commanded by Rear Admiral Hara, with

the little aircraft carrier *Ryuho,* a light cruiser, and two destroyers, was to accompany the Striking Force, then to pull away from it to create a diversion and draw off enemy attacks on the big aircraft carriers, so leaving them free to operate unmolested.

Admiral Kondo, commanding the Guadalcanal Supporting Force, had under his immediate command six cruisers and a seaplane carrier. He sailed far in advance of the Striking Force.

On the eve of the fleet departure, six submarines set out for their patrol stations. Three others had been sent to positions in the Coral Sea, west of the New Hebrides.

The 1500 men of the Guadalcanal army landing force were transported in the *Kinzu Maru* and four old destroyers. The escort for these vessels was furnished by the 2nd Destroyer Division under the command of Rear Admiral Tanaka, flying his flag in the light cruiser *Jintsu.*

This young flag officer deserves attention. Rather short and slim, with an elongated, solemn face, he had always been silent, even shy. He became the specialist of the operations to reinforce Guadalcanal. Imperturbable in the midst of the worst catastrophes, never retiring until he had accomplished his mission, and always ready to resume his perilous expeditions, he was respected by the Americans, who called him "Tenacious Tanaka."

He eventually lost his command for daring to tell his superiors that the losses entailed by the supply operations were out of proportion to the results attained.

The reinforcements carried toward Guadalcanal with this profusion of naval protection were very small, far from the three divisions envisaged by Admiral Yamamoto. The reason was that, for the army, Guadalcanal remained a secondary theater which did not merit a greater effort. A fleet was to be risked to land and abandon to their fate a handful of men, in the face of troops brought in regularly by the Americans with abundant equipment and adequate supplies.

The operational plan, as seems to have been the rule with the Japanese, was to divert the enemy toward the *Ryuho*'s group, while the Japanese carriers attacked their American opposite numbers. The heavy vessels were to shell Henderson Field to prevent intervention by the American land-based aircraft, and then the troops were to be landed.

On August 23 the weather was bad; heavy nimbus clouds filled the skys and rain squalls spread a compact veil over the horizon. At 0950 an aircraft arrived in sight of the transports, circled a moment, and disappeared.

Tanaka turned off course at 1300 toward the northeast, followed at 1800 by Kondo's force. The American air squadrons, which had been informed about the transports by their reconnaissance aircraft, accordingly failed to make contact. Before daybreak on the twenty-fourth, the *Ryuho* group left the Striking Force to take up an advanced position in the south, and soon the whole fleet set course for Guadalcanal. During this time, Fletcher sent the *Wasp* and the destroyers south to refuel.

At 0905, the *Ryuho* was 220 miles north of Malaita, sailing south, and was only 280 miles from Fletcher's Task Force when it was sighted by a reconnaissance plane.

At 1300, six bombers and fifteen fighters took off from the deck of the *Ryuho*. Joined over Guadalcanal by bombers from Rabaul, they steered toward Henderson Field, from which fighters climbed. Clouds of dust rose from the runway; aircraft circled, guns crackled, white puffs of smoke blossomed in the sky.

The bombing ended with the loss of twenty-one Japanese aircraft.

The American reconnaissance planes had evidently discovered the Japanese, because, at 1515, two of the *Enterprise*'s aircraft swung in the sky as they came out of cloud and dived on the *Shokaku*. One bomb fell in the water; the other burst on deck without piercing it.

Almost simultaneously two other aircraft from the *Enterprise* dropped on the *Ryuho*, which recognized them as torpedo planes and maneuvered accordingly.

Four other enemy torpedo aircraft were intercepted by Japanese fighters.

The *Ryuho* was turning into the wind to send off a group of aircraft, when an American formation came out of the clouds and dived on her. Anti-aircraft batteries opened fire, and fighters dashed at them, but too late. The whole hull of the aircraft carrier shuddered under repeated explosions which caused fires and slaughter, as six or seven bombs struck her. Profiting by the diversion, a flight of torpedo aircraft came in its turn and split into two groups to attack her on two sides. A well-aimed torpedo struck the little carrier which, her steering gone, circled as she burned. Soon she was listing twenty degrees and had to be abandoned. Her aircraft then aloft were ordered to land at Buka, northwest of Bougainville, and the vessel was then abandoned by her crew, who were taken on board by the *Tone* and the escorting destroyers.

Wall of fire

Meanwhile, at 1405, a seaplane from the *Chikuma* had sighted the American aircraft carriers.

An hour later, a first wave of dive bombers and torpedo aircraft escorted by fighters left the *Shokaku* and the *Zuikaku,* followed in an hour by a second wave. The wind had a strength of sixteen knots, and the sky in the area was full of high cumulus clouds, while the waves were little more than strong ripples.

At 1625, the *Enterprise* appeared. It occupied the center of a circle formed by her escorting cruisers and destroyers. A battleship, the *North Carolina,* kept station astern.

Twenty-five miles from his target, the commander of the Japanese formation fired a flare, and while the fighters climbed, the torpedo aircraft descended nearer sea level, and the dive bombers split into small groups.

The pilots felt as if they were running against a wall of fire, but nevertheless they dived for the kill. A bomb passed through part of the rear elevator, penetrating as far as the third deck, the hull was pierced, and the vessel took on a moderate list. But a fire hose was severed and by luck put out one of the most serious fires. It was the first bomb hit which this ship had taken in the war.

Another bomb landed in almost the same place; an ammunition magazine aft was ablaze. On deck the 5.1-inch guns were destroyed and splashes of blood marked the places where the gun crews had been. At 1645, a third bomb exploded on the flight deck without piercing it.

Some machines had broken away to attack the *North Carolina* but had been unable to break through the barrage of anti-aircraft fire.

An hour later the *Enterprise* was making twenty-four knots and, in spite of a serious incident which locked the helm, the ship was completely safe by 1900.

The second Japanese wave of eighteen dive bombers, nine torpedo aircraft, and three fighters did not find their enemy.

At 1735, Kondo's force was attacked by five torpedo aircraft, which were easily dodged. A little later two bombers dived on the seaplane carrier *Chitose*. The port engine was destroyed, the engine room ripped open to the sea, and other compartments set ablaze. The ship took a thirty-degree list but returned to Truk at sixteen knots.

Kondo sought a night battle; in night fighting, as noted earlier, the Japanese navy excelled. Joined at 1630 by the Vanguard Group, he set course toward Fletcher's position, supposedly twenty-three miles southeast of the Stewart Islands.

The search force comprised the battleships *Hiei* and *Kirishima,* ten cruisers, and a swarm of destroyers. While the latter scoured the sea around, the big vessels, ten thousand yards distant from each other, formed an immense rake preceded by the cruisers' seaplanes. This was necessary because the Japanese ships, unlike those of the Americans, were not equipped with radar.

At 2400, as he had seen nothing, Kondo decided to retire to the north at twenty-eight knots, because the light of day would put him at a disadvantage. On the twenty-sixth he kept station between Ontong Java and Truk. His reconnaissance aircraft still had nothing to report and, war weary, he returned to Truk on August 28.

What had happened? Fletcher, fearing a night battle, had retired southward to meet the *Wasp,* which was steaming north at high speed.

In spite of the departure of the Japanese fleet, Rear Admiral

Tanaka—the "Tenacious"—who commanded the escort of the landing corps, decided to continue on his course. During the night of August 24-25, five of his destroyers went ahead and bombarded Lunga Point, while the seaplanes of the *Chokai,* the *Kinugasa,* and the *Yura* attacked Henderson Field.

On the twenty-fifth, at 0930, a group of twelve American dive bombers arrived from Guadalcanal and the convoy began to maneuver, firing every gun. But a tall flame sprang from the cruiser *Jintsu,* which had been struck between the two forward turrets. Admiral Tanaka, on learning that the forward ammunition lockers were flooded and that the bulkheads were seriously shaken, calmly ordered the destroyer *Kagero* alongside, boarded her, and sent the *Jintsu* back to Truk, escorted by the destroyer *Suzukaze.*

As the *Kagero* began to move forward, the admiral saw a glow in the *Kenryu Maru.* The *Mutsuki* was given the order to run alongside to take on board the passengers and crew of the burning transport.

While the transfer was in progress, a flight of eight Flying Fortresses arrived at 1015. No one was alarmed, although anti-aircraft batteries opened fire. High-level bombers, they said, never hurt anyone.

Then the *Mutsuki* suddenly vanished in a cloud of steam and smoke. She had been struck well and truly by three bombs and sank at 1140, while the last destroyer present, the *Yayoi,* alone remained to pick up the survivors.

As he climbed on board, Commander Atano, captain of the late *Mutsuki,* grumbled, "Even the B-17s are starting to hit their targets!"

When everyone had been embarked, Tanaka once again started ahead, but not for long: at noon he received the order to fall back.

A report on the operation stated: "Partial reinforcement by small units multiplies the risk of having troops destroyed one by one. It is essential that big units should be ferried over."

"Tokyo Express"

While waiting for the chance to carry out a large-scale operation, the Japanese continued to send reinforcements and provisions to Guadalcanal in destroyers, under cover of darkness.

The Americans named these convoys the "Tokyo Express." The aircraft at Henderson Field were not sufficiently numerous for daily attacks, and their radius of action was not great enough to enable them to catch up with the retiring Japanese vessels at daybreak on the morning following the landings.

Some nights, the Japanese landed nine hundred men at Cape Espérance, at the northwestern extremity of the island. Generally, these operations were accompanied by a bombardment of Henderson Field by the escort destroyers or by aircraft, so as to prevent the American bombers from taking the air to harass the troops while landing.

On August 28, four Japanese destroyers set out from the Shortlands. At 1800 they were attacked by dive bombers, seventy miles north of Guadalcanal. The *Asagiri* blew up; the *Shirakumo* had to stop, her engines out of action; and the superstructure of the *Yugiri* was destroyed by fire.

The following day, five destroyers landed 450 men at Point Taivu, on Guadalcanal.

On August 30 the *Yudachi* brought troops, embarked at the Shortlands.

Eighteen Japanese aircraft bombed Henderson Field, and a bomb from one of them sank the transport *Colhoun*. During this time the *Yudachi* landed cargo at Taivu. On August 31 a further 1200 Japanese landed at Guadalcanal with General Kawaguchi, who was to assume command of the land operations.

On the night of September 4-5, while the transport destroyers landed a detachment, the *Yudachi* stood away with the *Hatsuyuki* and the *Murakumo* to attempt a diversion. At 0100 the vessels opened fire on the anchorage at Lunga. As it happened, a Catalina passing overhead fired some flares and, thanks to these, the Japanese discovered near them the old American destroyers *Little* and *Gregory*, which were cruising near Lunga Point and waiting for daylight. They were immediately selected as targets and sunk, and at 0135, after this success, the Japanese destroyers departed.

And so it went on. It was a stubborn and confused battle. All the belligerents' energy seemed concentrated on Henderson airfield; one opponent had established himself upon it, if somewhat precariously, and the other was absolutely determined to recapture it, because the one who finally possessed it would dominate with his aircraft one of the vitally important zones of the immense Pacific.

As is always the case in amphibious operations, ultimate success would depend upon mastery of the sea approaches, with the resultant ability to control the movements of troops and supplies to and from Guadalcanal. Mastery would depend primarily on the relative carrier strengths of the two navies, and it was to regain carrier advantage that the Imperial Navy had come again to offer battle. Now, what they had been unable to realize through their own planned efforts, was about to be thrust upon the Japanese forces by a stroke of good fortune, although only for a brief period.

Under water

On August 27, to the southeast of San Cristobal, the submarine *I-26* sighted the *Saratoga* in the pale light of the rising sun and immediately set her underwater course to reach attack position. The American aircraft carrier was steaming at a relatively low speed in the middle of her escort vessels, as she waited for orders.

At 0745 the *I-26* launched six torpedoes and dived deeply to escape. As she did so she had the satisfaction of feeling a shock against her hull which showed that one torpedo at least had hit the target.

In fact, the *Saratoga* had been struck on the starboard side, and although the blow was not mortal, the vessel was electri-

cally propelled and the water which flooded in caused short
circuits which made the operation of her propulsive machinery
uncertain.

On September 14 the submarines *I-19* and *I-15* sighted two
American aircraft carriers protecting a distant convoy proceeding from Espiritu Santo, in the New Hebrides, to Guadalcanal.

The *I-19* took up her attack position, and three of her torpedoes hit the *Wasp* with terrible effect. The ship was refueling
and rearming her aircraft. The ammunition blew up, the aircraft caught fire, and broken pipes allowed oil and gasoline to
escape and feed the blaze. At 1500, an elevator was blown into
the air by a terrifying explosion; twenty minutes later, the vessel had to be abandoned. She was sunk by an American destroyer the following evening.

The *I-15* was not so fortunate; she missed the *Hornet,* but
one of her torpedoes struck the *North Carolina,* whose speed
was not seriously affected. The destroyer *O'Brien* was also
struck, and broke in two off Samoa some time later, while trying to regain the American coast.

These two lucky strokes sank one American aircraft carrier
and put another out of action until repaired, so that only the
Hornet and the *Enterprise* remained in the Southern Seas.

War of attrition

Before attempting a new and important expedition to Guadalcanal, Yamamoto wanted to take Henderson Field. General
Kawaguchi, who now controlled the equivalent of a division,
tried to take the airfield by assault, but his equipment was
scant; he had only light arms, and his men, badly nourished,
were suffering from fever. In spite of great valor, Kawaguchi
was crushed on September 12 by the American defense.

But the "Tokyo Express" continued. Under these conditions,
the wear and tear was rapid. Each bombing of Henderson
Field was carried out at the price of heavy losses in aircraft.
The Flying Fortresses based there, ranging widely, caused frequent damage to the Japanese ships.

On September 14 the cruiser *Myoko* was slightly damaged. On the twenty-fifth the after turret of the *Myura* was put out of action. On October 5 the destroyers *Minegumo* and *Murasame* were seriously damaged by near hits.

There is nothing which weakens and exasperates a fleet so much as a war of attrition of this character.

OPPOSING FORCES AT START OF GUADALCANAL CAMPAIGN AND IN BATTLE OF EASTERN SOLOMONS, AUGUST 24, 1942

JAPANESE FORCES

Combined Fleet, Admiral Yamamoto

Guadalcanal Supporting Forces, Vice Admiral Kondo

Advance Force, Vice Admiral Kondo
    Main Body, Vice Admiral Kondo
    Cruiser Division 4: Atago, Maya, Takao   (3 CA)*
    Cruiser Division 5: Myoko, Haguro   (2 CA)
    Screen: 1 light cruiser, 5 destroyers
    Support Group, Commanding Officer of *Mutsu*
    Mutsu (OBB), seaplane tender Chitose, 4 destroyers

Striking Force, Vice Admiral Nagumo
    Carrier Group, Vice Admiral Nagumo
    Shokaku, Zuikaku (53 fighters, 41 dive bombers, 36 torpedo bombers)   (2 CV)
    Screen: 6 destroyers
    Vanguard Group, Rear Admiral Abe
    Battleship Unit: Hiei, Kirishima   (2 OBB)
    Cruiser Division 7: Suzuya, Kumano, Chikuma   (3 CA)
    Screen: 1 light cruiser, 6 destroyers
    Diversionary Group, Rear Admiral Hara
    Tone (CA), Ryuho (CVL) (16 fighters, 21 torpedo bombers), 2 destroyers

Southeast Area Forces, Vice Admiral Tsukahara
    Outer South Seas Force, Vice Admiral Mikawa
    Cruiser Unit: Chokai, Aoba, Kinugasa, Furutaka   (4 CA)

* *Abbreviations:* BB, modern battleship; OBB, old battleship; CV, aircraft carrier; CVL, light carrier; CA, heavy cruiser; CL, light cruiser.

Escort Unit: 1 light cruiser, 7 destroyers
Submarine Unit: 9 I-class submarines
Air Unit: 100 aircraft

UNITED STATES FORCES

Task Force 61, Rear Admiral F. J. Fletcher

Task Force 11, Rear Admiral Fletcher
    Saratoga (36 fighters, 36 dive bombers, 15 torpedo bombers) (CV)
    Minneapolis, New Orleans (2 CA)
    Screens: 5 destroyers

Task Force 16, Rear Admiral T. C. Kinkaid
    Enterprise (36 fighters, 36 dive bombers, 15 torpedo bombers) (CV)
    North Carolina (BB)
    Portland, Atlanta (1 CA, 1 CL)
    Screen: 6 destroyers

Task Force 18, Rear Admiral L. Noyes
    Wasp (28 fighters, 36 dive bombers, 15 torpedo bombers) (CV)
    San Francisco, Salt Lake City, San Juan (2 CA, 1 CL)
    Screen: 7 destroyers

15 Cape Espérance

On October 8, aircraft from Henderson Field were so active that convoys on their way from the Shortlands had to turn back. But on the ninth, the *Tatsuta* and five destroyers landed General Hyakutake and reinforcements at Tassafaronga.

A bigger operation was decided on for October 11. In the afternoon a force comprising the cruisers *Aoba, Furutaka,* and *Kinugasa,* escorted by the destroyers *Fubuki* and *Murakumo,* sailed down the "Slot" to shell Guadalcanal, while a transport and two destroyers, covered by a destroyer flotilla, landed their reinforcements near Cape Espérance, and while aircraft of the 11th Air Fleet of Rabaul neutralized Henderson Field.

Seen, but unseeing

This last operation was carried out by thirty-five bombers accompanied by thirty fighters. When they set out on the return flight, eight bombers and four fighters had been shot down but, thanks to their attack, the convoy had not been disturbed.

Nevertheless, at 1810, when the little squadron was less than a hundred miles from Savo, it was sighted by a B-17. The *Aoba,* flagship of Rear Admiral Goto, was leading the two other cruisers and was flanked by two destroyers as the convoy passed the northern point of Guadalcanal.

Twenty miles from Savo, the Japanese cruisers, which had no radar, sighted a brilliant light in the southeast, which was taken to be a signal from the transport group. A reply was called for, and the *Aoba* turned on a searchlight.

In fact, the light was that of an aircraft of the *Salt Lake City* which had caught fire while taking off.

A little to the northwest of Savo, Admiral Scott's Task Force was cruising in the night. It comprised the heavy cruisers *San Francisco* and *Salt Lake City,* the light cruisers *Boise* and *Helena,* and six destroyers.

For some time the radar of these vessels had been following the progress of the Japanese formation while the latter advanced without suspecting the presence of its adversary. The Japanese vessels' guns were trained fore and aft, as their sleepy crews awaited the time for opening the bombardment. Suddenly, at 2346, the gloom was pierced by rapid flashes, and a salvo fell alongside the *Aoba.* A cannonade crackled as the *Helena* opened fire. Soon a shower of sparks indicated that the Japanese cruiser had been hit. Then came a deeper rumble as the 8-inch guns of the *Salt Lake City* opened fire.

The Japanese gunners leapt to their guns and replied, while the noise of the ammunition hoists, the sounds of shells being rammed home, and the orders of the gun captains sounded everywhere. The vessels shuddered under the detonations of their guns.

The *Salt Lake City* was hit in her turn. Quite near to her, the destroyer *Duncan* turned to escape, but the *Furutaka* fired on her and she received a shell in a boiler room, from which torrents of steam escaped.

The American fire stopped suddenly. In the confused condition of the communications, Admiral Scott believed that he had been shooting at friendly vessels. Goto also suspended fire, wondering if the vessels before him were those of the landing group.

He had turned hard to starboard, when an avalanche of shells descended upon the *Aoba.* The Americans had reopened fire and, thanks to radar, their fire was very accurate. Tactically, the American force had "crossed the T" on the Japanese, and the point where Goto's vessels had to turn in succession became a target for their salvos.

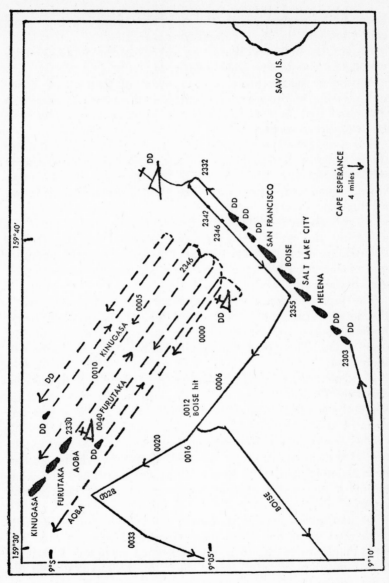

BATTLE OF CAPE ESPÉRANCE, OCTOBER 11–12, 1942

The *Furutaka* was struck and the two cruisers were ablaze. The *Aoba*, which had suffered some forty hits, could no longer fire. Goto lay on her bridge mortally wounded, and his chief of staff, Captain Kijima, lifted him and carried him to his sea cabin.

When he saw what was happening, Captain Sawa, commanding the *Kinugasa*, last of the line, turned to port, instead of following his companions, and thus saved his vessel.

The Japanese, first taken by surprise, took a grip on things.

The *Duncan*, in spite of her damage, returned to the attack and launched her torpedoes at the *Furutaka*, which dodged them and answered back. The American destroyer was then finally sunk.

The *Fubuki*, caught napping by the *Aoba*'s abrupt alteration of course, did not turn at once. She also believed that she was involved with the convoy and even switched on her identity lights. She was at once crushed by the fire of the whole American force.

It was 2355; the Japanese cruisers were steaming northwest in two columns. Admiral Scott came parallel with them and the American destroyers attacked.

The *Boise* closed in audaciously on the *Furutaka*, which was hit by a torpedo. One engine was stopped, but the brave Japanese vessel continued on her course in spite of the rising water and spreading fire.

However, a short time later, all hope for the cruiser was lost and, at 0040, the vessel settled and suddenly capsized, twenty-two miles northwest of Savo.

The *Kinugasa*, the only one intact, continued firing on the Americans and shifted to the *Boise* when the latter turned on a searchlight to identify an object whose presence was indicated on her radar screen. The *Aoba*, still on fire, had succeeded in getting some of her guns back in action and, together with the *Kinugasa*, also took that American light cruiser under fire. But the heavy cruiser *Salt Lake City* intervened, and a duel ensued between her and the *Kinugasa* in which both were hit.

At 0200 the Americans turned south-southwest and stood away.

The *Aoba* gradually mastered the raging fire and steamed at top speed, so as to be as far as possible from Henderson Field when day broke. The *Kinugasa* followed her, ready to give help.

Admiral Goto was dead. While he lay dying on the couch in the sea cabin, Captain Kijima entered. He read a mute question in the veiled eyes of the admiral and, leaning over the dying man, he told a pious lie: "Die satisfied, Admiral. We have sunk two big enemy cruisers." Actually, the Americans had lost the destroyer *Duncan,* and the cruiser *Boise* had been badly damaged but she was later repaired and restored to service.

At dawn the anti-aircraft gun crews were at their posts, and all precautions against air attack were taken. This attack, however, did not materialize until 0700 when, greeted by intense fire, some B-17s delivered a very haphazard bombing attack, which scored no hits.

In the morning of October 12, the two vessels anchored at the Shortlands, but the *Aoba* soon departed for a long period of essential major repairs.

Death before captivity

While the cruiser battle raged, Rear Admiral Joshima landed the troops and supplies near Kokumbona. He returned along the coast and escaped to the westward.

The destroyer *Murakumo*, which escorted the *Aoba,* emerged unscathed from the fight, thanks to the cover provided by the smoke which spread over the sea from the fire in the cruiser. After the Americans had left, the Japanese destroyer turned back to pick up survivors from the *Furutaka*. The *Natsugumo* joined her, and the two vessels recovered four hundred men. They then sighted an American destroyer moving toward them and set course to the northward in the hope that the enemy would follow them and thus come the next day within range of the Japanese aircraft. With this in mind, the two destroyers proceeded at moderate speed.

But the pursuer turned back and, at dawn, bombers appeared from Henderson Field to rain blows on the two little ships. The *Murakumo* became a wreck covered with dead and wounded.

Everything that could float was thrown overboard, and those men who were still able to do so tried to reach the nearest islands, while the engine-room force opened the sea cocks to scuttle the vessel.

Soon afterward, the same fate overtook the *Natsugumo*.

At 1430 the survivors of the *Fubuki*, still clinging to their bits of flotsam and their improvised rafts, saw a destroyer approach them. She was American.

The vessel stopped near the survivors. Lifebelts and lifelines were thrown to the men in the water. They had only to seize them to be rescued. That way lay salvation—and also captivity. Not one Japanese sailor accepted rescue at that price.

Captain Kijima, Admiral Goto's chief of staff, was summarily relieved of his duties by Admiral Mikawa for not having ordered the cruisers to maintain a condition of readiness for action during their mission in enemy waters, and so having permitted the enemy to surprise them.

Indeed, the rebuke was not without foundation, because war demands continuous preparedness. However, it should be remembered that the expedition which was under way was a routine operation and the squadrons that had bombed Henderson Field that afternoon had not signaled the presence of unusual enemy naval forces; the danger zone, confined to the strait of Savo, had not yet been reached.

Night operations involve great tension of spirit and crushing fatigue. Was not the Japanese command required to defer the undertaking of such efforts, within reasonable limits?

Finally, it must be emphasized that the Japanese had supreme confidence in their superiority in night combat, which the facts had not yet denied. Always, they counted upon being first to detect the enemy, and taking the initiative accordingly.[1]

It was the American use of radar which was the real cause of

---

1. *Moreover, it was Admiral Goto's responsibility to order the crews alerted for action. His chief of staff could only be held blameworthy if it were proved that he had failed to advise his admiral to order the alert for action, when he noted that this had not been done although the time for doing so had arrived.* (R.A.T.)

the surprise. This was to have great consequences, not only from the material but also from the morale point of view. Thenceforth, the confidence of the Japanese sailors was shaken. They always knew that their movements, even in zero visibility, would be disclosed long before the forces would come within battle range of each other. Even on the clearest night, the eyes of the best lookouts could not hope to compete with radar in the distant detection of enemy forces, either surface or airborne.

16   Santa Cruz

All the preceding operations were based on the Japanese plans for the reconquest of Guadalcanal. It was a question of obstructing the passage of the American reinforcements and of ensuring the arrival in the island of enough Japanese troops to try a decisive assault on Henderson Field. Once the airfield was taken, enough aircraft would be sent to keep the mastery of the air over the sector, and the complete elimination of the Americans from Guadalcanal must quickly follow.

It was in furtherance of the first part of the program that the submarines *I-4, I-5, I-7, I-8, I-22,* and *I-176* had been sent to the waters through which the American convoys had to pass to reach Guadalcanal.

A second group of submarines, composed of the *I-9, I-15, I-21, I-24, I-174,* and *I-175* under the name of Force B, later reinforced the first.

With air help, the aim had been considerably realized. The Americans suffered severe losses, and the difficulties of supplying the troops which they had on Guadalcanal were greatly increased.

The second part of the program was realized by the "Tokyo Express," which succeeded in landing an average of nine hundred men a night. In this way, the Japanese troops on Guadalcanal reached, by about October 14, an effective strength of twenty-six thousand men. But they had only one 105-millimeter fieldpiece, unloaded from the convoy of October 11, while their few light tanks were considerably handicapped in their operations by the swampy character of so much of the terrain.

The life of these men was frightful; without shelter, they camped in the midst of the jungle in pestilential mud, eaten by myriads of mosquitoes and threatened by snakes that blended with the lianas. For food they had only rice, which rapidly turned moldy, and soya beans, which, although limited in quantity, assured them, thanks to its excellent nutritional properties, the minimum of indispensable calories.

Ravaged by fever and sapped by dysentery, they were nevertheless full of zest and dreams of fighting.

To undertake the assault on Henderson Field, they needed only an additional detachment of three thousand shock troops.

As the Americans had only two aircraft carriers at their disposal, the equilibrium was temporarily reestablished in Japan's favor.

This was the decisive moment to concentrate all the available reserves and snatch success.

Nagumo to the rescue

On October 11, the most important squadron to be assembled since Midway weighed anchor at Truk. There were the battleships *Hiei*, with Admiral Abe on board, and *Kirishima*, which stood away to the eastward, surrounded by cruisers and destroyers. This was the Vanguard Group, the advance supports for the Carrier Force, which was to follow it at sixty miles' distance.

On the bridge of the gigantic battleship *Yamato*, Admiral Yamamoto, slim in his white uniform, returned the salutes of the veterans of Pearl Harbor and the Coral Sea, as the ships in succession rendered the usual honors when they passed his flagship—the *Shokaku* and the *Zuikaku*, followed by the little aircraft carrier *Zuiho*. Nagumo was still in command of the Striking Force, with his flag flying in the *Shokaku*.

The Advance Force, under the command of Vice Admiral Kondo, was the next to pass. From his flagship, the *Myoko*, he contemplated the three other heavy cruisers, the small aircraft carrier *Junyo,* and the escort destroyers led by the light cruiser *Isuzu.*

Then followed the 3rd Battleship Division which, with its destroyers, comprised the Support Group commanded by Vice Admiral Kurita. The battleships were the *Kongo* and the *Haruna,* with their powerful 14-inch guns. Their magazines carried nine hundred shells, three hundred of which were high-explosive shells for use in the bombardment of land objectives.

At the peak of the tower dominating the bridge, a grill-like antenna indicated that, at last, the two great vessels were equipped with radar.

While Nagumo took a cruising station one hundred miles to the northeast, Kondo set course to pass between Santa Isabel and the Florida Islands. The four screening destroyers, well in advance, were to challenge any vessel encountered and to torpedo them if they were not Japanese. Thus they would maintain secrecy regarding the movements of the main forces.

Shortly before midnight on October 13, the battleships led by the light cruiser *Isuzu* sighted Savo, which meant that they were entering the danger zone whose waters already covered so many wrecks and dead men.

The big vessels passed through the opening to the north of Savo. Guns were loaded and the gunners waited silently for the red lights to order "open fire." Gun layers were keeping the guns set at the desired elevation and azimuth of train by following the pointers on the luminous dials that transmitted the settings and movements of the director master sight in the fighting tops.

On October 14, at 0100, illumination flares blossomed slowly from the observation seaplanes flying over Henderson Field.

This was the signal. The great guns responded immediately, recoiled, and returned to battery; an enormous roar sounded through the night silence, to be echoed by faraway explosions. The seaplanes signaled the spotting corrections, and the settings of gun-director sights were altered accordingly. A second salvo caused immense flames to rise above the airfield, and continuous fire was at once ordered. The gun crews smiled happily as they guided the heavy shells brought up by the hoists, and then placed the powder charges onto the loading tray so that the rammers could thrust them in succession into the gaping breeches. The flames spread over the airfield, and whitish debris flew into the air and formed a pall which the easterly breeze moved without dispersing.

At 0230, the guns had used up their high-explosive ammunition, and the "cease fire" was rung. Admiral Kurita turned northwest, and left by the channel south of Savo.

A single gun made itself heard, modestly. It was the only fieldpiece the Japanese soldiers had on the island. Every quarter of an hour the gun fired one shell—and no more, so as not to use up precious ammunition.

The operation had succeeded perfectly. Everything was destroyed on Henderson Field. The runway was unusable, only one plane was intact, and there was no gasoline left.[1]

Rain of shells

The same day, the last echelon of reinforcements intended for Guadalcanal, which included the shock troops, sailed down the Solomons canal in six transports, accompanied by destroyers, and with fighters overhead.

Some American aircraft, probably from Espiritu Santo, sighted the convoy and passed to the attack, but only the *Samidare* was slightly damaged.

A speck appeared in the northwest and rapidly grew larger. Soon the *Chokai* and the *Kinugasa* could be distinguished, escorted by destroyers and moving at high speed. The soldiers, embarked in the transports, acclaimed the flag of Admiral Mikawa, who had insisted on leading the expedition himself. The two fine cruisers passed and soon grew fainter in the southeast.

---

1. *Actually, the runway was only temporarily unusable, and something over half the aircraft had been destroyed. The fuel was down to 400 drums, but by midmorning, transport planes were flying gasoline in from Espiritu Santo.* (R.A.T.)

They arrived at Savo in the night, slowed speed, and approached the spot chosen for the landings the following day. It was essential that the airfield should not be patched up so that it could serve as a base for the enemy's bombers during that decisive day. The sixteen 8-inch guns went into action and poured 752 shells upon the airfield and its neighboring installations.

When the convoy arrived in the morning of the fifteenth, it anchored immediately in the designated position and began the disembarkation of troops and supplies.

For some hours there was an extraordinary bustle in the bay with its green foreshores, on which emaciated and tattered soldiers had come to wait for their comrades. The few landing craft came and went. They were used mostly to carry supplies. The men left the transports in all the craft available, including some native pirogues which had been pressed into service.

But the Americans, in spite of the disaster they had suffered, did not remain inactive. From Espiritu Santo, a certain number of aircraft reached Henderson Field in spite of everything. Flying Fortresses, thanks to their long range, were able to take part in the defense, and gasoline arrived by aircraft in spite of Japanese interception.

At the end of the morning, aircraft circled above the roadstead amid tracer bullets and the puff balls of exploding shells, which blossomed in the sky. Bombs fell among the transports which were discharging, and the *Azumasan Maru,* the *Kyushu Maru,* and the *Sasako Maru,* badly damaged, had to be beached to avoid sinking. But the landing continued. At 1550 the three remaining unharmed transports set off without hindrance to return to the Shortlands.

Evening fell and the *Myoko* and the *Maya* entered the bay. That night, 1500 shells from 8-inch guns fell on the American defenses and installations.

Faulty maneuver

General Kawaguchi had asked for six days after the landing of the shock troops in which to prepare for the attack on Henderson Field, and the date was set accordingly for October 21.

As the preliminary operations, however, had not had the expected results, "J Day" was postponed to the twenty-second.

On that morning the Japanese troops attacked furiously. All day there was a continual din of rifle and machine-gun fire, broken from time to time by the deeper sound of artillery. A pungent vapor spread over the jungle, a vapor which seemed alternately to flow from north to south and then from south to north, following the fluctuations of the battle. The attackers ran up against a well-organized defense, backed by entrenchments and furnished with automatic arms and artillery. In his first day's assaults, Kawaguchi lost two thousand men and twelve of his light tanks.

A new attack was planned for the twenty-fourth but was postponed to the twenty-fifth. Admiral Nagumo grew impatient; he had emptied his oil tankers and would soon be under the necessity of returning to his base on account of shortage of fuel.

Kawaguchi stiffened his men and led them in a desperate assault on the airfield defenses. The scattered Japanese soldiers threw themselves forward, heedless of the fire which mowed them down, and penetrated to the edges of the camp. At 0230, when he saw his troops so near their goal, the general signaled: "Airfield taken."

Fourteen Japanese fighters and a group of bombers left the carriers at once and arrived above Henderson Field, which was to serve them as a base. They flew over the runway, giving their recognition signals, but there was no response.

The airfield was doubtless not yet serviceable, and they had to wait, especially as dawn was breaking.

But a furious counterattack by United States Marines had thrown back the Japanese. The aircraft circling unsuspectingly were suddenly attacked by a pack of American fighters which surged out of the shadows, and in a few minutes the Japanese were all shot down.

At 0700 on the twenty-sixth, Kawaguchi canceled his signal of the previous night. The propitious moment had passed, and the Japanese army was not destined to capture Guadalcanal.

The Hornet

Meanwhile, on receiving news of the Japanese attacks on Guadalcanal, the American commander had grouped his naval forces. Two carrier task forces, each containing one of the two carriers *Enterprise* and *Hornet*—the only ones available—skirted the north coast of Santa Cruz then turned toward the southwest. When they arrived east of San Cristobal, they waited for the chance to intercept the enemy advance. A third task force, grouped around the battleship *Washington* and the heavy cruiser *San Francisco,* cruised southeast of San Cristobal out of range of war planes.

The presence of their enemy was known to the Japanese, whose submarines and aircraft were watching the whole area.

A Japanese aircraft had sighted the *Enterprise* well off the Gilberts; but before air forces could intercept, the carrier withdrew to the eastward.

On their side, the American reconnaissance aircraft had spotted the Japanese forces on the twenty-third, and from that date on, the Vanguard Group of the striking force daily sighted patrol aircraft. On the twenty-fifth, about 1300, six B-17s passed high over the Vanguard Group and dropped bombs, which fell into the water.

The day following, at 0630, a Japanese scouting aircraft signaled the exact position of the enemy's carriers. At the same time, American aircraft made contact first with the battleships of the Striking Force and then with the carriers.

The weather was fine, with a few cumulus clouds stretching across the sky and a good breeze blowing from the southeast. About 0840, two American reconnaissance aircraft emerging from clouds dived unexpectedly on the *Zuiho,* which received two bomb hits aft. The deck was pierced and anti-aircraft guns overturned.

The vessel was no longer serviceable for landings but, luckily for her, her machines had already taken off, and this saved her from the terrible flames which had enveloped the carriers at Midway.

Indeed, after the signal of 0630, another of the *Shokaku's* aircraft had reported: "Numerous enemy in sight. One carrier, five other vessels."

The sixty-five aircraft of the big carrier, which had been waiting for the order, took off, circled overhead until formed, and flew toward the Americans, two hundred miles to the southeast.

The elevators immediately started to bring up the second wave of aircraft, which mechanics feverishly made ready and which took off very quickly.

The squadrons flying southeast sighted a long line of planes coming in the opposite direction. They were fifteen dive bombers, six torpedo aircraft, and eight fighters from the *Hornet;* three dive bombers, eight torpedo aircraft, and eight fighters from the *Enterprise;* and finally a further twenty-five aircraft from the *Hornet.*

These dispersed groups were a temptation to the Japanese fighters, who left their formation and shot down a few aircraft in the *Enterprise* flights.

There was the *Enterprise!* The big carrier was in the center of a circle formed by the *South Dakota,* the *Portland,* the anti-aircraft cruiser *Juneau,* and eight destroyers.

The *Hornet,* also in sight, was surrounded by two heavy cruisers, two anti-aircraft cruisers, and seven destroyers.

Fighters took off from the two vessels and tried to gain height; but it was too late.

At 0900 a lucky squall hid the *Enterprise.* The Japanese formation, which was about to split into two groups, accordingly continued in one unit toward the *Hornet* and deployed for attack at 0910.

In spite of the barrage of fire put up by the escorting vessels, the Japanese bombers dived on their prey. A bomb burst on the flight deck, and on the starboard side aft two near misses in rapid succession shook her hull. The commander of the dive bombers, whose plane was hit by fragments from a bursting shell, did not pull out of his dive.

With a horrible rending noise, the aircraft hit the stack, glanced off, and burst through the flight deck, where two of its bombs detonated.

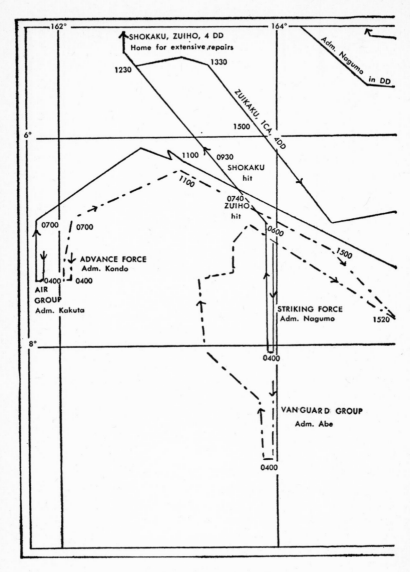

BATTLE OF SANTA CRUZ ISLANDS, OCTOBER 26–27, 1942

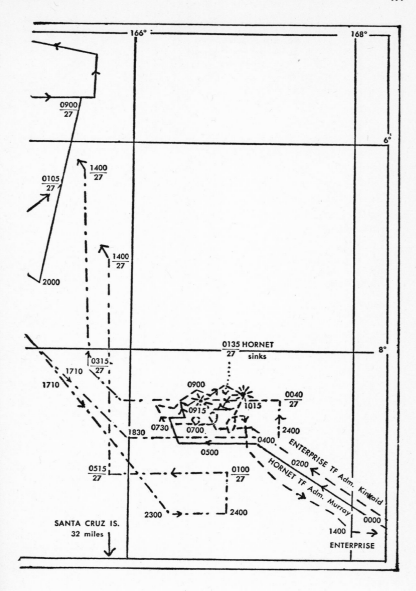

Simultaneously the vessel was shaken from end to end as two torpedoes burst in the engine spaces.

The *Hornet* lurched to starboard, stopped, and remained disabled; she no longer had power and her driving shafts were broken. Mercilessly the Japanese attack continued. A bomb burst on deck; a second reached the fourth deck before exploding; a third was equipped with a delayed fuse which exploded only after it had gone through four decks.

Finally, the pilot of a torpedo aircraft dashed his plane against the port forward gun gallery, and it blew up near the forward elevator, covering the bridge with splinters.

Ten minutes after this devastating assault, the attackers disappeared.

The Shokaku

What had been happening on the Japanese side meanwhile?

At 0930, fifteen dive bombers from the *Hornet* had attacked the *Shokaku* and the *Zuiho* which, forewarned, were surrounded by a swarm of fighters. These dashed on the assailants and shot down two bombers and damaged two others, but eleven bombers delivered their attacks. The *Shokaku* seemed to explode.

She had received four one-thousand-pound-bomb hits on the port side of the flight deck, forward and amidships, and two others near the after elevator. Guns were twisted, the upper hangar was riddled, and fires broke out but were soon brought under control. The ship was put out of action for nine months.

The attack was over when the *Enterprise* group arrived. The Japanese fighters surpassed themselves; the American planes, repulsed, and seeing the *Kongo* to the south, turned thither to attack her. The battleship, firing all her guns and supported by the fire of her escort, struck a zigzag course at top speed. Bombs and torpedoes surrounded her, but she was never touched.

The second wave of planes from the *Hornet* never found the Japanese carriers.

Too far from the others

Captain Komura, commanding the cruiser *Chikuma,* was separated a little from the group of which he was a part. He saw a formation of bombers heading toward him for an attack. He unloosed his fire and dodged vigorously, but in vain: a bomb burst on the bridge with a shattering explosion. The steel flooring shook so violently that an officer's leg was broken; nearly all the personnel on the bridge were killed or wounded. Komura himself was wounded in several places. But he was the commander: he must keep going! While he continued, pale and bloodied, to guide his ship, another bomb fell behind the bridge and burst in a stairway to the engine room; several men were killed and the speed of the ship diminished. Then two more bombs exploded in the water to starboard, so close that the ship staggered and water penetrated into the hold through parted steel platings.

"I was too far from the others," Captain Komura explained later. "I was without the benefit of their protection. And I no longer had any air cover."

The *Chikuma* still was able to set course for Truk. When she arrived in port, her captain, at the end of his endurance, collapsed. But he had saved his ship.

When luck is uncertain

At 0927, Admiral Nagumo learned that he was facing only one carrier and decided to dispatch all available aircraft to supplement the attacks on the *Enterprise* which had been initiated by the forty-four aircraft which had set out at 0822.

Before the aircraft of the first wave intercepted the carrier, the submarine *I-22,* which was prowling in these waters, sighted the *Enterprise* in her periscope and launched a salvo of torpedoes. The carrier maneuvered in time and completely avoided this danger, but the destroyer *Porter* stopped dead, both boiler rooms badly damaged by a torpedo hit, and had to be sunk by gunfire.

Then came the dive bombers. Carried along by their eager-

ness, they had overtaken the torpedo aircraft and attacked immediately. From above the carrier, in spite of the anti-aircraft
barrage, twenty-three bombs whistled down.

One pierced the deck near the bows and continued for more
than thirty-nine feet before exploding. A second fell beside the
forward elevator, pierced the deck, and broke in two. One part
burst in the hangar; the other pierced as far as the third deck
without exploding. A third bomb was a near miss to port and
ruptured the side plating; the bearings of one of the main turbines were damaged and the engine had to be stopped.

At last the torpedo aircraft arrived, but too late. Obliged to
attack alone, they suffered heavy losses. Nevertheless, nine of
them launched their torpedoes, but from too great a distance,
and the *Enterprise* maneuvered to avoid them all. The cruiser
Portland found herself in the waters covered by the spread of
these torpedoes and was hit by three of them, all duds.

One of the torpedo-aircraft pilots hurled his blazing plane on
the destroyer *Smith,* hitting number-two gun mount, causing
heavy fires, and killing or wounding over fifty of her crew. But
the badly damaged ship maintained her station in the task force
until the end of the engagement, when she was sent to Pearl Harbor for repairs.

A wave from the *Junyo,* which had joined the carrier groups,
then concentrated their efforts on the *Enterprise,* but her anti-
aircraft barrage broke up all the attacks, and the last American
carrier escaped every blow.

The disappointed Japanese survivors sought fresh prey. At
1127, some of them dived on the *South Dakota* and the *San
Juan.* A bomb exploded against the forward high turret of the
battleship but failed to penetrate the armor. The *San Juan*
was pierced deeply by a bomb, which burst almost at the bottom
of the ship. The rudder was jammed hard over, and the cruiser
began to turn in circles.

Fortunately, she was well clear of all the other ships as she
continued to circle until the engineers could restore the steering
gear to normal working order.

Stubborn ship

Before continuing the operation, Admiral Kondo reorganized his forces. Since morning the carriers had been sailing northwest. The *Zuikaku* was ordered to turn back. The *Shokaku* and the *Zuiho*, both badly crippled, held their course to seek the security of a base. As Admiral Nagumo remained in the *Shokaku*, the command of the remaining carriers passed to Rear Admiral Kakuta in the *Junyo*.

The morning's battles had already cost a hundred aircraft.

At 1315 Kakuta, who wanted to finish off the *Hornet*, ordered a wave of five machines from the *Junyo* and ten from the *Zuikaku* to take off.

The disabled American carrier was marked for the kill. The quarry could not resist, and at 1515, the *Northampton*, in order to be free to maneuver, let go her towline to the *Hornet*. The anti-aircraft cruiser *Juneau* had joined the *Enterprise* group by mistake.

The *Hornet* was again torpedoed and bombed, but she stayed afloat.

At 1515, a formation of six high-level bombers neared the wounded ship, and she was hit again in the flight deck aft. At 1702 a fresh attack was delivered by twenty-six aircraft, and a bomb burst in the hangar.

The Americans themselves now wanted to be rid of the ship, and for some time there was the extraordinary spectacle of the two opponents furiously attacking the same deserted target. The *Hornet* was torpedoed again and again; but she still remained upright and would not sink.

While the destroyers *Mustin* and *Henderson* continued to riddle her with shells and torpedoes, the Japanese vanguard and the Advance Force steamed toward the Americans, whose position had been reported by reconnaissance seaplanes.

At 2040 the *Hornet* was ablaze. The American destroyers made off, as Abe hove over the horizon on the *Hiei*. The Japanese admiral could have had no thought of seizing the carrier, which was nothing but a flaming mass. A destroyer division dashed in pursuit of the *Mustin* and the *Henderson,* and the *Makikumo* and the *Akigumo* finally dispatched the *Hornet,* which disappeared at 0135 on October 27.

Kondo withdrew to the northward. He decided to make a search followed by an attack the next day, but during the night he received the order to return to Truk, which he had left sixteen days before.

The same day, October 27, the *Washington* was able to dodge the *I-15's* torpedoes, but soon thereafter a second torpedo burst, some four hundred yards from her. The American battleship lost no time in getting clear of the unhealthy neighborhood.

After the battle

There is no gainsaying that the Imperial Navy won the battle of Santa Cruz, in which it inflicted heavy losses on the enemy and remained master of the battlefield. It would have been able to retain that mastery—because it was incontestably stronger than the American squadron—if it could have recaptured Guadalcanal and thus have eliminated the menace of the aircraft at Henderson Field.

It was regrettable, from the Japanese point of view, that after allowing the seizure of this essential position, they did not try to retake it much earlier by means of a big operation such as that just described.

The previous two months had been put to profit by the Americans. They were now solidly installed on Guadalcanal; their entrenchments were powerfully laid out, and they had at their disposal a considerable armament. Against this, the Japanese troops fighting on the island had insufficient means, and although they were reinforced in numbers, the lack of landing equipment had prevented them from receiving the guns and tanks without which they could only get themselves heroically cut to pieces.

The Japanese navy had paid dearly for its victory. The *Shokaku* had to undergo long-drawn-out repairs and the *Zuikaku* remained the only big carrier available, but on the other hand the *Enterprise* was also alone. Perhaps at that moment, in spite of everything, the Japanese had gained the greatest advantage from a naval point of view that it had enjoyed since the beginning of the Guadalcanal campaign. Pearl Harbor had brought them only an artificial superiority, since the American battleships which they had annihilated [2] did not have the importance ascribed to them: the real capital ship in this war was the aircraft carrier, and it was with respect to that type that, by October 1942, the Imperial Navy had done the most harm to its foe. For a short time, if other elements had not been playing a strong part in the strategic situation, it possibly could again have achieved its aims of the moment.[3]

But another important factor had shown itself in the interval, altogether to Japan's detriment: the growing insufficiency of transport and cargo vessels was slowing down supplies and acting as a brake on operations.

On the other hand, the results of the several battles in the vicinity of Savo Island (not the battle so named) and of that of Santa Cruz had introduced some precarious considerations for

---

2. *There is no desire to minimize the defeat inflicted upon the United States fleet at Pearl Harbor. "Annihilate," however, might be too strong a word. Four battleships were sunk, and four others were restored to active service after repairs which required about six months. Two of the ships sunk were raised and restored to active duty—the* California *by the summer of 1943 and the* West Virginia *several months later. As the author says, this would have been a far more crippling blow than it was, if the battleship had retained the importance it enjoyed in former wars.* (R.A.T.)

3. *However, the continued American possession of Guadalcanal was stopping any further advance of the Japanese in the Southwest Pacific, and the Japanese had just made an all-out effort to capture that position and had failed. Also, their final drive upon Port Moresby in Papua had been turned back. Furthermore, the Americans still had the* Enterprise *operating in the area, and the Japanese big carrier, the* Zuikaku, *the only one available for active service, had retired to the northward.* (R.A.T.)

the Japanese. Admiral Halsey, who at Noumea had recently taken command of the South Pacific forces, knew that he could count on early and increasingly powerful reinforcements.

Finally, the Japanese navy had lost more than a hundred aircraft in the last battle, and with them numerous trained pilots, veterans of Pearl Harbor, the Indian Ocean, and the Coral Sea.

A steadily rising flood of American air crews, always thoroughly trained, was arriving from America while, on Japanese airfields, it was necessary to limit strictly the hours of flight on account of the shortage of aviation gasoline.

Men and ships, the dead were not replaced.[4]

---

4. *In the battle of the Santa Cruz islands, the Americans lost the carrier* Hornet *and the destroyer* Porter. *The Japanese lost no ships, but the* Shokaku's *damage took nine months to repair. The* Zuikaku *and* Zuiho *were also damaged, as was the heavy cruiser* Chikuma.

Tactically, the battle was a Japanese victory. They remained on the scene of the fight after it was over, and their losses were not as great as those sustained by the Americans.

But the strategic consequences of the October operations, culminating in this battle, are another story:

1. The Japanese had failed to recapture Guadalcanal, and Henderson Field remained in American hands.

2. After this battle, the large Japanese aircraft carriers withdrew from the South Pacific theater and did not again appear in the operations there.

3. By the spring of 1943, long before the Shokaku *would again be ready for active service, the Americans would have, in addition to the* Enterprise *and* Saratoga, *two new aircraft carriers and four new light carriers in service.*

The American strategic situation in the South Pacific, although still critical, had shown a slight but unmistakable trend upward. (R.A.T.)

OPPOSING FORCES DURING HEIGHT OF LAND FIGHTING
ON GUADALCANAL EFFECTIVE ABOUT MID-OCTOBER, 1942

Gun Bombardments of Guadalcanal and Battle of Santa Cruz Islands

JAPANESE FORCES

Combined Fleet, Admiral Yamamoto

Guadalcanal Supporting Forces, Vice Admiral Kondo

Advance Force, Vice Admiral Kondo
        Cruiser Division 4: Atago, Takao (2 CA)*
        Cruiser Division 5: Myoko, Maya (2 CA)
        Screens: 1 light cruiser, 6 destroyers
        Carrier Unit: Junyo (CVL) (24 fighters, 21 dive bombers, 10 torpedo
           bombers), 2 destroyers
        Support Group, Vice Admiral Kurita
        Battleship Unit: Kongo, Haruna (2 OBB)
        Screens: 6 destroyers

Striking Force, Vice Admiral Nagumo
        Carrier Group, Vice Admiral Nagumo
        Shokaku, Zuikaku, Zuiho (63 fighters, 47 dive bombers, 47 torpedo bomb-
           ers) (2 CV, 1 CVL)
        Escort and Screen: Kumano (CA), 8 destroyers
        Vanguard Group, Rear Admiral Abe
        Battleship Unit: Hiei, Kirishima (2 OBB)
        Cruiser Unit: Tone, Chikuma, Suzuya (3 CA)
        Screens: 1 light cruiser, 7 destroyers

Outer South Seas Force, Vice Admiral Mikawa
        Flagship Unit: Chokai (CA)
        Bombardment Unit: 1 light cruiser, 5 destroyers
        Assault Unit: 3 destroyers

Advanced Expeditionary Force, Vice Admiral Komatsu
    Submarine Units: 11 I-class submarines

* *Abbreviations:* BB, modern battleship; OBB, old battleship; CA, heavy cruiser; CL, light cruiser; CVL, light carrier; CV, aircraft carrier.

Land-Based Air Force, Vice Admiral Kusaka
 About 200 planes of various types, based at Rabaul.

UNITED STATES FORCES

U.S. South Pacific Force, Vice Admiral W. F. Halsey

Task Force 61, Rear Admiral T. C. Kinkaid
 Enterprise (34 fighters, 36 dive bombers, 18 torpedo bombers) (CV)
 South Dakota (BB)
 Portland, San Juan (1 CA, 1 CL)
 Screen: 8 destroyers

Task Force 17, Rear Admiral G. D. Murray
 Hornet (36 fighters, 36 dive bombers, 15 torpedo bombers) (CV)
 Northampton, Pensacola, San Diego, Juneau (2 CA, 2 CL)
 Screen: 7 destroyers

Task Force 64, * Rear Admiral W. A. Lee
 Washington (BB)
 San Francisco, Helena, Atlanta (1 CA, 2 CL)
 Screen: 6 destroyers

* Task Force 64 did not participate in Battle of Santa Cruz Islands.

17 Guadalcanal

Nevertheless, the Japanese command did not give up the game. Admiral Yamamoto prepared a new operation. Twelve transports gathered in the Shortlands south of Bougainville and made ready to embark 10,000 men, reinforcements of the Hiroshima Division, and 350 specially trained marines. The convoy was also to carry heavy field guns.

At Truk and Rabaul, important surface forces made ready. Vessels fresh from the fighting erased the traces of their wounds. Engines were inspected, and gunners carefully verified the many items on which depend the regularity and efficacy of fire.

Unfortunately, the Japanese High Command did not think it possible to put the big aircraft carriers in the line. The losses in men and material in these ships had been so heavy that they decided to be content with land-based aircraft.

While waiting, the "Tokyo Express" continued its runs. Between November 2 and 10, sixty-five destroyers and two cruisers landed their cargoes on Guadalcanal.

The Americans also reinforced their base. Two transport groups steered toward Lunga. One group, under the command of Rear Admiral Turner, reached its destination early on the twelfth; the other, commanded by Rear Admiral Scott, made several round trips between Espiritu Santo and Lunga Point.

To avoid Japanese reconnaissance, Admiral Scott passed north of San Cristobal on November 10, but a seaplane saw him from afar.

Scott arrived at Guadalcanal on the following day and feverishly began to discharge supplies.

The coast guard again

Afraid of Japanese reaction, Halsey sent to the troubled spot
the *Enterprise* Task Force and Task Force 64 of Admiral Lee,
which included the battleships *Washington* and *South Dakota*.

Twenty-four Japanese submarines were watching the Solomons.

The little aircraft carrier *Hiyo,* detained at Truk by engine
trouble during the battle of Santa Cruz, prowled northwest of
Savo. Her commander judged, on November 11, that Scott's
transports had arrived at Lunga, and he ordered the pilots,
grouped in the briefing room, to attack the vessels of the convoys
at their moorings.

In spite of the fact that such operations had long since become
routine, hearts always tightened a little as the squadrons vanished over the horizon.

The formation flew in three groups. To the right of the
bombers and a little below them were the torpedo aircraft; much
higher, the fighters scanned the sky.

To the right lay Santa Isabel, a dark spot fringed with white,
then Savo appeared, with the transports and landing craft scur-
rying to and fro.

The flight commander fired a flare and let loose the onslaught.

Deadly fire was unleashed, and the aircraft from Henderson
Field hurried into the air. The Japanese dived into this hell,
climbed out, then dived again, each time fewer in number. Only
a few, riddled by splinters, returned excitedly toward the waiting *Hiyo*.

One American transport started leaking from a near miss and
left for Espiritu Santo in midafternoon after discharging the
troops and half her cargo. Among Rear Admiral Callaghan's vessels protecting the transport group, the destroyer *Buchanan* was
damaged by American anti-aircraft fire.

The following day, at 1317, a group of two-engined torpedo
aircraft passed near Buin and hurried toward Guadalcanal. A

Buin coast guard signaled the approach of this group to the
Americans, and when at 1405 the squadron arrived in sight of
the transports, these, covered by their escort, were zigzagging toward Savo.

Attack succeeded attack without result. The pilot of a damaged plane dived on the stern of the *San Francisco*, which vanished momentarily in a column of smoke, but although the
cruiser's deck was blasted, the rails twisted, and the sides blackened by fire, the ship was not seriously damaged.

The American transports, at dark on November 12, departed
for Espiritu Santo.

An inferno

It was the turn of the Japanese to attempt a landing. While
Admiral Kondo arrived from Truk at the head of a powerful
squadron designed to cover the operation, Tanaka made ready to
lead the transports to the landing site. The cruisers at Rabaul
were under full steam, ready to weigh anchor at a moment's
notice.

With the convoy on its way, Admiral Callaghan decided to
stay with the protecting forces present in the roadstead. He
formed a line composed of the cruisers *Atlanta*, *San Francisco*,
Portland, *Helena*, and *Juneau*, preceded by four destroyers in
column and four others, also in column, bringing up the rear.

At 2200 the squadron set course to the north. The radar
antennae turned to sound the night.

The Japanese aircraft had reported the movements of the
American convoys, and it seemed logical to assume that the support forces had left with them. Preceded by a distant screen of
ten patrol destroyers and four search submarines, the Japanese
forces, commanded by Vice Admiral Kondo, advanced.

On November 12 the raiding force of Admiral Abe was
ahead. The two battleships *Hiei* and *Kirishima* trained their turrets, protected ahead by the light cruiser *Nagara* and fifteen
destroyers. Some of these, which came from the Shortlands,
joined up at 1530, seventy miles north of the strait.

Abe set course to pass west of Savo, but at midnight, northwest of the island, he was caught by a violent squall and turned back. Twenty minutes later he returned southward, but he had lost time, and the three destroyers on the left flank, the *Asagumo,* the *Murasame,* and the *Samidare,* were astern to starboard and thus no longer in their proper stations in the formation.

At 0130 the Japanese course was 105 degrees, speed twenty-three knots. The guns were already loaded with special shells for bombardment, and the gunners were ready to open fire on Henderson Field.

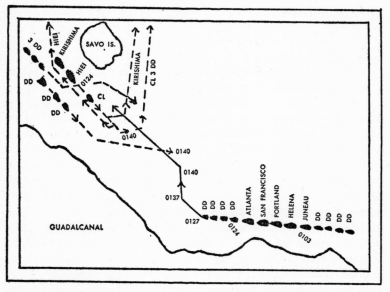

GUADALCANAL BATTLESHIP-CRUISER NIGHT ACTION, OCTOBER 13, 1942

The admiral had signaled the alert, and every eye was keeping watch. It did not seem that a surface enemy force would be met with, but it was essential to be ready for anything.

In the darkness, the cruisers of Admiral Callaghan and Admiral Scott followed the movements of the approaching Japanese by radar. The Americans steamed northward at twenty knots.

Luckily for their foes, the Americans kept no control over the radio voice transmissions; the simultaneous conversations over these circuits were numerous and continuous and so created total confusion.

At 0142 in the black night, the *Akatsuki* sighted a destroyer approaching from starboard, which turned abruptly right. Abe was immediately warned, and he ordered the destroyers ahead to turn on their searchlights. Surprised by the nearness of the Japanese, the American ships had maneuvered independently to avert collisions and were in utter disorder.

They opened fire on the searchlights, which went out, but bursts in other areas indicated that some of their fire had been directed at their own vessels.

The Japanese replied. In the *Atlanta,* Admiral Scott collapsed, struck down just as a torpedo hit the vessel and so disabled her that she was soon dead in the water.

It was a mêlée at close quarters.

The *Hiei* saw a destroyer close by; it was the *Cushing*. The American destroyer's six torpedoes went astray or failed to explode, and in a few minutes, under a rain of shells, she was reduced to a blazing wreck.

Another destroyer surged from the darkness. She was so near the *Hiei* that her torpedoes, unarmed by lack of sufficient run, rebounded from the hull without bursting. This attacker was wiped out also, by two gun salvos and a torpedo hit.

A third destroyer, the *O'Bannon,* launched torpedoes in her turn, but with no result. She was so near that the guns of the Japanese battleship could not be sufficiently depressed to hit, and the shells passed harmlessly over her.

In the reigning confusion, Abe could not tell where he was and ordered a slight turn to the left. The *Hiei* then became the target for all the enemy vessels. In the daylight, his guns would keep any cruiser at bay; the cruiser's 8-inch guns would be useless against his heavy armor at the longer ranges. But with the night's help, the enemy ships were much closer, at practically point-blank ranges, and the same shells caused the enormous vessel much serious damage. Her main battery fire was handicapped, inasmuch as she was forced to fire thin-walled high-explosive shells intended for land bombardment, and their low penetration against any armor made them insufficient against the hulls of warships.

The *Kirishima* was farther astern; she was not touched, and fired as if on maneuvers.

The American firing ceased for a moment, because Admiral Callaghan feared that his vessels were firing on one another, but the pause was very brief. The *San Francisco* was illuminated by a vessel firing on her, and the *Kirishima* also took her under fire. Admiral Callaghan fell among the bodies littering the bridge as the American cruiser became unmaneuverable.

The *Portland* and the *Juneau* were torpedoed.

This battle was a hell, a furious mêlée in which, as in the battles of old, the warriors fought individually. Tracer shells flew in every direction, flares dropped from the sky, hulls passed glowing, magazines exploded, fuel oil burned with somber flames, geysers spouted from the sea. And, over all, spread a bitter pall of smoke, swirling in a sickening mass.

Wounded ships

At 0200 on November 13, Abe ordered a sharp turn to port.

The *Hiei* turned with difficulty. She had been hit more than eighty times, her steering gear was in bad shape, her shafts functioned with difficulty, and her badly shaken boilers compelled her to reduce speed. She dragged herself to the north-westward, to pass to the south of Savo and try to reach a friendly haven.

The engineers were worn out. In the suffocating heat deep inside the vessel, intensified by the fact that insufficient ventilation was supplied by the damaged systems, they tried to plug leaks and to effect repairs on the steering gear. Electricians rigged emergency wiring. But as soon as one repair was completed, another injury was revealed.

During the night the *Akatsuki* had been sunk, the *Murasame* had her forward boiler put out of commission, and the *Yudachi*, penetrating to the middle of the American squadron, was put out of action by six salvos from the *Portland*.

At dawn, while the unscathed *Kirishima* sailed northward,

the damaged American survivors headed toward the New
Hebrides. There were only three cruisers capable of proceeding,
and these were badly crippled: the *Helena,* the *San Francisco,*
and the *Juneau,* with three destroyers. The same day, at 1101,
the *Juneau* was pulverized by a torpedo from the *I-26* and sank
instantly.

The *Portland* was towed painfully to Tulagi; the *Atlanta* had
to be scuttled that evening; the *Aaron Ward* was immobilized;
and the *Cushing* and the *Monssen* were still ablaze.

Admiral Yamamoto strode nervously up and down in his office
at Truk, in front of his dismayed chief of staff. The news of the
night had just arrived. The enemy squadron had suffered heavy
losses, but a Japanese battleship had been delivered to the close-
range fire of cruisers. Decisions were quickly made, and Vice
Admiral Abe was informed by radio that he had been relieved of
the command of the Vanguard Group operating with the Advance Force.

End of the Hiei

In spite of the check to the proposed bombardment, Admiral
Kondo did not countermand the transport sortie. Before everything, he hurried to help the *Hiei.* For his part, Mikawa weighed
anchor once more in the *Chokai* and took with him four heavy
cruisers, two light cruisers, and six destroyers to proceed to shell
Henderson Field.

The reinforcement group at Faisi took up station to carry out
the landing at dawn on November 14.

Meanwhile, to Guadalcanal Admiral Halsey sent Task Force
16 (Rear Admiral Kinkaid), comprised of the carrier *Enterprise*
and her escorting cruisers and destroyers, and Task Force 64,
composed of the battleships *Washington* and *South Dakota.*
He reinforced Task Force 64's screen with the *Pensacola* and
two destroyers.

The American carrier launched fifteen aircraft toward Henderson Field from a good distance off, but before they arrived, they
sighted the *Hiei* dragging her way painfully ten miles north of
Savo.

For the damaged battleship, each hour gained gave new hope. If she could hang on till night, she was saved.

At 1020, a group of aircraft emerged from a cloud and dived seaward, sending a spread of torpedoes at the *Hiei*.

Her commander tried to maneuver but her speed was slow. Two torpedoes burst at her stern, her steering became jammed, and the ship commenced to circle. A repair squad hurried into action, working the engines in an endeavor to hold the ship on her course. She was restarted on her hesitant progress northward. For honor alone—officers and crew now knew that their ship was lost.

At 1430 her executioners reappeared. In spite of the fire from all the guns capable of service, two torpedoes shook the *Hiei*. The engine was flooded, and steam escaped with a piercing whistling. The proud battleship was only a wreck drifting slowly toward Savo.

But this was not all. The sky echoed to a fresh roaring, as fourteen Flying Fortresses came from the east and fifty-six bombs fell. This time, however, the high-level bombers did not perform counter to their well-known reputation, and the *Hiei* was only swept by the spray which the wind whipped from the fountains rising from the sea.

Finally, at 1800, the fact had to be faced that there was no hope left of saving the battleship, and she must not fall into the enemy's hands.

Those of the ship's boats and rafts still usable were lowered into the water; everything capable of floating—tables, benches, beams—was thrown overboard. Those men who were able to, crowded on them or clung to them. Mute with horror and weariness, they watched the enormous hull settle in the water. She took 450 of the crew with her as she sank beneath the waves.

Morning visitors

During this time, Mikawa was passing north of Choiseul and Santa Isabel to escape air reconnaissance. He arrived at Savo a little before midnight and signaled Rear Admiral Nishimura's bombardment group to carry out its task.

Mikawa stayed at the entry to the southern channel of Savo with the *Chokai* and the *Kinugasa*, for which the light cruiser *Isuzu* and two destroyers acted as scouts.

Covered by the *Tenryu* and four destroyers, the heavy cruisers *Suzuya* and *Maya* went deeper into the bay. The 8-inch guns were pointed ahead, slightly on the starboard bow. They were loaded with special shells for bombardment.

The cruisers' seaplanes had been catapulted, and circled at cloud level waiting for the signal.

A word over the telephone, and rockets burst in the sky, and flashes lit up the cruisers' fore parts. Flames sprang up on land, not far from the airfield which, under the pallid light, was etched against the darker forest of palm trees.

"Short. Increase range by 275 yards."

Again the guns boomed. This time the pilots signaled joyfully: "On target!"

In thirty-seven minutes, five hundred 8-inch shells struck Henderson Field.

The Americans were holed up. Under the deluge of fire they could only seek shelter as well as they could, and wait. The Japanese ships were out of field-gun range, and the Henderson Field aircraft were powerless to act.

At 0205 on November 14, everything stopped and Nishimura, his bombardment ammunition exhausted, withdrew north of Savo and rejoined Mikawa. The squadron slipped off to the northwest at full speed, and the seaplanes withdrew in the same direction to land at the Shortlands.

At Henderson Field, a dive bomber and seventeen fighters had been destroyed and twenty-three fighters damaged, but there still remained many untouched aircraft, and the runway was usable.

Mikawa's group did not have the time to get far enough away. At 0800, the swarm of aircraft that had escaped the carnage arrived over the retiring Japanese force. In spite of the intense anti-aircraft fire and the rapid maneuvers of the ships, the *Kinugasa* was shaken by the explosions of torpedo hits that tore great holes in her bottom, and the *Isuzu* was struck by a bomb.

Two hours later, the *Enterprise*'s aircraft circled over the little squadron, seizing every chance to attack. The unfortunate *Kinugasa* took a bomb hit in the aviation-gasoline tank aft, and flames leapt upward as it exploded. The blaze spread irresistibly and water flooded in through holes in her hull.

When the assailants at last withdrew, the *Kinugasa* had sunk. The *Chokai, Maya,* and *Isuzu* had gaping wounds in their sides and decks, and the plates of their superstructures were blackened and twisted.

But here were the Shortlands. With inexpressible relief, the worn-out crews heard the anchor chains rattle through the hawse pipes.

Carnage of cargo ships

When the *Enterprise* had gathered in her aircraft she set off toward Noumea. Rear Admiral Lee, with the *Washington* and *South Dakota,* was a hundred miles to the south-southwest of Guadalcanal.

"Tenacious" Tanaka had sailed from the Shortlands on a course through the Solomons channel. From the bridge of the destroyer *Hayashio,* he surveyed the convoy. The eleven merchant ships in three columns were proceeding at best speed with eleven destroyers disposed in a circle around them, every gun at the ready.

An umbrella of fighters from the small carrier *Hiyo* circled in the sky overhead, while the carrier kept well to the north. It was a useful precaution, because at 0900 an American squadron arrived from the southwest and deployed. But, caught between the fighters and the heavy fire from the ships, the discouraged pilots turned back without having caused any damage.

But others came, and throughout the day attack succeeded attack. The aircraft from Henderson Field appeared in a group at 1150, 1245, and 1530, when they were joined by the aircraft of the *Enterprise,* which were on their last strike before returning to Noumea.

The group of transports was sixty miles northwest of Savo and to the north of Russell. The number of protecting fighters had

dwindled continually, because the *Hiyo* had only a limited com-
plement.

In the end, it was a veritable massacre. The transports maneuvered in vain and the destroyers vainly fired their hot and glowing
guns as the American aircraft dived, climbed, and dived again
among the white puffs of bursting shell.

One after another, the transports were hit. Some were struck
by torpedoes and sank quickly. Others blazed under the explosions of bombs. There was nothing but dazzling flashes, flame,
and smoke. The ships spun around, colliding with one another,
and the group thinned out.

Tanaka, from the bridge of the *Hayashio,* helplessly watched
the carnage which spared the warships. The admiral heard
around him successive shouts: "The *Arizona Maru* is sinking!"
. . . "The *Kumagawa Maru*'s on fire!". . . "The *Sado Maru* can't
steer. . . . She's collided with the *Nagara Maru!*"

At last the Americans withdrew, and their escort, running
short of fuel, turned back with them. The *Hiyo* sent off a small
group of fighters, which attacked the remaining bombers and
shot down three.

"We go on."

The attack was over. Only four transports remained; three
were sunk and four were in sinking condition. In the water,
among the flotsam of every description, nearly three thousand
men clung to bits of wreckage or floated supported by their life
belts.

Lieutenant-Commander Yamamoto asked Tanaka:

"Admiral, should I signal to turn back?"

The admiral thought a moment.

"No. We go on. The mission must be carried out. Order the
Takanami to take command of the 31st and 30th destroyer
divisions. Let these ships pick up the troops and rejoin me. I am
setting a course of eighty degrees."

Some destroyers threw lines to the soldiers; others ran alongside the burning transports and embarked the troops and as
much equipment as possible. Then they formed line and sailed

at full speed toward their chief, leaving behind them a torch that, in the night to come, served as guide to the friendly and enemy forces converging on Savo.

Tanaka continued on his course until midnight and then turned south to pass west of Savo to gain the landing area. Soon after he had turned, he saw astern and to port a discreetly winking light; it was the Japanese identification signal. Tanaka replied immediately and went on with a lighter heart. He now knew that he was to be supported and that he could hope again.

Contest of giants

Indeed, Kondo was there. Some hours earlier, while waiting near Ontong Java, he had gathered up the *Kirishima* and the light vessels that had survived the battle of the thirteenth and was now hurrying to protect the landing.

At 1000 on the fourteenth, he was east of Santa Isabel.

Abruptly the *Atago* altered course; the lookouts had reported the wakes of torpedoes. The squadron stood away, by a simultaneous ship-turn maneuver, and the destroyers opened fire on the spot from which the threat had come. When the danger had passed, the squadron resumed its course, but Kondo knew he had been sighted and reported and would find his enemy on guard. His plan was to evade the American forces which barred the passage and again to bombard Henderson Field to prevent aircraft attacks on the transports the following morning.

Kondo's forces were divided into three groups: first, a screen formed by the light cruiser *Sendai* and three destroyers, under the command of Admiral Hashimoto; an inner screen of six destroyers and the light cruiser *Nagara*, flagship of Rear Admiral Kimura; and a bombardment group composed of the *Kirishima* and the heavy cruisers *Atago* and *Takao*.

The ideal timing would be to bombard Henderson Field at the moment when Tanaka began debarkation operations from his transports.

At 2210, the *Sendai* sighted a group of vessels entering the channel to the north of Savo. She followed them without showing

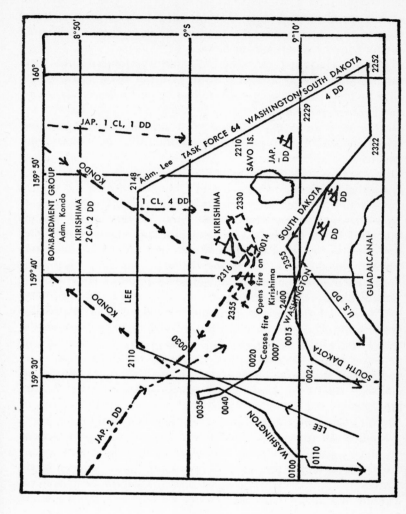

GUADALCANAL BATTLESHIP NIGHT ACTION, NOVEMBER 14–15, 1942

herself, with the *Shikinami,* and dispatched the *Uranami* and the *Ayanami* to reconnoiter the pass to the south of Savo.

The *Nagara,* with three destroyers of her screen, was to enter that north channel at full speed behind her two vessels of the outer screen; the three other destroyers of the inner screen would continue with the bombardment group, which would pass west and then south of Savo.

At 2316 a rumbling sounded. It came from the Americans who had picked up the *Nagara* by radar. The *Sendai,* thinking she had been discovered, started a smoke screen and turned abruptly to port, followed by the *Shikinami.*

Further south, the *Ayanami* and *Uranami,* leading on a westward course, sighted destroyers to starboard. The two destroyers were seen at the same time because one of the enemy at once launched flares. On the silvery sea, the silhouettes of the *Nagara* and the Japanese destroyers stood out, and fire was immediately opened upon them. At 2330, the two Japanese destroyers launched a salvo of torpedoes, and five minutes later Admiral Kimura's vessels followed suit.

The aim of the Japanese gunners was good. The *Walke* was heavily hit. The *Preston* was disabled and dead in the water. A boiler in the *Gwin* emitted steam; a shell burst on her deck and released some of her torpedoes, which fell inert in the sea.

At 2338 the Japanese torpedoes arrived and added new explosions. The *Walke* was badly damaged forward, as was the *Benham.*

Kimura's section of the inner screen made off toward Savo. The *Uranami* and the *Ayanami,* which had suffered somewhat heavily from enemy fire, zigzagged in an effort to avoid the salvos. The *Sendai,* which had turned back again, hurried south to the rescue.

A few minutes later the *Benham* sank, together with the *Preston,* abandoned by her crew.

Kimura made out a big ship approaching—the *South Dakota.* The Japanese admiral at once warned Kondo and then escaped, after launching thirty-four torpedoes at the American battleship, all of which went astray.

At 2348, Kondo's vessels were in column on a course to the

southwest, eight miles north of Cape Espérance. When he received Kimura's signal, the admiral immediately altered course to southeast.

The Kirishima

Meanwhile Kimura, in turning, had lost sight of the Americans. At that moment the *Asagumo* sighted to starboard a big silhouette arriving off her beam and turned a light on it. It was the *South Dakota*. The two big Japanese cruisers *Atago* and *Takao* and the *Kirishima* fired almost at once on the American battleship. The latter sailed amid a forest of fountains—the misses—and dull-red flashes and showers of sparks—the hits. The *Asagumo*, at the head of the Japanese line, fired her torpedoes, but they did not reach the target.

Suddenly, a little farther west, some flashes showed as a salvo of 16-inch shells scored hits and near misses on and about the *Kirishima*. It was the *Washington*, which, undetected until that moment, had, with the range and bearing obtained by her radar, been able calmly to prepare this devastating intervention.

In seven minutes, the *Kirishima* was put out of action. Her superstructure was a shambles, two of her turrets were wrecked, her steering gear was jammed, and her main sources of electricity had been cut off. She was badly crippled and unable to maintain station on her group.

Kondo saw the *Washington*, which turned to the northwest and then to 340 degrees. To escape encirclement, the Japanese admiral himself turned to the northward, followed by Kimura, who hurried up from the southeast.

At 0025, Kondo ordered those vessels not engaged to withdraw and turned smartly north-northeast, laying a smoke screen to conceal his movements.

Tanaka had heard the gunfire. In spite of his recent ordeals, he longed to hurry to the rescue. He could not himself abandon his transports, but he sent two of his destroyers as reinforcements, the *Oyashio* and the *Kagero*. In the gloom, these two ships sought the enemy while Kimura's screening vessels searched the sea.

They saw a battleship near the Russell Islands on a course to the northwest. The two groups launched a torpedo attack, but the *Washington* evaded them and, turning hard to port, disappeared to the southeast at full speed.

The echoes of battle died. West of Savo the *Kirishima*, mortally wounded, made desperate efforts to gather way. She literally staggered along, slowly, her crew haunted by the memory of the *Hiei* which, two days before, had suffered so much before finally succumbing.

Kondo approached the battleship, and the *Sendai* and the *Shikinami* also closed her.

What were they to do? The dying ship could not draw away quickly enough and, in daylight, would be destroyed by aircraft from Henderson Field. What purpose was there in waiting?

The decision was made: her crew was transferred to the other vessels, and at 0300 on November 15 the *Kirishima* settled in her watery grave, northwest of Savo, and went to join her comrade in battle, in the depths where so many valiant ships were already resting.

Epilogue

Tanaka, meanwhile, arrived at Tassafaronga. At 0400 the transports anchored near shore, and the landing craft immediately started their coming and going. Speed was needed, since Henderson Field had not been neutralized, even temporarily. At daybreak the merchant ships would be bombed and certainly destroyed. It must not be forgotten that all these immense air and naval operations, in the course of which so much daring had been expended and so many victims sacrificed, had been originally conceived by the Japanese solely to land a few men and a little equipment on this inhospitable island.

The destroyers approached the shore as closely as they could, and the men were crowded into the small craft, which whipped landward.

The destroyers could and must be saved. Their speed and small size allowed them to escape or avoid aerial attacks. Shortly before sunrise, even before they had finished putting their car-

goes ashore, they weighed anchor and steamed to the northwest
at their best speed.

There remained the four transports, the *Kinugawa Maru, Hiro-
kawa Maru, Yamaura Maru,* and *Yamatsuki Maru.* Their last
martyrdom began with the growing light. Bombed and gunned,
they slipped their anchors and beached themselves in order to
continue landing their cargoes as long as possible or until, torn
apart and burned, they were nothing but melancholy wrecks.

At midnight on November 15, Tanaka's destroyers at last
moored at the Shortlands.

The battle of Guadalcanal was decisive and solidly detrimental
to the Japanese. Their losses had been too heavy for their fleet
to attempt an extensive operation in this region again. The carriers were being repaired in Japan; the grand battle of squadrons, so long the dream of Yamamoto, would not be possible until they were returned to active service, and by that time the
Americans would enjoy a carrier superiority which would continue to increase rapidly with the passage of time. Moreover,
operations confined so strictly to a precise and limited geographical theater would not provide much scope for maneuver and
surprise.

Without the power to reconquer Guadalcanal, the only alter-
native for Japan was to establish an intermediate base in the
Middle Solomons, at New Georgia, for example, to neutralize the
effects of the Guadalcanal base upon any later United States
operation against Japanese positions to the northward.[1] Even
then, in the most favorable hypothesis, action from that new
base, designed to hinder the enemy communications, would be
opposed by the close presence of powerful American naval and
air forces solidly installed and constantly reinforced.

And, in fact, it was these forces that would take the offensive.

---

1. *This represented a radical change in Japan's strategy. She now
envisaged a holding strategy in place of that of expansion, which
had animated her wartime moves up to this point.*

*This would soon be reflected by the transfer of the offensive to
the American forces, although the start of the all-out U.S. war
offensive was still a year away.* (R.A.T.)

LOSSES IN THE BATTLES OF GUADALCANAL, NOVEMBER 12-15, 1942

JAPANESE LOSSES

Hiei, Kirishima (2 OBB),* *Kinugasa* (CA), sunk
Akatsuki, Yudachi, Ayanami (3 DD), sunk

UNITED STATES LOSSES

Juneau, Atlanta (2 CL), sunk
Barton, Monssen, Cushing, Laffey, Preston, Walke, Benham (7 DD), sunk
South Dakota (BB), moderate damage
Portland, San Francisco (2 CA), heavily damaged

* *Abbreviations:* OBB, old battleship; CA, heavy cruiser; CL, light cruiser; DD, destroyer; BB, modern battleship.

18 Tassafaronga

During the period of waiting, the unfortunate troops still fighting on Guadalcanal could not be abandoned. Until the end, they had to be supplied and reinforced. Again it was "Tenacious" Tanaka who was charged with these ticklish missions.

At the end of November, the Japanese troops on Guadalcanal gave proof of a renewal of activity, and American reconnaissance aircraft reported a recrudescence of traffic in the Shortlands area. For these reasons, Task Force 67, under the command of Admiral Wright, arrived from Espiritu Santo.

From Tassafaronga, where the Japanese troops clung to their positions, they could see through the mangroves of the foreshore the *Minneapolis, New Orleans, Pensacola, Northampton,* and *Honolulu,* escorted by six destroyers, file past and out to sea.

On his side, Tanaka weighed anchor from Buin on November 30 at the head of eight destroyers. The cruiser *Jintsu,* damaged on August 25, was still being repaired, so the admiral flew his flag in the *Naganami.* Six of the destroyers were loaded with troops and supplies, which had to be disembarked at Tassafaronga to the northwestward of Lunga Point.

To avert a long halt and the necessary comings and goings that the lack of landing barges made so difficult, the material had been packed into 1100 barrels, which encumbered the decks. These barrels were to be thrown into the sea near the shore and fished out by the soldiers.

The three destroyer divisions composing the squadron had

received a magnificent training in night fighting. On this occasion they were to show their remarkable suppleness in maneuver.

Eyes and radar

Tanaka had been warned by a signal from Rabaul that the enemy cruisers were present at Guadalcanal.

To avoid being located in the "Slot," he set course to the eastward by Bougainville Strait, a passage north of the Solomons. At 1100 there was an alert as an aircraft appeared in the distance, but it continued on its course and appeared to have seen nothing.

In the afternoon came a new signal. Rabaul reported that the American cruisers were steaming toward Savo; Guadalcanal stated that a dozen American destroyers were off Lunga Point, keeping an eye on the discharge of a convoy.

Tanaka took the news calmly and warned his vessels: "Enemy forces at Guadalcanal. Get ready for a night battle." Evening fell as the destroyer column turned south toward Cape Espérance. The night was still and dark, and the bows cut through a smooth sea in which the wakes glowed with phosphorescence.

At 2245 Tanaka turned south, to the west of Savo, and skirted the north coast of Guadalcanal at twelve knots.

He saw nothing; but he knew that the enemy was in these waters and was equipped with radar. By hugging the shore, the admiral hoped to confuse the echoes. The *Takanami* kept station a little ahead and to port of the admiral's ship. At 2320 she sighted two wakes of torpedoes passing ahead of her. At the same time, the enemy opened fire.

The Japanese destroyers respected the admiral's orders: "Do not use guns so as not to give away your position. Launch torpedoes at the flashes from the enemy's guns."

Only the *Takanami*, whose station brought her nearest the Americans, replied with her guns, and she was immediately crushed by gunfire and sank between the two lines.

Tanaka maneuvered to dodge the torpedoes which were still arriving. He signaled: "Twenty-four knots, turn by divisions one hundred and eighty degrees to port. Attack!"

The *Naganami, Oyashio,* and *Kawakaze* turned to port to the northwest, followed in succession by their subordinates. The *Kagero,* surprised, continued on her course for a little too long and now found herself at the tail of the division led personally by Tanaka.

This maneuver, difficult even in daylight, demonstrated the skill acquired by the Japanese sailors. To prevent disorder and collisions at such a moment, the leaders of each division must turn at exactly the same time, with the same turning radius, and the following vessels must turn exactly in the wake of their guide.

Feast for torpedoes

Now came a feast for torpedoes. The flashes from the enemy guns made excellent targets. Only the *Kagero,* encumbered by her barrels, which she strove to throw into the sea, was unable to use her tubes.

At 2327 the torpedoes reached their goal. The leading enemy vessel, which had just fired her ninth salvo, was hit twice, forward and in her second boiler room, and she began to burn; but the spray that fell back on her put out the principal fires.

The *New Orleans,* which followed, had all her forepart blown away, up to the second turret.

Finally, at 2339, the *Pensacola,* which had turned to port and whose outline was clearly limned against the light of the flames, was struck level with the mainmast. An engine was flooded, and her fuel oil gushed through a gaping opening. Incapable of firing further, the cruiser turned slightly to starboard and dragged herself toward Tulagi.

The sky was lit up as seaplanes from the American cruisers dropped flares, but it was too late.

The *Honolulu* and *Northampton* had turned to starboard—the former to continue her course round Savo by the west, the latter to return to a westerly course. Then, at 2339, the *Oshio* let fly her last eight torpedoes at the *Northampton,* and again the faces of the Japanese sailors lit up with grins as two explosions resounded. Fire broke out on board the American cruiser, which rapidly took a list to port.

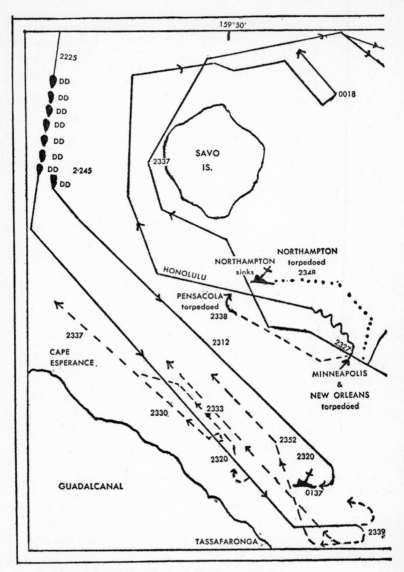

BATTLE OF TASSAFARONGA, NOVEMBER 30, 1942

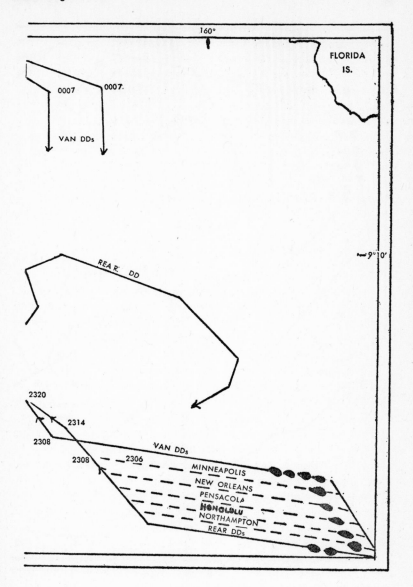

The *Kagero* and the *Kuroshio* returned to attack the damaged cruiser again, but now they were picked out, and their torpedoes, launched at too great a distance because of the enemy fire, failed to carry. As to the *Oyashio,* she searched for the *Takanami's* crew and then returned at full speed to the northwest.

Tanaka left at 0130 and made the Shortlands by noon.

The American cruisers, victims of the encounter in spite of their great superiority of strength, position, and means of information, were in pitiful state. The *Minneapolis,* the *New Orleans,* and the *Pensacola* dragged themselves as far as Tulagi. The *Northampton,* listing farther and farther, had to be abandoned, and sank at 0304.

"Tenacious" Tanaka keeps going

After the operation, Tanaka made his report. It ended:

"The enemy knew our plans and our movements. He sent aircraft to drop flares, took up position for an artillery engagement, and had the advantage of opening fire. But his fire was erratic and, moreover, many shells failed to explode. Either the enemy's skill is not remarkable or his fuses are of poor quality."

The battle of Tassafaronga must be counted as an incontestable Japanese tactical success, to the honor of Admiral Tanaka and his subordinates. But the goal of the operation—to supply the troops on Guadalcanal—was not attained. The barrels still littered the destroyers' decks. Three other raids were needed to carry this material to its destination.

On December 3 Tanaka led ten destroyers, carrying part of these supplies. The barrels were placed on deck in such a manner that they would not obstruct the fire power.

Covered by Japanese aircraft, the little squadron escaped an attack by fifteen aircraft from Henderson Field and was able to throw its cargo into the sea near Tassafaronga.

Tanaka returned again on the seventh with eleven destroyers; then on the eleventh with ten destroyers. At 0100 on the twelfth, he was attacked by twelve motor torpedo boats. The Americans had just brought into the region these little craft which were admirably suited to the narrow waters of the archipelago. Struck by a torpedo, the destroyer *Teruzuki* blew up at 0440.

Half a loaf

In the meantime the Japanese, having abandoned all thought of Guadalcanal as their base, decided to build an airfield on another of the Solomon Islands.

They chose Munda, on the southwest corner of the island of New Georgia. In fact, supply vessels could set out from the Shortlands, discharge their cargoes in the northwest of the island, and return to their departure point, all in one afternoon. The supplies then had to be forwarded overland or by Hathorn Channel, which separates New Georgia from Arundel.

The runway at Munda would be supplemented by an airfield which was being built at Vila in southern Kolombangara.

Work was begun at the end of November 1942, camouflaged by coconut palms, but American aircraft were warned and, after frequent appearances, they finally spotted the site of the works. In spite of the ensuing raids, the airfield was ready on December 12 to receive fighters to protect the "Tokyo Express." This was still running, although suffering losses. On December 16 the *Kagero* was hit. On December 25 the *Nankai Maru* was torpedoed and collided with the *Uzuki.* On the twenty-sixth the *Ariake* suffered from a near bomb miss.

On their side, the American submarines were very active in the Rabaul zone, where there was a constant movement of ships. The light cruiser *Tenryu* was sunk, together with many merchant ships.

On January 2 there was a new expedition to Guadalcanal. There could be no letup in supplies to that island. Tanaka was now wary. Almost every barrel containing rations, arms, and ammunition which was intended for the last defenders of the bloodstained island and was dropped into the water, was sunk by enemy machine-gun fire the following day.

On the night of January 5 all were asleep on Munda except

the patrolling sentries. Suddenly the Japanese soldiers halted. There had just been an explosion amid the palm trees, and far away sounded the rumbling of guns.

Men dashed to the aircraft and hauled them as far from the runway as possible. The Japanese air crews, powerless, watched the spectacle beginning. For fifty minutes, a hurricane of fire descended on the runway and its surroundings. Great sparks sprang from the forest of palms, and debris flew in all directions. Whole trees were struck down. The island seemed to be shaken to its depths, and enormous shell holes pitted the airfield. It seemed as though the thunder and chaos would never end.

When the American squadron sailed away, after carrying out its radar-controlled bombardment, the Japanese commander re-assembled his men. Squads were formed, and mechanics went out to repair the aircraft which, despite their distance from the airfield, had been hit by splinters; laborers busied themselves on the runway, where innumerable holes had to be filled in. Thanks to this antlike labor, the airfield was usable again by the end of the morning.

Fuel oil level

On January 4, the Imperial Navy at last obtained the order to evacuate Guadalcanal. The army, which had long opposed this, had finally recognized that it was impossible to continue the hopeless fight on this faraway island.

Again, on January 11, Tanaka entered Savo Channel, and during the night of January 14–15 landed nine hundred men to cover the evacuation.

The Americans now had on Guadalcanal nearly fifty thou-sand combatants. The best of the Japanese, who were still hang-ing on, were in a frightful physical state.

For these men, although they were as hardened and inured to war as it is possible to be, the interminable battles that had torn the famous island had been a terrible ordeal. Without food, almost without munitions, they had to fight in the swamps, where a burning mist persistently floated; half of them had perished, eaten up by fever, starved, and cut to pieces by American machine guns. The survivors, who looked like ghosts, still found the courage to defend themselves, but they were at the end of their strength.

The evacuation was begun by submarines which approached the land in Kamimbo Bay west of Cape Espérance. Little craft, into which the soldiers were crowded, put off from the shore and the submarines moved away submerged to return northwest.

While this was going on, the Americans recommenced their bombardments of Munda and extended them to Vila. These did not have much effect; the holes in the runways were quickly filled in, and the air activity was hardly diminished.

Yamamoto, still at Truk, learned that the American navy was very active in the Guadalcanal zone. According to information received, important convoys were on their way to the island with relieving troops.

The admiral at once proposed to Tokyo an interception operation, and he listed the quantity of fuel oil required. The reply was negative; at such a moment, such an expenditure of fuel could not be allowed.[1]

The admiral looked abstractedly at the telegram in his hands. So Japan had reached that stage already! After one year of war!

But Yamamoto was not a man to lose himself in vain regrets. Something had to be done. If the navy was immobilized, the air force would act!

Japanese submarines kept watch in the passage between New Georgia and Guadalcanal, and on the twenty-ninth at 1850 they sent the following information:

"American force six cruisers, twelve destroyers, fifty miles north of Rennel Islands, course northwest to enter Solomons Channel."

Thirty-one aircraft took off from Munda, formed up, and sped

---

1. *In any case, with no large carrier present and with no possibility of giving a surface force adequate air support and protection, he could hardly have been seriously considering the use of important fleet units in waters where they would be subjected to air attacks by land-based aircraft and planes from the* Enterprise. (R.A.T.)

southeast. They skirted the southern coast of New Georgia, flying over Vanguru; the sun was already low when the group commander sighted the enemy. He studied them rapidly while making a wide detour.

The destroyers formed a half circle ahead of the cruisers, which advanced in two parallel columns—the heavy cruisers *Wichita, Chicago,* and *Louisville* and the light cruisers *Montpelier, Cleveland,* and *Columbia.*

The Japanese aircraft formation moved away a little to the west, so that the enemy ships stood out wonderfully with the rays of the setting sun reflected from their sides.

An order was given, and the group split in two and dropped to a low altitude. Then the engines roared, and the attack started.

The first wave launched its attack on the destroyer *Waller* and machine-gunned her. The deck of the *Wichita* was similarly swept. The Americans, who could make out the attackers only indistinctly against the sun, fired erratically.

The second wave passed between the *Chicago* and the *Wichita,* then launched its attack on the *Louisville,* but the cruiser maneuvered and escaped damage.

The sun had set. A magnificent fireworks display lit up sky and sea. The American force, lit by dazzling yellow and white rockets, proceeded between two rows of luminous buoys, white, green and red, which seemed to mark out an immense channel.

At 1931 new torpedo aircraft arrived from the east. The *Chicago* was missed. The aircraft formed a pack again, and charged through automatic fire at the starboard column. An aircraft in flames crashed on the *Chicago,* which looked like a great torchbearer. At 1945 a torpedo burst against her and the vessel slowed, out of control. Another torpedo stopped her.

The *Wichita* was also shaken by an explosion and altered course smartly to starboard at full speed. The new Japanese attack found only empty space.

The following day, twelve Japanese aircraft carried out a search toward Rennel Island to take note of the results of the battle. The *Chicago* was there, towed by the tug *Navajo,* but even more tempting a prey, further on, appeared the imposing outline of the *Enterprise!*

The aircraft turned enthusiastically toward the carrier, only to see circling fighters far off, with other aircraft taking off from her deck. Without protection, it would be madness to persist, but at least they must have the *Chicago.*

She also was guarded by a patrol of fighters as the struggle began. Three Japanese planes fell broken into the sea, but the others flew down to sea level and the pilots' hands dropped to the levers to fire the torpedoes. The fighters dived while, sparkling with flashes, the *Chicago* fired every gun.

Seven more Japanese aircraft vanished in enormous splashes, but they had launched their weapons. At 1624 the *Chicago,* hit by four torpedoes to starboard, was lost.

Only one Japanese airman remained to give an account of the mission's success.

Return of the vanquished

The big evacuation from Guadalcanal began in the night of February 1-2, 1943.

The Americans, noting the daytime activity of their adversary, believed that reinforcements were coming to the troops on Guadalcanal.

They deployed every means of action. The Solomons Channel was watched over by patrols, ready to dive on convoys making their way down to the southeast. The coasts of Guadalcanal were mined, and the motor torpedo boats, tiny craft armed with torpedoes, invisible in the gloom, circulated in the waters round Savo, seeking a chance to hurl themselves at forty knots on suspicious shadows.

The efforts were in vain.

The airfield on Munda played its part, and the Japanese fighters efficiently protected the expeditions crossing the "Slot."

Each night, bombers and scouting aircraft harassed Henderson Field, while destroyers, thanks to their excellent watch, detected the motor torpedo boats and cut them down.

As soon as the light vessels were moored, embarkation began in haste, as groups of men clambered up the rope ladders that hung down the sides. Relieved to have escaped at last from the fetid mud, the unhealthy humidity of the jungle, and the snakes, the rugged soldiers, emaciated by privation, lay down on the decks and slept heavily, after they had put down beside them the little boxes of whitewood containing the ashes of those comrades for whom they had been able to perform the last rites.

On February 7, a last echelon of eighteen destroyers went for the soldiers who had remained as rear guard, and the following day the operation was over.

Of more than 30,000 men who had been landed successively in the famous island, only 11,700 had been saved. The others had perished in the swamps and the brush, from fever, disease, starvation, and the relentless actions of their enemy.

No one knew what became of the solitary gun.

February 1943

The battle for Guadalcanal—August 7, 1942, to February 3, 1943—had been a long, wasting struggle, at the end of which the Japanese had to admit themselves defeated.

The Imperial Navy had suffered heavily in the battle. It had lost two battleships; one light aircraft carrier of 8500 tons; three heavy cruisers; one light cruiser; eleven destroyers, six submarines.

The small vessels, above all, had had a hard time. Many of them had suffered damage, and all had been used without rest for months, almost always at full speed and with the minimum of maintenance overhauls and repairs. Modern machines are precision tools which require assiduous care and periodical inspection, without which wear and tear take their toll rapidly. Accordingly, general repairs were then finally ordered.

A considerable merchant tonnage had been lost, just when operations required a growing number of these ships for both the army and the navy, as is always to be expected in war. To

afford a comparison, the tonnages available at the conclusion of
the first and third phases are set forth herewith:[2]

	April 1942	February 1943
Army	1,382,900	1,623,400
Navy	1,771,500	1,814,000
Civilian service	3,112,400	2,629,300
TOTAL	6,266,800	6,066,700

The over-all downward trend was not great, but the diminution
of 483,000 tons in the shipping available to civilian needs was
cause for serious reflection at that moment in the war. Japan's
merchant shipping had not been subjected to intensive enemy
action up to that point, although United States submarines were
active in Far Eastern waters. There is nothing more vital to an
island nation's warmaking capabilities than the maintenance of
an adequate seaborne commerce.

It was essential to Japan to maintain her imports at a high
level: coal from China and Tonkin; rubber from Indo-China;
gasoline and fuel oil from the Dutch East Indies; metals from
every available source—every natural resource needed to keep
the war industries going, in which Japan was so lacking.

From that time on, further new adventures were forbidden,

---

2. *The war's first phase embraced the Japanese campaigns to the
successful conclusion of their invasion of Java. The Midway
operation was to initiate for them the second phase. Brief as it
was, the Midway adventure bears no relation to the operations
which preceded or followed it, and must stand alone as phase
two. The South Pacific operations to the definite end of the Japanese offensive in February 1943 was the third phase. Phase four
embraced the campaigns for consolidation of the allied positions
by progressive gains in the South Pacific and was followed by the
fifth and final phase, the allied major offensive. These last two
overlapped, as phase four did not terminate until April 1944,
while the occupations of Kwajalein and Eniwetok in January
and February initiated the fifth phase in the Central Pacific.*
(R.A.T.)

and the Japanese were ordered to maintain a prudent defensive, to conserve their forces, and to put them back into shape, striking only when a good opportunity presented itself.

In spite of the enormous labors and painful sacrifices demanded of it, the air force had held its own and even increased in size. At the end of 1942, the number of aircraft was nearly three thousand, but the quality did not improve quickly enough.[3]

The Val dive bomber had no retractable undercarriage and was easily shot down. The Kate torpedo aircraft lacked speed and endurance in comparison with the American Avenger. The two-engined torpedo aircraft Betty was an excellent machine but caught fire too easily.

At the beginning of 1943, the Japanese planned to build fifteen vessels of the *Hiryu* class and five of the *Shokaku* class, and to convert the big battleship *Shinano*, sister ship of the *Yamato*, into an aircraft carrier. Only one of these vessels was completed before the war ended.

Above all, in every department there had been frightful wastage of human life. Airmen were often inadequately protected. All too frequently, there was no organized effort to save them when they fell into the sea. Lack of aviation gasoline prevented the development of the required numbers of adequately trained replacement pilots. The veterans of the first months of the war

---

3. *This estimate of the Japanese air force situation might be a bit on the sanguine side. Japan had then lost four large and two small carriers. Her aircraft losses had been very high when the plane losses at Midway are remembered. With the damage to the* Shokaku, *which had returned home for lengthy repairs, the Japanese large carrier was withdrawn from the Solomon Islands area and did not again appear there—a clear indication of the concern that the Japanese naval command felt over this situation. Also, in weighing the air situation, the relative prospects of reinforcements have to be taken into account and, from that angle, the Japanese air future did not look too bright. This fact must have been apparent to the Japanese admirals, even if they were prepared to discount it in their comments.* (R.A.T.)

had disappeared, and their successors were far less efficient. In consequence, losses increased ceaselessly, and although the number of pilots under training had had to be increased considerably, each pilot in the training centers had fewer flying hours to his credit than sound training demanded. It was a vicious circle —an incurable disease. The constant decrease in the number and efficiency of the air crews led to terrible losses among them in return for results which became progressively less commensurate.

Only one thing did not diminish. It showed itself stubbornly to the end of the war, and that was courage.

PART FIVE

Kahili Rendezvous

19 "There Was Only One Yamamoto"

The battle of the Coral Sea, May 1942, had halted the amphibious operation whose goal was the conquest of Port Moresby.

Nevertheless, the Japanese command did not renounce its project. The possession of this base, the most important in New Guinea, served the aims of the High Command exactly, and accordingly it worked out a new plan. Port Moresby would be taken by a pincer movement; one of the arms would stretch down from Buna, on the east coast by the Kokoda Pass, and trail through the mountains, and the other would start from Milne Bay. This was a fjord twenty-six miles long at the southeastern extremity of the main island, and an excellent base of operations in spite of its unhealthy climate.

On July 18 and 22, Buna was reinforced in spite of American air reaction.

Japanese reconnaissance aircraft reported, meanwhile, that the Australians were installing an airfield at Gili-Gili, just west of Milne Bay, and that they were actively fortifying the region of Milne Bay.

On the twenty-fourth, the cruisers *Tenryu* and *Tatsuda* weighed anchor from Rabaul, with three destroyers, two submarine chasers, and two transports, carrying 1900 men.

The convoy left by St. George Channel and set course for Milne Bay, passing well to seaward of the Goodenough Islands. During this time, Japanese fighters flew over Gili-Gili, to prevent enemy aircraft from taking off.

At midnight on the twenty-fifth, the Japanese were in the bay, only six miles from the airfield. They moored and began the disembarkation. But the danger came from elsewhere. With the daylight, there appeared a squadron of Flying Fortresses. The sky was dappled with puffs of white, but the big aircraft paid no attention to them. A column of black smoke rose from the transport *Nankai Maru*. The attacks followed each other so steadily that anchors had to be weighed before all the troops were ashore.

The Japanese troops started their attack almost at once, and with their usual fury.

The natives of New Guinea—among the most primitive people of the world—saw with amazement these strangers of different races throwing themselves upon each other, wielding weapons of sudden death. The Japanese soldiers' assaults succeeded one another untiringly, in spite of considerable losses. Their attacks all broke on the Australian fortifications.

From then on, the operation was lost, especially as the assaulting troops received almost no reinforcements: all those who survived to return to Rabaul were thereafter used in the battle of Guadalcanal. For Japan, New Guinea thenceforth became a secondary theater of operations.

The Japanese advance and fight over the Kokoda Pass was a fierce, heroic effort, which was not turned back and defeated until it had driven to within 22 miles of Port Moresby.

In the night of September 5, a cruiser and three destroyers evacuated the final contingent of survivors from Milne Bay.

Goodenough Island, to the west of the Entrecasteaux group, served as refuge for some of the survivors from sunken ships, but the Australians landed there on October 22, and four days later a submarine arrived to evacuate the last Japanese.

On January 2, 1943, came a new discomfiture: MacArthur's Americans attacked and took Buna after fierce fighting. On the eighteenth it was the turn of Sanananda.

At last, the Japanese command grew disturbed by these successive setbacks, and it was decided that the line Munda-Rabaul-Lae should be reinforced. Troops landed at Wewak, 382 miles northwest of Lae; others occupied Hollandia in Dutch New

Guinea and began to build a strategical road from Madang to Finschhafen. These movements were carried out by numerous boats which skirted the shores of islands and crossed the narrow passages separating them at night. The most rapid traffic was assured by submarine.

The level falls quickly in the fuel tanks

The garrison of Lae numbered only 3500 men. It was decided to send them a reinforcement of 6900 men of the 18th Army, because an attack by the Australians was feared, and the enemy position at Wau was only thirty miles from Salamaua.

A convoy assembled at Rabaul at the end of February. Eight transports embarked the six thousand men; the *Kembu Maru* was full of aviation gasoline, and the *Nogima Maru* carried an additional thousand men. Each item of cargo had been carefully divided among the several transports, so that the sinking of one or two ships would not cause the entire loss of any particular category of material. The landing was to be completed in six hours.

The captains of the destroyers were old campaigners of Guadalcanal, and Admiral Mikawa had promised to neutralize Gili-Gili and Port Moresby; if the weather allowed, two hundred fighters would provide cover.

The convoy weighed anchor on March 1, when the leaden sky and the fall in the barometer indicated the approach of stormy weather—an excellent opportunity to escape enemy aircraft.

The bad weather did arrive. The winds reached gale strength and kicked up heavy seas, but in spite of all this, at 1600 a big American bomber approached, made a wide tour of the formation, and vanished in the southwest. The Japanese followed the north coast of New Britain. The wind decreased, the tempest died down more quickly than had been expected, and on the morning of the second the sky was clear. The convoy arrived at 0815, thirty miles north of Cape Gloucester, and again several Flying Fortresses appeared in the distance, but made off after a short observation.

An attack had to be expected, and accordingly the anti-aircraft batteries were kept fully manned. Admiral Kimura warned Rabaul and asked for the promised air coverage.

At 1015 a big formation of bombers arrived from the southwest; they were twelve B-17s and seventeen B-24s. The Japanese fighters, just arrived, dived on the enemy, but they were unpleasantly surprised, because the fire power of the American aircraft had been considerably augmented. The fighters were far from their base, and they consumed fuel rapidly from their moderate-capacity tanks. Soon they had to withdraw, leaving the ships without air protection against the persistent attacks of the big enemy aircraft.

From thirteen thousand feet, where the silvered craft shone in the sunlight, bombs fell. But high-level bombings against maneuvering ships have always been ineffective. For two hours the attacks succeeded one another without result, but finally, at noon, a transport's siren bellowed, and a swirl of smoke enveloped her as she sank. Hurriedly, the destroyers *Yukikaze* and *Asagumo* rescued the survivors from the water and proceeded with them toward Lae. During the night, they landed 950 soldiers and then rejoined the convoy.

They found it in a terrible situation.

A *bitter demonstration*

All day, the American fighters had plunged to strafe the quarry. Now fast bombers arrived in waves, preceded by more fighters which machine-gunned the decks and decimated the anti-aircraft defenses as they passed at mast level. Armor-piercing bombs of one thousand pounds burst in the bottoms, rending the hulls, and near misses staved in the side plating. It was a wiping out, an uninterrupted massacre in the din of the apocalypse.

The Japanese fighters had returned to engage and pursue the attackers, but they found themselves no match for Corsairs and Hellcats, which easily dominated them.

Night came, but it brought no respite in the tension which had reigned for so many hours. Over the waves dashed some speedy motor torpedo boats, and now the Japanese gunners were far less numerous and were weary after this day of hell.

Most of the nocturnal attacks were repulsed, but a few explosions that shook the night showed that some torpedoes had struck home.

At daybreak on the fourth, the attacks were resumed. By evening, of the sixteen vessels that had left Rabaul three days earlier, there remained only four destroyers, the *Shikinami*, the *Yukikaze*, the *Asagumo*, and the *Uranami*. They landed the survivors of this interminable massacre at Lae and escaped at full speed to return to Simpson Harbor.

The Japanese were certainly handicapped in the emergency by the extreme slowness of the convoy, which made only nine knots, and the weather too had not favored them, but a striking demonstration had been given. The American air arm was assuring for itself the mastery of the skies, thanks to the qualities of its latest-model aircraft and the capabilities of its pilots, whose training had not been handicapped by any thought of conserving gasoline as had that of the new crop of Japanese aviators.

Reinforcements for New Guinea thenceforth could be shipped only in the weak detachments that could be accommodated in small craft and submarine. Transport by large ships under the navy's protection had become too costly.

Continent and ocean

In Tokyo, an entente between army and navy men was still difficult to realize. The former, who seemed not to understand that the destiny of their country was at stake in the Pacific, persisted in giving the menace of Russia the first priority in their wartime planning and dispositions. General Tojo was all-powerful, and Admiral Shimada, Minister of Marine, had been chosen by Tojo because he shared his views.

Industry had no say in the conduct of the war, and no adequate coordination existed between the army demands upon production and those of the navy.

The ordeal which had begun only exacerbated the dissensions. Yet it was on the Imperial Navy that the essential task of protecting the left wing of the Japanese disposition in the Solomons

primarily rested. The naval staff saw with despair that the
forces which were so necessary to the continuance of this task
were being turned toward inert and passive sectors.[1]

At the beginning of 1943, the Japanese were far from having
lost all the advantages they had gained in the first months of
the war. In the South Pacific zone, they still held advantageous
positions. The airfields of Rabaul, Buka, Kahili, Vila, Munda,
and Rekata Bay, newly installed, formed a continuous chain
which facilitated reliefs of operating units and brought aircraft
nearer their operational zones.

Certainly Munda was often bombed by American aircraft, but
without much effect. The men lived underground; the planes
were dispersed under the palm trees; the craters made by
bombs were quickly filled in. The periods when take-offs could
not be made were very rare.

At Christmas, 1942, Vice Admiral Kusaka, who commanded
the 11th Air Fleet at Rabaul, had taken over the direction of the
southeastern zone and had two hundred aircraft to hold the central Solomons.

He it was who had to fight against the American offensive

---

1. *There are always differences of opinion between the army
and navy when the two services are closely associated in amphibious operations, and in this instance the differences were
heightened by the definitely changing complexion of the naval
situation in the active theaters of the South Pacific. To a very
considerable degree, the Japanese navy had been forced to yield
in its fight for command of the sea. The main sea defense was
then being supplied mostly by land-based air forces. The Japanese navy had been forced to transport army reinforcements in
the Bismarck Sea in submarines, an unsatisfactory makeshift for
moving troops by sea. The progressive capture of Japanese bases
in the Solomon Islands was steadily consolidating the American
position in that area, and the Japanese navy was not even slowing up the successive advances. And, before the end of the year,
Admiral Yamamoto's prewar estimates were to be fully verified,
as reinforcements for the American navy then began to arrive in
ever-increasing numbers.* (R.A.T.)

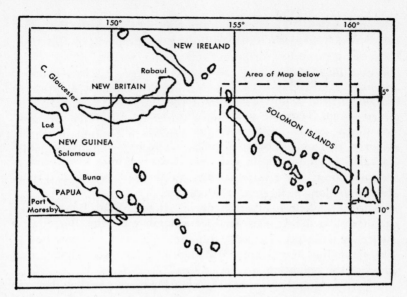

EASTERN NEW GUINEA, NEW BRITAIN, SOLOMON ISLANDS

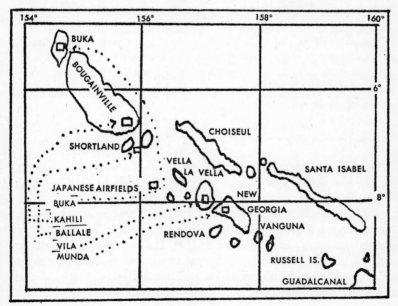

which, starting from Guadalcanal, was to climb toward Rabaul by cautious advances from island to island.

Unequal duel

The Russell Islands are thirty miles to the west-northwest of Guadalcanal. They are renowned for the rain which waters them constantly and turns them into enormous bundles of mud, and also for their magnificent coconuts. These islands were occupied by small Japanese contingents and had sometimes been used as staging points for reinforcements on the way to Guadalcanal, during the long struggle of the autumn.

After a violent bombardment of Munda, Vila, Bougainville, and the Shortlands, the Americans landed on the Russells on February 21, 1943. The little Japanese garrison escaped during the night, but it was not until March 6, two weeks later, that news of the operation reached Rabaul.

Soon the offensive against the new Japanese positions became clear. While the bombardment of airfields continued, the Americans launched raids by cruisers and destroyers against the vessels supplying Vila and Munda.

On March 6, in Kula Gulf, which separates Kolombangara from New Georgia, two Japanese destroyers which had just landed their cargoes at Vila were wiped out in the deepest darkness without being able to answer back. Once again, radar had given them away.

Wishes and realities

Admiral Yamamoto, uneasy about this American offensive which threatened the Solomons bases, decided to hit back energetically.

The production of aircraft in Japan had now reached an average of five hundred a month, and the admiral called for and obtained growing aerial reinforcements. He had just installed himself at Rabaul, with Vice Admiral Ozawa commanding the 3rd Fleet, at the headquarters of Vice Admiral Kusaka, the local commander.

The Combined Fleet had to be restored to fighting trim, but was no longer to be used in detailed operations which had already cost it so dear. It was the air arm which was to attack in strength.

At the end of March the carriers *Zuikaku, Zuiho, Junyo,* and *Hiyo* brought to Rabaul ninety-six fighters, sixty-five dive bombers, and some torpedo aircraft. These were added to the eighty-six fighters, twenty-seven dive bombers, and seventy-two two-engined aircraft and torpedo aircraft based on land.

From Rabaul, these aircraft were distributed among Buka (to the northwest of Bougainville), Kahili, and Ballale.

On April 1, a convoy sailed down to Vila while fifty-eight fighters patrolled the Solomons Channel.

The Americans, who continued to be kept informed of Japanese movements, wished to attack the convoy, and a big air fight occurred in which eighteen Japanese aircraft were shot down as against six American.

On April 7, sixty-seven Japanese dive bombers, covered by 110 fighters, descended on Guadalcanal. When they arrived over the roadstead at about 1400 and found that the warships had vanished, they had to be satisfied with a few oil tankers and cargo ships, some of which were sunk in spite of the fighters from Henderson Field. This meager success cost the Japanese twelve bombers and nine fighters. On April 12, Port Moresby was visited by 131 fighters and forty-three bombers but, forewarned as always, the ships had left in time. The fighters gave fierce battle to the intercepting aircraft while the bombers went on, but they did not find the objectives they sought.

Two days later, a similar operation, carried out by 188 aircraft, was repeated, this time against Milne Bay, and again the success was slight.

On April 16, Yamamoto stopped the operations, believing that he had caused the enemy considerable damage, because he trusted too strongly the reports of his aviators. In all good faith, the pilots, who only saw the objectives from high above or for a few seconds during the moment of attack, in the smoke from explosions, the flashes from bombs, and spray that the wind spread like a curtain, made reports about the raids which were very inaccurate. A destroyer became a big cruiser, an oil tanker an aircraft carrier, a vessel hidden by spray would be taken for sunk, and one slightly hit, which emitted black smoke, would have blown up.

In reality, the victims of the great Japanese air offensive were limited to a destroyer, an oil tanker, a corvette, and twenty-five aircraft.

He was always on time

On April 18, Admiral Yamamoto left by air to visit the upper Solomons bases. Traveling with another bomber as consort, he was protected by nine fighters. The formation steered for Kahili (Buin), and at 1135 the two big aircraft lost altitude as they prepared to land. The escort, its mission apparently ended, turned back and disappeared.

Suddenly, from out of the clouds, descended a swarm of seven American fighters which hurled themselves on the two big aircraft before they had time to land. The fight did not last long. Torn apart, with wings shredded, the bombers twirled downward, one into the sea, the other into the jungle.

Later the admiral's body was found deep in the forest by naval Captain Watanabe. The body was burned with solemnity and the ashes taken to Tokyo in a wooden casket, where they were interred with great pomp on June 5 in Hibya Park, in the presence of members of the government and before an immense and silent crowd.

Vice Admiral Ugaki, chief of staff, had been taken out of the second bomber seriously injured.

Who was to replace Admiral Yamamoto? The choice of the powers above fell on his disciple, Admiral Koga Miniuki.

In contrast to his predecessor, the new chief of the Combined Fleet was a heavy man, with a massive head. He was not ignorant of the difficulties to which he had fallen heir, and his proclamation was a warning:

"Our enemy is preparing to seek final victory in developing his means of offensive and in preparing plans for the strategic application of new weapons. There was only one Yamamoto and no one is able to replace him. His loss is an insupportable blow to us."

This fateful blow can be explained by the fact that, once again, the American services had intercepted and decoded the messages in which the tour of inspection of the Japanese admiral had been announced. Nimitz's headquarters knew the exact hour that the aircraft carrying the most redoubtable of America's enemies was to reach Kahili. But this spot was at the extreme limit of the American fighters' radius of action. If they laid an ambush in the hope that Yamamoto would fall into it, they could stay in the neighborhood only for a few minutes. But they also knew that the chief of the Combined Fleet, wherever he went, was always on time.

Defense of Munda

During the following weeks, the Americans thrust forward energetically in New Guinea and the Solomons.

On June 30, MacArthur's troops landed at Nassau Bay, whence their guns belabored Salamaua. To the east, Munda, Vila, and the Shortlands suffered repeated bombardments. On June 30 the enemy occupied Rendova, five miles from Munda, without difficulty, and the same evening opened fire on the airfield. The Japanese reply was delayed and ineffectual.

Munda was now always supplied by night from Vila. The Americans proposed to stop this, and on July 5, three cruisers and four destroyers penetrated into Kula Gulf just as Rear Admiral Akiyama was steering toward the Vila anchorage with three destroyer groups, two of which carried troops.

The cruiser *Helena*, of ten thousand tons, was sunk by a torpedo, but the *Niizuki* was destroyed by gunfire, and the *Nagatsuki*, which became stranded during the night five miles north of Vila, was blown up the following day by enemy aircraft.

Vila received the expected supplies and reinforcements.

On July 12 there was a new battle at the same place. Rear Admiral Izaki, who replaced "Tenacious" Tanaka, in the *Jintsu* which had at last been repaired, entered the gulf with nine destroyers, four of which carried 1200 soldiers. This time the Japa-

nese possessed radar, which at least allowed them to recognize
the presence of an enemy force, and they were not surprised by
Rear Admiral Ainsworth, who approached with a squadron of
three cruisers and ten destroyers.

As soon as the action started, the *Jintsu*, which had switched
on a searchlight, was overwhelmed by a hail of shells, and a
torpedo cut her in two. The unhappy vessel disappeared about
0200 with the admiral, her captain, and 482 officers and men.

The Japanese used excellent torpedoes driven by oxygen.
They had a range of twenty-two thousand yards at forty-nine
knots and of forty-four thousand yards at thirty-six knots. The
three American cruisers were struck, and the destroyer *Gwin*
exploded at 0214.[2]

The 1200 men were landed in the gulf of Vella.

All these efforts were in vain. The Americans, powerfully reinforced, landed at the end of July in New Georgia, at Rice Anchorage on the west coast and at Zenana on the north coast.
From the two sides, they advanced toward Munda, which was
taken in the first days of August. The airfield was to serve them
as a springboard for a new leap forward.

The Japanese fleet continued to suffer. A few weeks earlier,
Admiral Koga, fearing for the Shortlands, had sent the little aircraft carrier *Nisshin* from Truk to Rabaul to transport to New
Georgia additional infantry and artillery. At the exit from Bougainville Strait, the Japanese aircraft which, with three destroyers, protected the carrier, were crushed by an American attack and the *Nisshin* sank.[3]

---

2. *The Japanese placed their main reliance in night actions upon
the torpedo, and while the Americans also used that weapon,
they placed more reliance in the fast-firing 5-inch and 6-inch
guns. The range, speed, and explosive power of the Japanese
torpedo accounted for a large measure of their successes in these
actions.* (R.A.T.)

3. *Again, despite decided tactical reverses in the two early July
night actions, the strategic situation continued to improve for the
Americans. But, if the American High Command had not been
aware of the oncoming new-construction reinforcements, those*

Hymn of the dead

On August 6, a convoy of four destroyers under the command of Rear Admiral Sugiura had to take 900 soldiers and a quantity of matériel to Kolombangara. The convoy entered Vella Gulf at 2330. It was a black night, with visibility not more than two miles —ideal conditions for avoiding detection.

Nevertheless, at 2342 the alarm sounded as the *Hagikaze* sighted to port first a black outline and then four destroyers altering course to starboard.

The Japanese maneuvered immediately but too late. Torpedoes launched from close range arrived together, and in a few minutes the three first vessels of the Japanese line sank amid the thunder of explosions. Only the *Shigure*, last of the line, escaped northward.[4]

Once again radar had proved fatal to the Japanese sailors.

More than 1500 sailors and soldiers were in the sea, far from land, in a desperate situation. The American destroyers approached them, and their searchlights glittered on the surface of the water where floated dark heads which stood out in dramatic shadow.

---

losses might have caused a reappraisal of the 1943 campaign of consolidation—especially its tactics. (R.A.T.)

4. This was the first night action since the destroyer attacks upon the Japanese transports off Balikpapan in January 1942, in which the American destroyers had been released to act independently to perform the type's most important wartime function, the night torpedo attack. Three of the four Japanese destroyers were sunk in a matter of minutes. This success emphasizes a tactical mistake that had long characterized United States night actions. The destroyers had been tied as screens ahead and astern of cruiser formations which proceeded not only to enter the lion's den but also to stick their heads in the lion's mouth by steaming straight into waters which the Japanese destroyers filled with torpedoes. All actions against purely Japanese destroyer forces should have been turned into slugging bees between opposing destroyers. (R.A.T.)

The victors threw out ropes and lifebuoys, and the swimming men had only to raise a finger to escape drowning. But not a hand was stretched toward the life-saving equipment. Eyes gleamed with savage resolution, and mouths opened to sing the poignant "Hymn of the Dead":

> *If I perish at sea*
> *Water will dissolve my body.*
> *If I perish on the mountain*
> *Moss will cover it.*
> *I shall have no regrets,*
> *Having died for the Emperor.*

The Japanese completely evacuated New Georgia by means of launches which ran into Bairoko by night.

Their intention was to hold Kolombangara and to occupy Vella Lavella, which would constitute a supplementary staging point; but the Americans forestalled them by landing at Vella Lavella on the morning of August 15, and the Japanese air attacks were repulsed with heavy losses.

Threat of suffocation

Tojo watched the American advance in the Solomons without great uneasiness. Essentially preoccupied with the continent, he thought that the main allied attack would be made via India. He accordingly proposed a withdrawal to a perimeter, running from the Marianas to Wewak, via Truk, and the reinforcement of the East Indies barrier.

Koga was startled. It was from the sea that Japan was vulnerable, he said. The Pacific must be defended at any cost. The admiral, by his insistence and protests, managed to get his views taken into consideration to a certain extent, and it was decided to hold on everywhere and, sheltered by this stubborn defense, to prepare an offensive for 1944.

The army and the navy were to fight the enemy advancing in the southeast; but at the same time they would build bases for subsequent counterattacks.

The new defensive perimeter would pass by the Marianas,

Truk, the central Solomons, New Guinea, and Timor. While depending principally on Rabaul, the Japanese would use the garrisons dotted throughout the Bismarck Archipelago, at Bougainville, in the Gilberts and in the Marshalls, to delay and wear down the American attacks.

In eastern New Guinea, seventeen new airfields would be built. Special efforts would be made to hold Dampier Strait and the north coast of the main island.

The fleet would await an opportunity to engage in a decisive action, preferably when the enemy launched an amphibious operation.

Throughout the country a formidable campaign was inaugurated to reinforce the air strength. In less than six months, the big Japanese textile factories were transformed, and the thousands of spinning-mill workers of Osaka began to manufacture aircraft. New factories began to sprout between Osaka and Tokyo, and Manchuria was made to contribute actively.

To multiply the number of pilots, the universities were required to disgorge their students, who were directed to new schools. An immense amount of propaganda was disseminated. The glory of aviation was emphasized by the government and the press, employing the profusion of poetic metaphor with which the Japanese soul adorns the objects of its admiration. Formerly, heroes redressing wrongs and *samurai* with flaming swords exalted the imagination of Nippon. Then it became the "flying eagles"—the young pilots inflamed by a spirit of sacrifice. Nothing was neglected in this campaign; the building of model airplanes became the national hobby.

Unhappily, although the production of aircraft increased in quantity and quality, the lack of aviation gasoline prevented the requisite training of pilots.

All the gasoline came from the Sunda Islands and Borneo, and to the last drop had to be brought by tankers. But the lines of communication were long, and the number of available ships progressively decreased. Before August 1943, the American submarines had caused only limited losses; their torpedoes were mediocre, and the merchant navy did not fear them. By then, however, the American torpedoes had been greatly improved, and suddenly the peril from under the sea became a matter of grave concern.

On September 1 the share in tonnage was as follows:

Army: 1,179,400 tons.

Navy: 1,687,900 tons.

Civilian needs: 2,692,500 tons.

Total: 5,559,800 tons.

To supply the materials for fortifications which had been decided upon, the civilian services had to surrender to the army an additional 250,000 tons. To make this good, efforts were made to hold the annual losses to a million tons.

In spite of everything, the work did not go forward as expected, because of a lack of ships and consequent shortage of materials. The ship losses, in the month of September alone, rose to 172,082 tons.

The Empire was threatened with a stifling of the national war effort through alarming losses to its seaborne communications.

20   The Octopus Contracts

In spite of some losses from Japanese air attack, the Americans continued to land on Vella Lavella. On September 14, they took Horaniu in the northern part of the island. An airfield was installed at Barakoma on the southeastern coast of Vella Lavella, a point from which it was easy to intercept the launches supplying Kolombangara. These now passed via Choiseul, but it became necessary to abandon Vila which, hemmed in as it was by two enemy airfields, was no longer of any use.

On September 20, a hundred launches went to Point Tuki to take off the garrison of Vila. In the night of the twenty-seventh and twenty-eighth another convoy continued the task. During this time, Japanese seaplanes harassed five patrolling American destroyers by means of rockets and illuminated buoys.

Every night there were continual skirmishes. On a smaller scale, it was the drama of Guadalcanal over again.

By the first days of October, Kolombangara was completely abandoned. In five trips, 9400 men had been evacuated.

The Japanese still held Choiseul and the extreme north of Vella Lavella, but this last base was no more than an advanced post, difficult to supply and incapable of playing any part. This also had to be evacuated, and Admiral Ijuin was given the order to carry out the operation with ten destroyers, three of which were to serve as transports, and twelve small vessels.

On October 6, at 2230, reconnaissance seaplanes located a group of three American destroyers which were steering toward Marquana Bay, where the disembarkation was to take place. They flew over them and surrounded them with flares and illuminated buoys.

Ijuin engaged the enemy. Soon the *Yugumo* drifted in flames, in a sinking condition, but on the other side the *Chevalier*, struck by several torpedoes, blew up, and the *Selfridge* was temporarily immobilized, but later returned to base under her own power, although the entire forepart of the ship was a shattered mass.

The Japanese reconnaissance aircraft then reported a new enemy force arriving from the south, and the destroyers stood away for Rabaul. The little vessels, which had not been warned, continued their mission. Without a blow being struck, they brought back 589 men to Buin.

Where will the next blow fall?

A parallel American advance continued in New Guinea. Salamaua fell, then Lae. Finschhafen was taken on October 2.

At Truk, the Japanese had premonitions of an approaching menace hovering over the Solomons. Admiral Koga flew his flag in the big battleship *Musashi* and sent to Rabaul, at the beginning of October, all the aircraft from his carriers. The submarine *I-36* had arrived near Pearl Harbor and the planes she sent off had sighted an important concentration in the port, notably four battleships and four aircraft carriers. The enemy seemed on the point of launching a big offensive, and Admiral Koga accordingly weighed anchor for Eniwetok in the Marshalls, where it would be easier to watch over events. Nevertheless, a week later he returned to Truk. All these marches and countermarches, orders and counterorders, meant that the fleet commander was conscious of lack of information. He expected a blow but did not know where that blow would fall.

The air reinforcements that had just arrived at Rabaul were composed of eighty-two fighters, forty-five dive bombers, forty torpedo aircraft, and six reconnaissance planes.

The crews were clearly superior to those of the land-based aircraft, and so the American raids, which had multiplied against both Rabaul and Dobodura, met an energetic defense. A single attack cost the enemy nine bombers and ten fighters.

All the same, the High Command preferred to use these picked men sparingly, when possible, in minor operations. They were the fruit of meticulous selection, and their concentration in the carrier air squadrons had called for many sacrifices of strength in other organizations.

When it was wished to replace the casualties in the aircraft carriers, the losses were felt cruelly, because the new trainees could not match the standards of efficiency set by the carrier aircraft crews of the early days of the war.

Little by little, Nimitz's airmen regained the advantage, thanks to the power and the valor of the Airsons (Air Solomons Command). The Japanese camps were so badly bombed that they were constantly unusable.

The hovering menace ended by becoming precise. In the last days of October, the Americans feigned a landing on Choiseul and on November 1 landed troops at Cape Torokina, which commands the north side of Empress Augusta Bay on the southwest coast of Bougainville.

And so a new struggle began. The immediate air resource from Rabaul remained inefficacious.

Blind attack

Admiral Koga ordered Vice Admiral Sentaro Omori, commanding the 5th Cruiser Division based on Rabaul, to attack an American force on its way up the Solomons Channel. This force had actually bombarded Buka and retired without having been seen.

When he returned to Rabaul, Admiral Omori received an order to escort five destroyers, carrying about a thousand soldiers, to contest the landing on Bougainville. He had under his control two heavy cruisers, the *Myoko* and the *Haguro,* while Rear Admiral Ijuin covered the left flank with the *Sendai* and three destroyers, and Rear Admiral Osugi the right with the *Agano* and three destroyers.

This Japanese formation encountered the squadron protecting

the American transports, in the early hours of November 2. Overwhelmed by the radar-directed enemy fire, the Japanese attack miscarried, and Omori returned to Rabaul; the *Sendai* was not with him—she had sunk during the battle.

The admiral was severely censured and relieved of his command—a heavy penalty! To fight blindfolded against an enemy who can see you is a mad enterprise, even for the strongest will.

On the other hand, the repeated actions in which the opposing destroyers had engaged during the many Solomon Islands battles and in which those light vessels had suffered so heavily in the past months, had led to haphazard groupings, which lacked the homogeneity so indispensable for night battles.

Surprised in the nest

Koga was alarmed by the news he received, but some days later, Admiral Kurita arrived at Rabaul with a fleet of seven heavy cruisers, a light cruiser, and four destroyers. The graceful ships cleared the water, their bows boldly uplifted, passed before Kavieng, skirted the coasts of New Ireland, and entered Rabaul, where they anchored in widely separated berths. It was the first time that such a force had appeared in these waters, and it seemed as if luck was going to change.

Alas! this hope was not to last long. On November 5, at 0900, an enormous swarm of aircraft appeared in the southeast. The alarm sounded, fighters were already airborne, and soon fire was opened.

One fact showed up immediately—the Americans seemed to know exactly where the anti-aircraft battery emplacements were located. Still grouped, they maneuvered to pass out of range of the guns. Trails of smoke and explosions in the sky showed that the fight was a fierce one.

Suddenly the formation deployed, and the American machines hurled themselves at the ships. For several minutes which seemed like centuries, bombs fell and torpedoes dived toward their targets. Heavy rolls of black smoke covered the harbor, and the sea seemed to boil into a thousand bursting white bubbles as the guns maintained a continuous fire.

When the attacking squadrons had disappeared, Admiral Kurita received the reports. They were discouraging:

The *Maya* had received a bomb hit in her main engine room.

The *Takao* had a serious leak.

The *Atago* had been shaken by three near hits.

The *Mogami* had some serious damage.

The light cruisers *Agano* and *Noshiro* had also been struck and were no longer battleworthy.

In under a quarter of an hour, the magnificent squadron which, bristling with guns, had appeared invincible, had ceased to count. The damaged ships were all able to withdraw under their own power. While none was sunk, several needed long periods of navy-yard repairs, and this was the end of important Japanese fleet units in the Solomon Islands area.

This strike was from the carrier *Saratoga,* back after her period of repair, and from the light carrier *Princeton,* the first of this class to appear in the Southwest Pacific, the first of many.

Raft of despair

Admiral Kusaka had only 270 aircraft remaining at Rabaul, of which 100 belonged to aircraft carriers. Thirty-nine of the airmen put ashore had been shot down, and their loss was irreparable.

From then on, Rabaul was subjected to a pitiless succession of air raids. New names were passed around, the names of new American aircraft carriers just entering service—the *Princeton,* the *Essex,* the *Bunker Hill,* and the *Independence.* What was there to oppose them? The three last-named carriers arrived in the area on November 11. New construction had really begun to appear.

The attacks delivered from Rabaul broke against the defenses of these vessels. Uneasy for his last carrier air crews, Admiral Koga withdrew them from the battle and sent, as reinforcements in their place, aircraft and men of poorer quality who came from the Marshalls.

To gain time to reinforce the new perimeter, the loss of Bougainville had to be delayed as long as possible. Rear Admiral Osugi who, at the head of the right wing, had played a useful part in the clash of November 2, was given the task of reinforcing the handful of troops who were fighting the Americans at Buka and Torokina.

The two operations were carried out without difficulty. But when, on November 24, Admiral Kagawa sought to repeat them, he ran up against some American destroyers. The run of luck was against the Japanese; they lost the destroyers *Onami, Makinami,* and *Yugiri.*

All these tragedies at sea were repeated in minor and obscure human dramas which formed a pathetic background. On November 9, a raft which was bringing back seven Japanese soldiers to New Britain was met by the American destroyer *Spencer.* Once more, the Americans wanted to save these forsaken men, exposed to all the caprice of the ocean. Boats were lowered and, making signs of friendship, the Yankees neared these unfortunates, half dead with hunger and thirst. The Japanese rose when they saw their saviors. A salvo sounded. The seven men grimly fired a burst of automatic fire into their mouths. Better to die than to be taken prisoner! The last man, the officer, fell on the disfigured bodies of his comrades.

Rabaul burns

During the month of December, Admiral Kusaka kept up the bombings on Empress Augusta Bay, where the American transports were moored, but the results were practically nil.

On December 25 the Japanese troops, still holding out on Bougainville Island, were finally chased out and the Americans installed an airfield for heavy bombers at Piva.

Elsewhere, General MacArthur's forces, who went up the northeast seaboard of New Guinea, landed first at Cape Gloucester and then, in spite of Japanese reaction, at Arawe in New Britain. This was on December 26.

From the twenty-ninth, Rabaul suffered continual attack from the southeast and southwest by aircraft whose bases were now quite near; Torokina was only 210 miles away.

At first the Americans suffered appreciable losses. A hundred and thirty-three naval aircraft from Truk on January 25 brought to 300 the number of aircraft at the base, and the anti-aircraft fire became more effective. Between January 23 and 30, thirty-seven Japanese and twenty-three Americans were shot down in the sector.

Under the enemy pressure, Rabaul grew weary. Reinforcements grew scarcer from February 1 on, and the harbor finally was empty.

Fifteen days later, the Americans occupied the Green Islands. A big air battle again took place on the nineteenth, and of the fifty Japanese aircraft which took part in it, twelve did not return.

General Tojo came himself on a flying visit to inspect the position, accompanied by the chief of the General Staff, General Nagano, and Admiral Shimada. Speaking to Admiral Imamura, the prime minister said:

"Rabaul must be held without fail. It is the key to our barrier in this region. Unfortunately, I cannot do much for you just now. As soon as I have sufficient means at my disposal, I shall not forget you."

And he set off again.

Rabaul was almost completely isolated. One after another, the anti-aircraft guns were destroyed in spite of their excellent camouflage. After March, the attacking bombers were no longer escorted, so rarely were defenders met. The town burned continually under the never-ceasing rain of blows.

The perimeter is pierced

Now Rabaul was neutralized. Its defense had been costly, and its downfall permitted the American threats to develop. MacArthur was going to be able to start his advance along the north coast of New Guinea toward the Philippines while Nimitz advanced in the central Pacific.

In mid-December, it was decided to reinforce Kavieng, at the northwestern extremity of New Ireland. Because of lack of tonnage, the battleship *Yamato* took part in the operation. She was torpedoed by a submarine on Christmas Day and had to return home for repairs.

The position was attacked by American aircraft carriers which sought to isolate it from Truk.

On March 20, the Americans took Emiriau, between Kavieng and the Admiralty Islands, which enabled them to observe the entire north coast of New Ireland.

On April 3, the Admiralty Islands, after a vigorous defense, fell in their turn, and the perimeter planned for the protection of the Japanese zone of early conquests was finally pierced.

Wall in the factory

In November 1943, a General Headquarters High Command for escorts was created to exercise control of the naval stations and the two escort groups. Its direction was confided to Admiral Oikawa Koshiro. As the result of continual effort, this energetic and patient officer managed to improve the situation somewhat, although the means at his disposal were decidedly insufficient. In particular, escort vessels were few in number and often in a miserable state of repair. This aspect of the naval war, commerce protection, had been entirely neglected by those who had prepared its plans.

Four little aircraft carriers were provided for escort service. They were so dilapidated that the first of them was not usable until July 1944, and not one could be kept in active service for more than one or two voyages, at most.

Of the airmen used to watch over the commercial routes, all those who acquired a recognized efficiency were quickly transferred to the Combined Fleet.

In spite of everything, Admiral Oikawa Koshiro put the finishing touches upon a plan of action:

1. Minefields were to be laid between the Nansei Shotos, Formosa, the Philippines, and Borneo. The places which could not be mined would be provided with radar capable of directing

aircraft and destroyers. Inside the zone protected in this manner, ships could circulate freely.

2. The girdle passing by the Nampo Shotos (including the Bonin Islands and Volcano) and the Marianas was to be guarded by means of destroyers and radar. Convoys would navigate inside this protecting line.

3. The shipping routes along the southern coast of Honshu between Yokohama and Kobe, and along the east coast between Yokohama and Hokkaido, would be defended alike by destroyers and aircraft, helped by radar. Ships would circulate freely.[1]

Unfortunately, there were only four minelayers available, and the operation was so long drawn out that, at the end of the war, only the west China Sea and Formosa Strait were partly mined. Before the fall of Okinawa, only one radar station had been installed.

Another 300,000 tons of shipping were withdrawn from civilian use to enable reinforcements to be sent to the Marianas and Carolines. The merchant-ship losses in January and February 1944 were 240,840 and 256,797 tons, respectively.

The creation of a ministry of munitions did not stop the rivalry between anchor and star, between the navy and the army. With reason, the navy accused the ministry of being partial to the army and, for this reason, jealousy kept its own factories. The recently built workshops should have delivered their aircraft in equal shares to the army and the navy, but in some of them, walls with iron doors had to be erected to cut the whole factory in two, and prevent the raids which sailors and soldiers had been making on each other's arms, machines, and munitions. Between these defenders of the same country, real battles sometimes broke out, and the prize was the material which in any case was to be used against one and the same enemy. The wall was a symbol.

In practice, the army stocked in its depots a large quantity of

---

1. *This whole plan needs no extended comment. It is so fabulously fantastic that it is difficult to see how it was ever proposed in full seriousness.* (R.A.T.)

material which the navy needed urgently. And this practice continued until the end.[2]

---

2. *As has already been said in previous notes, wartime differences
of opinion between the army and navy are frequent occurrences.
But these usually are and should be entirely based upon honest
differences of viewpoint produced by variance in training and
experience. But this picture and those in two or three other passages in this book depict a most unfortunate atmosphere for the
production of the maximum, soundest national effort in a vitally
important war.* (R.A.T.)

21 Farewell to the North

Attu and Kiska, which had been in Japanese hands since June 1942, depended for the whole of their supplies and protection on Admiral Hosogoya, whose quarters were at Paramushiro. This post was 650 miles from Attu, with Kiska another 378 miles farther away.

These distances and the prevailing weather conditions in the region made warlike operations difficult. Besides, Admiral Theobald's squadron was at Kodiak, and the value of the Aleutians did not justify actions of wide scope.

The landing operations and then the movement of supplies had at first been accomplished without difficulty, but American public opinion grew disturbed and, overestimating the real importance of the northern islands, it demanded their reconquest.

From then on, aircraft attacked the Japanese convoys. To supply Kiska, Admiral Hosogoya, a cautious old sailor, obtained the help of the *Zuikaku* and three small carriers.

In July, American submarines joined in the game and sank the destroyers *Nenoki* and *Arare*.

In August 1942, Guadalcanal began to draw the Japanese forces southward, leaving Hosogoya only a skeleton naval force. To replace the vessels that had been taken from him, he wanted to build airfields at Attu and Kiska, but the nature of the ground, especially at Kiska, made this work almost impossible with the means at his disposal. Besides, in these regions, aircraft were only a makeshift unless equipped with radar which could make light of the mists.

Kiska is shaped like a caterpillar, its head formed by a 3,936-foot volcano. The port opens on the east coast. In the late afternoon of August 7, the garrison was alarmed by a violent bombardment from the sea. In the grayness, five cruisers could be made out, their sides lit by yellowish flashes. The shells burst on contact with the earth without penetrating it. To shelter from the inclement weather, the Japanese had installed themselves in grottoes or else had dug shelters which defied the guns, and the destruction was insignificant.

But the Americans seemed to want to maintain their pressure on the island and, according to information gathered, were building an airfield at Adak, where the soil lent itself more readily to this work.

It was thus thought preferable to concentrate at one point the weak forces dispersed over the two islands, and at the end of August 1942, the garrison on Attu reinforced that of Kiska.

The enemy occupation of Adak had, however, caused uneasiness in Japan. The threat of an invasion coming from the Kuriles had often haunted the imagination of some Japanese leaders. Hosogoya suddenly received troops and was able to reoccupy Attu and reinforce Kiska at the same time.

On January 12, 1943—the evacuation of Guadalcanal by the Japanese had just been decided—the Americans occupied the deserted island of Amchitka between Kiska and Adak.

Attu in its turn suffered continual bombardment, and the supplying of the two islands became impossible because of the blockade which isolated them.

Lost opportunity

Hosogoya, determined to break this blockade, left Paramushiro on March 22 on board the *Nachi*, followed by the *Maya* with the light cruiser *Tama* and two destroyers as escort. Transports, protected by the light cruiser *Abukuma* and two more destroyers, sailed behind the covering force.

The weather was good and the thermometer low; at this season in this latitude the sun is still lazy.

The convoy set course northward to catch up with a transport which had left before the others, the *Sanko Maru.*

On March 26, about 0800, the red signal lamp of the *Asaka Maru* winked; the officer of the watch had sighted an enemy force thirteen miles to the south. Signals ran up the halyards, and klaxons and bugles sent the crews to action stations. The warships altered course to the southeast, while the transports stood away northward.

Soon the American line appeared to starboard of the *Nachi.* The intelligence officer tried to identify the enemy vessels, with the help of cards on which sketches indicated the characteristics of foreign vessels. At the head was the *Richmond,* then the *Salt Lake City;* four destroyers surrounded them.

It was an extraordinarily clear day. At 0840 the enemy was thirteen thousand yards away, and the admiral ordered: "Open fire as soon as circumstances are favorable."

There came the thunder of guns in reply, and soon the Americans were surrounded by spray. They answered back. The *Nachi* was struck by a 6-inch shell from the *Richmond,* but the fire it caused was quickly put out.

About 0900 the admiral's ship suffered from the well-regulated fire of her adversary. A shell burst against the mainmast, destroying the transmission cables; a second struck the bridge to starboard, a third pierced the decks and penetrated into a torpedo-tube compartment.

The admiral was at the front of the bridge. Lieutenant-Commander Miura, a staff officer, was leaning against the hand rail of the starboard aileron. The second shell burst just beside him and he was thrown to the deck. A rain of shell splinters whistled around him, but he got up unscathed and resumed his interrupted watch.

Almost at the same moment an explosion occurred in the *Salt Lake City.* The aircraft, made fast to its catapult, had just been hit, and the gasoline caught fire and threw immense, clear flames skywards.

For a moment the Japanese line hesitated, especially because at 0900 a shell from a destroyer had unluckily penetrated the forward turret of the *Nachi*. The men there were chopped to bits by splinters, the cartridges in the lockers caught fire, and through the shattered deck head, thick smoke poured forth and spread southwestward.

The *Richmond* seized the opportunity to bear off to the northward, where the transports were hurrying. The small cruiser *Tama* left the line and resolutely interposed herself, but the *Nachi* had regained control of her steering and at 0930 proceeded at high speed in pursuit of the enemy, crossing its course at 0950. She was still five miles astern.

The admiral ordered that fire be concentrated on the *Salt Lake City*, and the big American cruiser began to yaw confusedly, her steering evidently damaged. She was again hit at 1010, as the smoke escaping from her hull indicated.

The American destroyers laid a smoke screen, and the *Richmond* altered course to 240 degrees, then to 210 degrees.

Deceived by the artificial fog, Hosogoya for a moment continued on his course, then altered course in his turn and gained ground, thanks to his two knots' superiority in speed.

At 1103 the *Salt Lake City* slowed. She was visibly in a bad way and was about to stop.

Victory was within reach.

The American destroyers detached themselves from their group and steamed at full speed to make a desperate attack, but Hosogoya had just made inquiries about the fuel level and the state of ammunition. He ordered: "Course westward."

The Japanese gunners saw disappearing over the horizon the prey which had needed only the *coup de grâce*. They silently cursed the caution of their chief, which had deprived them of a victory already won.

The squadron found the transports safe at Paramushiro.

Hosogoya was severely censured for the lack of audacity which had caused the failure of his mission and, deprived of his command, he went to Sasebo in the *Nachi*, which was to be repaired there.

Through a rift in the mist

On May 11 the Americans landed on Attu at three points. The defense had only 2,630 men at its disposal, and its arms and supplies were deficient, so much so that it could not reply effectively. Admiral Kawase, now in command at Paramushiro, had no resources and could only make desperate appeals to Tokyo.

Koga sent him urgently the heavy cruisers *Myoko* and *Naguro,* and he himself left Truk with three battleships, the small aircraft carrier *Hiyo,* two light cruisers, and five destroyers. In Tokyo Bay on May 22 he attached to his force the aircraft carriers *Zuikaku, Shokaku,* and *Zuiho,* three heavy cruisers, two light cruisers, and eleven destroyers.

It was too late, however, to save Attu, and the absence of this fleet allowed the Americans to land at Rendova without difficulty.

Attu was finally taken on May 20. The last defenders, tracked down, launched a desperate attack led by Colonel Yamasaki, but they broke against the American defenses. The survivors committed suicide by exploding grenades against their heads or hearts. The Americans were horror-struck before this heap of frightfully torn bodies.

Now it was Kiska's turn to suffer continual bombardments, sometimes by aircraft equipped with radar, sometimes by the fleet.

After considering the matter, the Imperial General Staff decided against sending the Combined Fleet north. It stayed in the Inland Sea for a training period.

Left to himself, Admiral Kawase began the evacuation of Kiska by submarine. However, engine breakdowns and damage due to weather compelled all the vessels to give up their tasks.

Kawase sought to bring matters to a conclusion. He weighed anchor in the *Tama* with a screen of five destroyers. Rear Admiral Kimura commanded a transport group, protected by the light cruisers *Abukuma* and *Kinu* and six destroyers.

On July 22 the meteorological service forecast thick

weather. Kawase set course to the southeast to prevent discovery from the air, and on the twenty-sixth arrived five hundred miles south of Kiska.

He turned northward. When he arrived fifty miles from his goal, he sent Kimura ahead and maintained station in that vicinity to cover the transports and their escorts.

Kimura anchored at Kiska at 1840 and fifty-five minutes later departed with all the garrison. At the moment he left the harbor, the mist rolled away, and the evacuees were able to cast a last glance at this inhospitable land they were leaving forever.

On August 1 Kawase was back in Paramushiro.

The Aleutians had been abandoned.

Allied consolidation*

This story of the Japanese navy at war is naturally concerned with the more dramatic features of that navy's participation in the conflict. After the battle of the Santa Cruz Islands, on October 26, 1942, the principal units of the Japanese fleet do not actively appear upon the scene until the battle of the Philippine Sea, described in the next chapter. Consequently, the requirements of perspective have caused the narrative to move rapidly through the accounts of the light-force clashes and shore operations which comprised the Solomon Islands and New Guinea campaigns.

With the conclusion of this chapter, the war reaches the end of its phase of consolidation; the period extends from February 1943 to early April 1944—from the firm establishment of the Allies in Guadalcanal and in the Port Moresby-Buna-Gona areas to their complete domination of the Solomons and eastern New Guinea, including the Bismarck Sea.

And, before the completion of this phase, the first big Pacific amphibious operation, the capture of Tarawa in the Gilbert Islands, had been successfully accomplished. While this was the precursor of the similar later undertakings of the Central Pacific offensive, strategically it was an operation of consolidation

* This section was written by Admiral Theobald.

and thus a part of that phase of the war then nearing its completion. For Tarawa was the natural staging base to the Fiji and Samoan Islands, and although the need for its capture was not too apparent in November 1943, its possession by the United States was the final link in the denial of the South Pacific to Japan.

The capture of Kwajalein and Eniwetok opened the American offensive in the central Pacific and, a little later, General MacArthur's seizure of Hollandia in northern New Guinea started his march-back. From then to the end of the war, the Japanese danced strategically to the tunes provided by the Allies.

Much has been written about leap-frogging versus island-to-island advance in the prosecution of the Pacific offensives. Most of these comments have left the impression that General MacArthur employed the former while Admiral Nimitz used the latter. Nothing could be further from the truth as far as the central Pacific operations were concerned.

Actually, the first appearance of the leap-frogging principle in the American operations of this war occurred in the Aleutian campaign of May 1943, when Kiska was by-passed in favor of lightly held Attu, after which Kiska was taken without a blow being struck, as the Japanese had evacuated the island before American attack forces arrived.

In the Marshalls-Marianas campaigns of 1944, the same principle was employed. The powerful Japanese bases in the eastern Marshalls—Wotje, Majuro, and Jaluit—were left to wither on the vine, while their supporting links to the westward, Kwajalein and Eniwetok, were captured. In the next move to Saipan, Tinian, and Guam in the Marianas, Ponape was by-passed. And throughout the Pacific campaign, the strongest mid-Pacific Japanese base, Truk, was never threatened with attack by surface forces.

Of course, in the preliminary preparations for a by-passing operation, the Japanese bases to be left behind were usually subjected to heavy neutralizing bombings and bombardments. These served two important purposes: they lessened the menace from the air forces of those bases; they helped to disguise from the Japanese, as long as possible, the real objective of the later main attacks. (R.A.T.)

22 The Buffalo Charges

In the late fall of 1943 and the opening months of 1944, the Americans increased their forces in the Pacific to overwhelming proportions. The industrial power of the United States had now fully equipped them to make war in two oceans.

With their 3rd Fleet, which was composed of four task forces (38-1, 38-2, 38-3, 38-4), each provided with two big aircraft carriers, two light aircraft carriers, two new battleships, and fourteen destroyers,[1] covered on their left wing they were to advance westward, conquering the Gilberts, then the Marshalls, the Marianas, and the Carolines.

The landing forces had at their own disposal fourteen escort

1. *This probably accords with the Japanese records. Through the campaigns mentioned here, however, Admiral Spruance's command was designated as the Central Pacific Force; its covering force in the Marianas and Carolines campaigns, including the Philippine Sea battle, was Task Force 58. This comprised four carrier task groups (58.1, 58.2, 58.3, and 58.4) and the battleline task group (58.7) of seven modern battleships with attendant cruisers and destroyers. In the Leyte and later campaigns, the battleships were distributed among the carrier task groups as stated above.*

The numbers of the task groups set forth here were the ones in use in the Leyte campaign. (R.A.T.)

aircraft carriers, seven old battleships, seven heavy cruisers, five light cruisers, and 122 destroyers.

The operations unfolded in a logical and unchangeable manner. Photographic missions flew over the islands to be attacked. The photographs revealed in detail the Japanese defenses. Then the task forces, helped by land-based aircraft, undertook the bombardments which sometimes lasted for several weeks. When the fruit seemed ripe, the transports closed in. After a final bombardment by aircraft and warships, innumerable landing craft and amphibious vehicles dashed toward the chosen beaches.

The defense, always vigorous, nevertheless was weakened by the tons of steel that had been poured on it and sooner or later succumbed to the power of the assault. And the conquered island served as a staging base for aircraft to prepare the attacks on the succeeding objective.

The Japanese could only supplement the defense of their bases in Oceania by means of the fleet. But enemy aircraft dominated the operations, and the available Japanese aircraft carriers were not adequate in quantity or quality for such an operation to have any chance of success.

The only hope was for land-based aircraft to intervene in the battle in sufficient numbers. For this, Admiral Koga must wait until the American forces had arrived in those western waters where these bases were more numerous and closer together.

The continual loss of islands, spread out over the immense Pacific, was not in itself disastrous nor in its early stages altogether disquieting. In a few weeks, the Japanese had conquered an area so wide that the American offensive still had only clipped its edge, after eighteen months of gigantic effort. But what was serious was that Japan had not been able in this struggle to carry the battle to the heart of the enemy fleet and that, on the contrary, the naval war had, little by little, been oriented to her disadvantage. Moreover, at certain places the enemy's advance threatened, or neutralized, vital points without which it was impossible to maintain the difficult economic and military balance on which depended not only the "Co-prosperity Sphere" but even the existence of the Empire.

But matters had not yet reached an acute stage. Kwajalein in the Marshalls, Truk in the Carolines, and Saipan in the Marianas were the centers of a defense system easy to supply from Japan.

The Gilberts and the Marshalls are coral archipelagoes which lend themselves to the construction of airfields.

The naval bases were at Saipan in the Marianas; Truk, Ponape, and Palau in the Carolines; Wotje, Majuro, Jaluit, Kwajalein, and Eniwetok in the Marshalls.

The islands were in general well fortified and equipped with radar, except for Eniwetok, in the western Marshalls. The garrisons were few in number, averaging some 1,000 to 3,000 men; air strength, almost always skeletonlike, generally comprised only some thirty aircraft, except at the more important bases, where there were about sixty planes, including reconnaissance seaplanes.

Tarawa

In August 1943 the Americans had occupied the Ellis Islands, and in October, forces based there harassed Nauru and the Gilberts. On November 20, the 4,800 men garrisoning Tarawa were wiped out by the Americans, who lost twenty percent of their effectives in the battle.

Eniwetok occupied

Nine hundred aircraft from carriers took part in the operations, not counting land-based aircraft. Japanese reaction was more spirited than effective. The light aircraft carrier *Independence* was hit by a torpedo, and the escort aircraft carrier *Liscome Bay* sunk by a submarine.

By the end of December, four American airfields had been completed in the Gilberts and were to serve the attack on the Marshalls.

In this archipelago, the Japanese had 130 aircraft available. On January 29, 1944, seven hundred American carrier aircraft began the preparations. The same evening the Japanese air

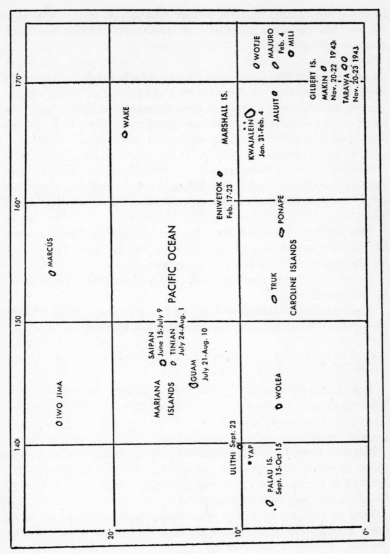

CENTRAL PACIFIC OPERATIONS, NOVEMBER 1943–OCTOBER 1944

forces were destroyed. The sequel was not delayed: the Roi-Namur Islands were in American hands on February 2, and two days later it was the turn of Kwajalein.

The Eniwetok islands were to become celebrated, six years later, by tests of the new atomic bomb which would be the main weapon of a future world war: in February 1944 these islands were defended by 11,400 Japanese infantrymen. Attacked by a force of 50,000 men, they fell between February 19 and 23. The frenzy of the defenders was such that their losses rose to a total of 11,044 killed.

During the operations against the Marshalls, the fast aircraft carriers attacked Truk and Jaluit, and twenty-six merchant ships, six warships, and 270 aircraft were destroyed at these bases.

The 1st Air Fleet had sent, for the defense of the Marianas barrier, a first echelon of 120 aircraft, but an American attack on February 22 wiped out this reserve.

By March, the Americans had acquired excellent bases 2200 miles west of Hawaii.

Truk also was unusable, and the bombardment of the Marianas proved that the inner defense line was threatened.

Fledglings in the storm

The Japanese realized that their strategy needed review. Their present means were so limited that only exceptionally favorable conditions would allow them to regain the ascendancy.

Admiral Koga had ordered the fleet to evacuate Truk, on February 10, to avoid further enemy attack. He went to Tokyo with his staff to confer with the Imperial General Staff.

One can imagine this meeting, held at a time when serious doubts were already insinuating themselves into the minds of these responsible leaders and military chiefs. But they allowed nothing of this to show in their outward demeanor. Until the end, they all maintained passive faces, according to the rules. They continued to argue and act as if there were still hope.

It was decided that the 1st Mobile Fleet would be based

partly in the Singapore zone and partly, for training, in Japanese waters. The commander in chief, on board the *Musashi,*
would base at Palau.

When he returned, Admiral Koga published his Order 73, under which the principal operations were to be localized in the
central Pacific, and the eastern boundary of the zone of interception was defined by the Kuriles, the east of Honshu, the
Nampo Shotos, the Marianas, the Carolines, and the west of
New Guinea. The enemy aircraft carriers would be attacked by
air concentrations; the surface forces, in cooperation with the air
arm, would carry out raids to weaken enemy convoys, and the
rest of these convoys were to be destroyed at the moment of
landing.

The High Command itself published directives in which
Operation TO was foreseen; any enemy fleet approaching
Japan would be intercepted and destroyed by land-based aircraft which the commander of the air group of Yokusuka would
command.

But it was impossible to establish complete and detailed plans,
because neither the training of the aircraft carriers and their new
groups of aviators nor the restoration of land-based air forces
had been achieved.

In March 1944, the 3rd Aircraft Carrier Fleet was formed into
three divisions, each composed of three carriers. All these vessels
were of modest tonnage, except the *Shokaku,* the *Zuikaku,* and
the *Taiho,** the three which comprised Carrier Division One. On
the other hand, the *Zuiho* and the *Chitose* were converted oil
tankers and the *Chiyoda* an old naval auxiliary.

In May, the three divisions were concentrated at Tawi-Tawi,
after a training period as intensive as possible.

Indeed, there remained hardly any pilots in the air group of
the 1st Division who had taken part in preceding operations.
Sent from Truk to Rabaul at the beginning of November 1943,
this group had been almost completely destroyed. The group of
the 2nd Division had suffered similarly in January 1944. The

---

* This big carrier, sister ship of the *Shokaku* and the *Zuikaku,* had just
entered service.

group of the 3rd Division had been formed only in February
1944.

The pilots of the Japanese carriers had received only two to
three months' training in all—that is, a half or a third of what it
should have been. Without experience or sufficient knowledge,
they were to participate in some of the most difficult maneuvers
of naval warfare. To meet the demands of their coming ordeals,
these young men had only their gallantry. They were fledglings
in a storm.

Squall

After it had abandoned Truk, the Japanese fleet's principal
base was Palau. At dawn on March 30, eleven fast aircraft carriers attacked the island and, after a day of pitiless aerial dog-
fights, all the Japanese air forces of the base were put out of
action. But reinforcements arrived during the night of March 30-
31, and the battle was resumed at daylight. It lasted until the
Japanese aircraft were completely annihilated. From then on,
the harbor was easy prey.

When the American force set off again, after it had mined
the approaches to Palau, the Japanese had lost two old destroyers, four escort vessels, and twenty auxiliary and merchant
vessels totaling 104,000 tons, of which six oil tankers accounted
for 47,000 tons. This time, the other vessels had left in time.

On March 31 it was the turn of Yap, Ulithi, and Ngulu to be
bombarded. On April 1, it was Woleai. One hundred and fifty
Japanese aircraft were shot down, against thirty-five American.

Admiral Koga then declared that he would hold the line Mari-
anas-Palau to the death, because if the inner line were pierced,
Japan was lost. In the event of an attack from the north, the admiral intended to install his command post at Saipan; if the attack were launched in the south, at Davao.

The reconnaissance of March 29 gave warning of a direct
attack upon Palau. It was announced that a landing force was on
a course to the west of the Admiralty Islands and that an American task force was advancing westward. The admiral concluded
from this that western New Guinea was to be attacked.

He decided to rally all the air forces in the Marianas at Palau and to send to Davao all the aircraft of the carriers based on Singapore, under the command of Admiral Ozawa. The pilots lacked carrier training; they were capable of daylight landings but not of those at night. In the meantime, they could be used from land bases.

Koga himself left for Davao in the evening of March 31 in a two-engined plane, and his chief of staff, Admiral Fukudome, followed him in a second machine.

On its way, the convoy ran into a violent storm. The chief of staff's aircraft skirted the disturbance and tried a night landing near Cebu, but the aircraft crashed not far from the beach and Fukudome, wounded, fell into the hands of the Filipinos.

This worthy and respected leader found himself at their mercy. He had to share their life, wandering in the caves and remote valleys of the savage island. Some months later, Japanese troops rescued the prisoner. Not for a moment had his dignity deserted him.

Admiral Koga's aircraft disappeared and was never seen nor heard of again.

A link in the chain

From April 21 to 24, the Americans continued their landing operations at Hollandia on the north coast of New Guinea. On the twenty-ninth and thirtieth, Truk was again attacked. Of the 104 aircraft based there, fifty-nine were shot down and thirty-four destroyed on the ground, while the Americans lost twenty-seven planes.

Admiral Toyoda became commander in chief of the Combined Fleet on May 3, 1944. He was a man of great experience and vast intelligence. Chief of the Navy Department during the two years preceding the war, he knew the limits of Japan's industrial potential and, for that reason, first had strongly opposed his country's entry into war and then many of the wartime projects of expansion which he considered far too ambitious. When he took up his command, the Imperial General Staff gave him directives according to which the air and naval forces were to prepare for a decisive action to take place at the end of May, but only under favorable conditions.

Toyoda did not hide the fact that the strategic position was bad. The defense was stretched over a huge area which the enemy could attack in force at any point he selected. The lines of communication were becoming more and more vulnerable under ever more vigorous attacks by submarine and aircraft, and the air bases were suffering very heavily from raids carried out by American carrier or land-based aircraft.

For the Japanese, it was a problem of launching a concentrated attack by their fleet supported by the land-based aircraft. The new commander in chief, in his proclamation, did not hide his anxiety:

"The war is approaching areas vital to our national security. Our situation is one of unprecedented gravity. There is only one way of deciding this struggle in our favor."

Indeed, the Marianas were an ultimate barrier. Moreover, they permitted the Japanese aircraft to hop from island to island and to concentrate at the chosen point in the event of a plan of action based upon their cooperation with the fleet.

The loss of the Marianas would be tragic. It would open an important breach in the inner area of defense and would cut the strategic lifeline of the Japanese empire.

Meanwhile, the preparatory operations were in full swing, and there was little room for doubt about American intentions. On June 11, some 225 American aircraft bombed Guam, Rota, Tinian, and Saipan. One hundred and forty-seven Japanese planes were destroyed. For three days, raid succeeded raid on these islands. On the thirteenth, seven aircraft carriers bombarded Iwo Jima, wiping out 130 aircraft on the ground and destroying installations. Finally, on June 15, with a tremendous deployment of forces, the foe landed on Saipan, in spite of 150 Japanese aircraft which had survived and had made desperate attacks from Guam, Rota, Tinian, and the Carolines.

The head of the American bridgehead spread out rapidly. One of the links in the Japanese inner chain had parted.

Armed watch

On June 10, 1944, the main part of the Japanese fleet was still at Tawi-Tawi, under the command of Vice Admiral Ozawa. This base had been chosen to parry an attack by the American fleet on Palau or to the south of Palau. The zone suited coordination between the movements of the fleet and the air force.

At Tawi-Tawi there was a force of nine aircraft carriers organized into three divisions, and the Battle Force under the immediate command of Vice Admiral Kurita, which controlled five battleships (two of them around 65,000 tons), eleven heavy cruisers, two light cruisers, and twenty-eight destroyers.

On June 13, the fleet left its anchorage and steamed in the direction of the Philippines to carry out a series of combined exercises, planned for a long time. The vessels passed Guimaras Strait between Panay and Negros islands and took on supplies.

On the fifteenth, the admiral received the following orders: "About thirty enemy transports to the east of Saipan started to disembark. From 1400 part of the Task Force attacked Iwo Jima, then Chichi Jima. Apply Plan AGO."

The halyards of the *Taiho*, the admiral's vessel, were filled with signals. By groups, the fleet made its way toward San Bernardino Strait, while the light cruisers and destroyers covered the waters ahead and on the flanks of the formations in search of submarines.

In the aircraft carriers, mechanics were busy getting the planes ready; the pilots, who for the most part had never been under fire, waited near their aircraft, dreaming of following in the footsteps of their elders and of giving the enemy a severe lesson. Their minds made up to any sacrifice, they recalled the verse of *Ikusa no Niwa* ("Garden of War"):

> *It is when you succumb*
> *That the highest praises are yours*
> *And your glory is the purest.*
> *If your hour has come,*
> *Fall, wild fledgling!*

After having refueled at sea on June 16, the squadron was ready for battle. Supported by the air forces from Palau, Yap, and Guam, the aircraft carriers were to destroy the American air forces. Admiral Kurita would afterward account for the transports.

On June 18 it was fine and clear as the hunt began. Information which arrived, from hour to hour, without being precise, showed the admiral that about 380 miles from him were three task forces, each comprising aircraft carriers and battleships and steaming forth to meet the Japanese fleet.

Wall of fire

On June 19 the sun rose in a magnificent sky, and visibility was unlimited, while a fourteen-knot wind blew from the east, slightly rippling the surface of the sea.

The morning reconnaissances confirmed the presence of three task forces. That of the north was composed of three carriers; that of the center, of three carriers and four battleships; that of the south, of three carriers and three battleships.[2]

The Japanese fleet itself sailed in several groups, centered on the three carrier divisions.

The admiral had decided to take the initiative in attack, profiting from the proximity of Guam to the American forces. There, the Japanese aircraft could land to refuel and effect quick repairs after they had completed their attack missions. At 0730, seventy-three aircraft took off from the carriers of the 3rd Division and flew toward the enemy. They were still forty miles from their designated targets when a swarm of Grummans, the best American fighters, dived from the clouds, and in an instant the formation was thrown into disorder as sinister trails of smoke plunged seawards. Suddenly, those aircraft which had held their course ran into a barrage of anti-aircraft fire.

Eighteen Japanese fighters did their best to check their power-

2. *According to the American official records, there were four carrier task groups in the Philippine Sea battle, plus one battleline task group, but one of the four carrier task groups was assigned to operate in support of the battleline task group.* (R.A.T.)

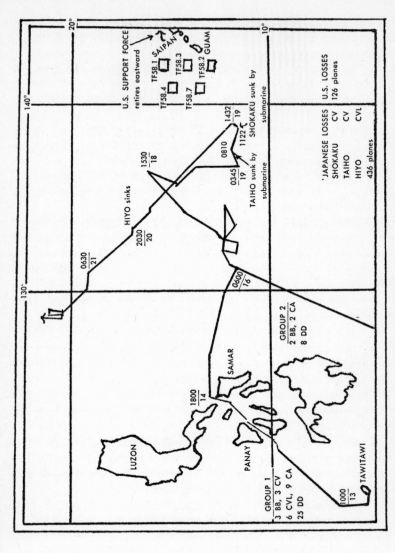

BATTLE OF PHILIPPINE SEA, JUNE 19–20, 1944

ful adversaries. The bombers turned and looked for a break in the barrage of fire. About forty succeeded in getting through, clipping the wave tops. It was 0945.

In the distance, an enemy surface fleet appeared: it was the center force. Four large battleships and a multitude of cruisers and destroyers were ranged in a circle around three aircraft carriers.

It was the moment to attack. The bombers prepared to strike, the torpedo planes lowered themselves toward the sea. The pilots were novices whose tactical skill did not match their courage. They pressed on without cohesion, and the enemy anti-aircraft batteries had ample time to concentrate their fire successively on the more menacing groups.

Despite all this, the Japanese attacked furiously. The *South Dakota* shuddered under the shock of a 500-pound bomb, but the powerful ship nonetheless held her course. The *Indiana* had some plates stove in, and near misses caused minor damage to several vessels.

Few Japanese aircraft survived. These retired toward their own formation or else followed orders and landed on Guam. But there, the pilots, who took things more easily when they left the battle area, again had to make fresh calls on their fighting spirit as they had to meet the furious attacks of American fighters circling the airfield like hawks waiting for their prey.

Those who, by skill and luck, managed to break through this barrage were chased to ground level by their tenacious foes and landed fighting to the end.

At 0800, one hundred and twenty-nine aircraft of the 1st Division set out in their turn. They also set course for the central enemy group but, in spite of prodigies of valor, they did not succeed any better than had their predecessors.

Forty-nine machines of the 2nd Division took off at 0830 and also steered for the central enemy Task Force but, halfway there, a signal altered their course toward the northern group.

There the enemy remained invisible, and fuel was getting low. The leader of the squadron made the only possible decision. Waggling his wings, he again led his group toward the central Task Force.

Forty Grummans jumped them, and a fight raged. No Japanese plane could break through the fighter barrier.

The Taiho *and the* Shokaku

The first wave of Japanese aircraft had scarcely vanished when the *Taiho* was shaken by a violent explosion, as a torpedo from a submarine struck her.

The blow had fallen upon a vital spot. Through broken piping, aviation gasoline poured into the hangar and the 'tween deck filled with the explosive vapor, and at 1100 the vessel blew up.

Before this, Vice Admiral Ozawa had ordered a destroyer alongside and had transferred his flag to the heavy cruiser *Haguro,* in which he continued to exercise his command.

At 1120 two fountains of water from torpedo hits climbed the side of the *Shokaku.* During the repairs she had undergone after the fight of October 26, 1942, the vessel had been modified in accordance with lessons learned in the war, but she could not withstand two such blows. She caught fire, gigantic clouds of smoke obscured the sky, water poured into her underwater compartments, and the breaches grew larger. At 1401 this big ship also sank beneath the waves.

The aircraft in the two carriers, which were preparing to take off in a new attack wave, disappeared with the ships.

At 1300 a second wave, of about eighty aircraft, left the *Zuikaku* and carriers of the 2nd Division, and headed for the southern enemy Task Group, but they vainly circled the estimated enemy position without sighting anything.

About 1345, a little formation of eight aircraft of the 2nd Division at last encountered two enemy groups which were approaching each other. This formation recklessly prepared to attack, but it was quickly wiped out by the enemy fighters.

Most of the survivors of the various assault waves took refuge on Guam, where thirty American fighters continued their patrol; the fight went on relentlessly, so that the landing and wreck squads had a never-ending job clearing the runway of the tragic wrecks that littered it in such rapid succession.

Ozawa reckoned that he had only a hundred or so aircraft left, fifty of them in the *Zuikaku*. He decided to withdraw toward the northwest, with the intention of taking on supplies and reorganizing his forces to return to battle on the twenty-first.

The end of the missing aircraft

On June 20, the admiral again shifted his flag, this time to the *Zuikaku*. An intercepted signal informed him that the enemy was in pursuit. The supply ships almost immediately were ordered to clear the formation, and the force continued its withdrawal, without being able to pause for breath or dress its wounds. The groups of vessels were strung out over a distance of 250 miles, as everything pointed to further violent attacks from the air.

Indeed, at 1820, a flight of American planes arrived from the southeast. The 2nd Carrier Division received the main brunt of the ensuing attack. Thirty-five interceptors were in the air, and the anti-aircraft batteries went into action, putting up a dense barrage around the precious ships. While the fighters engaged their adversaries in a ferocious fight, the ships maneuvered rapidly to baffle the attacks. But the assailants were numerous and skilful. Torpedo aircraft dashed in from all sides, while bombers dived at top speed. The Japanese gunners, in spite of their excellent training, were surprised by the multiplicity of targets. The light carrier *Hiyo* stopped, her steering jammed by the explosion of a torpedo, and while a squad of mechanics busied itself, another torpedo fired by a submarine struck home. At 1932 the vessel blew up.

The *Junyo*, another light carrier, received two bombs, and six near misses dislocated some plates in her hull; but, although seriously damaged, the ship was able to continue on her course.

The three carriers of the 3rd Division sailed in triangle, the *Chiyoda* ahead.

At 1732, fifty American aircraft deployed and attacked violently. They ran into the barrage, dived, and climbed again with a deafening throbbing of engines, returning to the assault until their stock of bombs was exhausted.

Two other light carriers, the *Ryujo* and the *Chiyoda,* were damaged by near misses, and the battleship *Haruna* and the heavy cruiser *Maya* also suffered damage.

Twenty-two aircraft had fallen while defending the fleet, and some twenty Americans had been shot down. Eighty other Japanese planes had a worse fate. Lost over the ocean, short of fuel, they ended by being swallowed up, one after the other, falling from the sky like ripe fruit. Still others crashed while landing, in the middle of the night.

Two Japanese supply ships, the *Genyo Maru* and the *Seiyo Maru,* had been sunk.

There was now no question of restarting the fight. All the Japanese fleet continued its course and anchored at Okinawa on June 22 and 23.

Battle of the Philippine Sea

After it had refueled, the fleet returned to Japan. For a dozen days or so the navy yards worked feverishly to get the damaged vessels into shape again. The battleships and cruisers at last received radar sets. The staff officers watched over their installation with great care, because they knew that, in the next battle, air patrols could hardly be counted on.

The carriers stayed in Japan. They had lost about 300 machines of the 450 they carried, and had to be rearmed with new aircraft and fresh crews, which could only be done in the motherland. Later they were to set out with pilots who, fatally, were even less well trained than those who had just paid so dearly in the battle of the Philippine Sea for their lack of preparation.

The other vessels under the command of Admiral Kurita returned to Lingga in the Singapore zone. In fact, the losses of oil tankers had been such that fuel was scarce in the homeland. The squadron could not keep itself supplied there for long, and had to get nearer the Dutch East Indies, the source of fuel.

The battle of the Philippine Sea, on which certain Japanese leaders had founded such great hopes, demonstrated once again that the Japanese could no longer hope for success in air operations against the overwhelming enemy superiority. Their aircraft were of good quality, but the maintenance was not all that could be desired because of a lack of spare parts. And the Japanese pilots, insufficiently trained, were up against adversaries admirably trained and flying planes maintained at peak level.

From April 1943 to April 1944, Japan had built 9952 aircraft; 6334 of them had been lost.

Nimitz joins MacArthur

On June 24 and on July 3 and 4, Iwo Jima was again bombed by carrier planes and bombarded by the guns of vessels.

A task force attacked Chichi Jima and Haha Jima.

On July 21, after long and devastating preparation, the Americans landed on Guam, and on August 8, air groups were installed on its airfield to carry out patrols.

Tinian, near Saipan, was occupied on July 24.

On August 4 and 5 a task force operating near Iwo Jima sank 35,000 tons of merchant shipping.

During this time in the southwest Pacific, the American advance along the north coast of New Guinea had reached Sansapar in the extreme west on July 30, and Morotai was marked as the next point of enemy attack.

Now the Japanese were faced with a critical strategic situation. Part of their inner defense line was occupied. Shipping, already violently attacked by submarines, was to suffer equally from the air, especially as the best airmen had to be withdrawn from convoy protection to reinforce the fleet.

The fall of Saipan, which the fleet was unable to prevent in spite of its desperate efforts, had been a stunning blow. Tojo himself announced: "Japan is threatened by a national crisis without precedent." On July 18, the cabinet was overthrown and the government which replaced it was charged with giving "all its fundamental attention" to the problem posed by the prosecution of the war.

The Carolines bases, although less useful, still formed a salient between the allied forces which had pushed west and north, with their lines of communication resting on the New Hebrides and Australia, and the forces of the central Pacific whose communications ran by Hawaii, the Gilberts, and the Marshalls.

Palau was bombarded continually from June to September.

On September 12 and 13, an American raid on the Visayan group in the Philippines cost the Japanese more than 300 aircraft, thirteen big merchant ships, and twenty small ones.

Then it was the turn of Luzon. This big air base, which served as a training center for pilots, was attacked on September 21 and 22 by carrier aircraft. Three hundred Japanese planes were destroyed, and three destroyers, twenty merchant ships, and three oil tankers were sunk.

Between August 31 and September 24, 1944, the Japanese lost more than 1000 aircraft, against 114 for the Americans.

In September, Peleliu, Angaur, and Ulithi in the western Carolines were occupied.

At this time, the Americans had bases which formed a junction between the central Pacific forces and those of the southwest Pacific.

From the naval point of view, the Empire of the Rising Sun was in the situation of a besieged stronghold.

The submarine campaign*

With the capture of Saipan and Guam, the defeat of Japan was an assured fact. The increased effectiveness of the United States submarine campaign guaranteed that. By the summer of 1944, the submarines had become a very powerful force in the Pacific. Now, overnight, its effective strength in the vital Japanese shipping areas had been doubled. This was so because, based on Guam or Saipan, the round trip of every submarine from base to operating area had been reduced by 6600 miles—a tremendous saving in time and fuel. Throughout the war, while surface and air action made inroads upon Japanese merchant-marine tonnage, the bulk of the losses was inflicted by American submarines. Not only were these submarines most efficiently

* This section was written by Admiral Theobald.

handled, but the Japanese defense of its seaborne commerce was easily the most ineffective feature of the nation's warmaking. In the modern sense, it was practically nonexistent, except in the close approaches to its principal seaports.

The Japanese merchant marine had suffered heavily up to the summer of 1944. Thereafter, its losses rose sharply, so that, just over a year later, 91 percent of its tonnage had been destroyed. An island nation cannot exist, much less wage war, without its seaborne communications. And Japan was about to be bereft of its navy and its merchant marine. (R.A.T.)

UNITED STATES FORCES IN THE SAIPAN, TINIAN, GUAM OPERATIONS, JUNE-JULY, 1944 *

Central Pacific Force, Admiral R. A. Spruance

Task Force 58, Vice Admiral M. A. Mitcher
(Covering Force, which fought Battle of Philippine Sea, June 19-20, 1944)

    Task Group 58.1, Rear Admiral J. J. Clark
    Hornet, Yorktown, Belleau Wood, Bataan   (2 CV, 2 CVL)†

* As there was no seaborne Japanese opposition to the operations for the capture of Tarawa, Kwajalein, and Eniwetok, the author treated these very briefly, and there was no purpose in including tables of opposing forces. The organization of the United States naval forces for the capture of Saipan, Tinian, and Guam was standard for all major Pacific amphibious operations. The main task force was always the covering force, which prevented enemy interference with transports during passage and with the landing operations. The transports, cargo ships and their supports were under the direct command of the amphibious force commander, during the advance and throughout the landing operations until the forces were fully established ashore. The supports comprised the old battleships, escort carriers, light cruisers, destroyers, and minesweepers.

† *Abbreviations:* CV, aircraft carrier; CVL, light carrier; CVE, escort carrier; CA, heavy cruiser; CL, light cruiser; CL-AA, anti-aircraft light cruiser; BB, modern battleship; OBB, old battleship.

Boston, Baltimore, Canberra, Oakland (3 CA, 1 CL-AA)
Screens: 14 destroyers

Task Group 58.2, Rear Admiral A. E. Montgomery
Bunker Hill, Wasp, Monterey, Cabot (2 CV, 2 CVL)
Santa Fe, Mobile, Biloxi, San Juan (3 CL, 1 CL-AA)
Screens: 12 destroyers

Task Group 58.3, Rear Admiral J. W. Reeves Jr.
Enterprise, Lexington, San Jacinto, Princeton (2 CV, 2 CVL)
Indianapolis, Montpelier, Cleveland, Birmingham, Reno (1 CA, 3 CL, 1 CL-AA)
Screens: 13 destroyers

Task Group 58.4, Rear Admiral W. K. Harrill
Essex, Langley, Cowpens (1 CV, 2 CVL)
Vincennes, Houston, Miami, San Diego (3 CL, 1 CL-AA)
Screens: 14 destroyers

Battle Line Task Group 58.7, Vice Admiral W. A. Lee Jr.
Battleship Division 6: Washington, North Carolina (2 BB)
Battleship Division 7: Iowa, New Jersey (2 BB)
Battleship Division 8: Indiana (BB)
Battleship Division 9: South Dakota, Alabama (2 BB)
Cruiser Division 6: Wichita, Minneapolis, San Francisco, New Orleans (4 CA)
Screens: 14 destroyers

Amphibious Forces, Vice Admiral R. K. Turner
Fire Support Group 1, Rear Admiral J. B. Oldendorf
Tennessee, California, Maryland, Colorado (4 OBB)
Indianapolis,* Louisville, Birmingham, Montpelier, Cleveland (2 CA, 3 CL)
Fire Supports and Screens: 17 destroyers

Fire Support Group 2, Rear Admiral W. L. Ainsworth
New Mexico, Idaho, Pennsylvania (3 OBB)
Wichita,* Minneapolis,* San Francisco,* New Orleans,* Honolulu, St. Louis (4 CA, 2 CL)
Fire Supports and Screens: 9 destroyers, 2 destroyer-type transports, 1 minesweeper

* These 5 heavy cruisers are listed in both Task Force 58 and in the Amphibious Support Forces because they were to operate with either of these forces in accordance with the demands of each particular tactical situation.

Carrier Support Group 1, Rear Admiral G. F. Bogan
Carrier Unit 1: Fanshaw Bay, Midway, 3 destroyers (2 CVE)
Carrier Unit 2: White Plains, Kalinin Bay, 3 destroyers (2 CVE)

Carrier Support Group 2, Rear Admiral H. B. Salada
Carrier Unit 3: Kitkun Bay, Gambier Bay, 3 destroyers (2 CVE)
Carrier Unit 4: Corregidor, Coral Sea, 3 destroyers (2 CVE)
Transport Screens: 15 destroyers, 1 destroyer-type transport

JAPANESE FORCES IN BATTLE OF THE PHILIPPINE SEA, JUNE 19-20, 1944

First Mobile Fleet, Vice Admiral Ozawa

Carrier Force, Vice Admiral Ozawa
     Carrier Division 1 ("A" Force): Taiho,* Shokaku, Zuikaku   (3 CV)
     Carrier Division 2 ("B" Force): Junyo, Hiyo, Ryuho   (3 CVL)
     Screens: 1 light cruiser, 15 destroyers

Main Body ("C" Force), Vice Admiral Kurita
     Battleship Division 1: Yamato, Musashi, Nagato
     Battleship Division 3: Kongo, Haruna (2 BB, 3 OBB)
     Cruiser Division 4: Atago, Takao, Chokai, Maya (4 CA)
     Cruiser Division 5: Myoko, Haguro (2 CA)
     Cruiser Division 7: Tone, Chikuma, Kumano, Suzuya, Mogami (5 CA)
     Carrier Division 3: Zuiho, Chitose, Chiyoda (3 CVL)
     Train: 8 supply ships, 4 destroyers

LOSSES IN BATTLE OF THE PHILIPPINE SEA

JAPANESE LOSSES	UNITED STATES LOSSES
Taiho, Shokaku (2 CV) sunk	126 aircraft
Hiyo (1 CVL) sunk	
2 oil tankers sunk	
424 aircraft	

* *Taiho* was a *Shokaku*-class carrier.

PART SIX

Under the Sign of the Kamikaze

23 The *Sho* Plan

By this time, beyond doubt, the attack on the Philippines was near, and the possession of the Philippines was now, for Japan, a matter of life or death. It was in fact the last barrier between the Americans and the China Sea; if the enemy broke through it, his aircraft and ships would finally cut the already precarious lines of communication that had brought to the motherland the riches of the south, and quick stifling of the nation's life must follow.

To the Americans, the occupation of the Philippines meant the possibility of attacking Indo-China and Malaya and would procure for them excellent bases to operate against Formosa.[1]

In the month of August, the General Staff had foreseen that this most decisive of all episodes would take place at the end of October. The High Command indicated in the following terms the way in which it intended to act:

---

1. *This is a Japanese appreciation of enemy possible moves after recapturing the Philippines. Actually, it is not believed that the American High Command ever gave serious thought to undertaking the reconquest of Malaya and a campaign in Indo-China. Victory in the war would take care of all that. There was, at one time, some talk of invading Formosa, but that was discarded in favor of Okinawa, closer to the Japanese Home Islands, and hence to the foci of such seaborne commerce as then still remained to Japan.* (R.A.T.)

"Everything possible must be done to discover the enemy invasion forces at the maximum distance (about seven hundred miles) by searches by land-based aircraft. Then we can determine the probable place and hour of the landing, and so allow our troops to take up their battle stations. The 1st Attack Force will proceed to Brunei, north Borneo, in sufficient time to pounce on the enemy transports and destroy them at sea, before the landing. If this Force cannot accomplish its task and if the transports start their disembarkation, the Attack Force will engage the enemy at the anchorage, at the latest in the two days following the landing.

"The 1st and 2nd Air Fleets will attack the enemy aircraft carriers by surprise to weaken them; then, two days before the arrival of our surface forces, they will thrust with all their strength on the carriers and transports to open the way for the 1st Attack Force, which will close in and engage the enemy."

In response to these directives, the fleet exercised with the same ardor and devotion that it had always shown. The ships knew now that to protect themselves from aerial attack they could no longer count on anything except their own fire power, and so they prepared to use everything that could shoot—even rifles.

Commanders carefully studied evasive maneuvers.

Finally, training in night warfare with the use of flares and radar was especially concentrated on, not only in matters affecting torpedo attacks but also in regard to accurate gunnery.

There were conferences to study the probable landing places. The conclusion was that there were three of these: in the north, Lamon Bay; in the center, the Gulf of Leyte; in the south, Davao Gulf.

Exercises were undertaken to discover the tactics which would enable them to approach the anchorage and methodically to destroy the transports, after having scattered the protecting screen.

The senior officers of the Imperial Navy thought with melancholy of the aircraft carriers, of which so few remained. Without these vessels, the finest fleets in the world, according to Admiral Koyanagi, were only tin cans.

Nonetheless, it was hoped that the last available carriers would be able to assemble at Lingga by the end of November. But would this not be too late? With great effort, enough fuel could be got together to allow them to set out, but they would weigh anchor only on a mission of sacrifice.

In September, a last reinforcement in men and material for the air bases was escorted from Japan to Manila by battleships. The convoy did not penetrate Philippine waters—the cargo was transshipped in Brunei Bay, Borneo, seven hundred miles from its destination, and then carried by small craft which worked their way between the islands, too modest a prey to tempt a torpedo or a bomb.

Other regions were stripped to reinforce the chain of islands. Indeed, as Toyoda had said, "If we are beaten in the Philippines, and even if the fleet remained to us, the southern sources of supply would be isolated. Returned to Japanese waters, the squadron could not be refueled; left in the south, it could not be supplied with arms and ammunition. It would not be reasonable then to save the fleet while losing the Philippines."

Waiting at Leyte

In consequence, the *Sho* ("Victory") plan was conceived. It stipulated that the American landing forces should be attacked by surface vessels, conforming to the directives already given by the General Staff. According to all the forecasts, the American attack would develop before the training of pilots permitted the aircraft carriers to reach Lingga; consequently, these vessels would constitute a diversionary force, which would try to draw the principal American task force away from the operational zone.

The *Sho* plan also foresaw the eventuality of an attack in the zone Formosa-Nansei Shoto-Kyushu meridian, the possibility of a threat to the zone Kyushu-Shikoku-Honshu and, finally, the likelihood of operations against Hokkaido.

Of all these possibilities, the attack on the Philippines was evidently the most probable. The Japanese army concentrated its efforts on the archipelago, fortified the coast, and prepared itself for a counterattack. Every available means of transport was put at the disposal of the local commander, and served mainly to reinforce Leyte, which seemed to be the most threatened spot.

The Japanese had learned that for defenses to fight without mastery of the air, the decision must be obtained in the early stages of the landing. It was a question of hours. Indeed, the critical moment for an invader exists when he has landed weak elements which are clinging to the ground to constitute a bridgehead. The defenders should profit by their momentary superiority to crush the adversary; if they delay, with their transport paralyzed by enemy aircraft, the balance of forces quickly becomes unfavorable to them, and they risk being overwhelmed.

Okinawa was bombed on October 10, Luzon the following day, and from the twelfth to the sixteenth fast aircraft carriers persistently attacked Formosa. From the airfields of the big island, more than seven hundred Japanese aircraft took off, and in the course of the fantastic four-day battle the Japanese seriously damaged two American cruisers and lost more than six hundred machines against seventy-five lost by their adversary.

All the same, the pilots of this force so exaggerated the results obtained by them that the High Command sent to Formosa—in the hope that a decisive blow would be dealt the enemy—a big proportion of the air groups intended for the aircraft carriers. These contingents, insufficiently trained, were decimated, and so the carriers were deprived of a goodly percentage of their air crews to no avail.

The reports received were so positive in their thoughtless optimism that a Japanese squadron was dispatched under the command of Vice Admiral Shima to proceed and finish off the remains of the American fleet, alleged to be in the process of destruction. This "2nd Diversion Attack Force" comprised two heavy cruisers, one light cruiser, and seven destroyers. It had just left the Inland Sea when more exact information arrived to report the presence of very important enemy forces. Shima was ordered to proceed to Amamio Shima and there await instructions.

Rendezvous with fire

At 0800 on October 17, the commander in chief received the
news that the Americans were landing on the islets which close
the gulf of Leyte. Immediately an order was given: "Alert Plan
Sho No. 1."

The defense of the Philippines was about to begin.

The operations which were to follow, very simple in conception, were complicated enough in their execution and development. That is why it is so necessary to distinguish the
three, and even four, different forces that the Japanese were to
put into the game. One was named the 1st Diversion Attack
Force but, contrary to what this name seems to imply, it was
not that force which was charged with the real diversion, but
the Main Body—an apparent striking force—commanded by
Vice Admiral Ozawa. Finally, there was another attack group
designated as the Third Night Combat Unit, commanded by
Vice Admiral Nishimura, which was to cooperate with the 1st
Diversion Attack Force, although the approach routes of the
two forces to the area of attack were widely separated. There remained the force commanded by Vice Admiral Shima, the role of
which had not yet been decided upon, but which was later
assigned to support Nishimura's forces in Surigao Strait.

Vice Admiral Kurita, who commanded the 1st Diversion Attack Force, was the model of a Japanese warrior. Taciturn and
short in stature, he was regarded as one of the best torpedo
specialists in the Imperial Navy. He had spent two thirds of his
thirty-two years of service at sea.

On the sixteenth, he received from Admiral Toyoda the order
to prepare to weigh anchor and immediately made all final
preparations. On the eighteenth, at 0100, he set out from
Lingga for Brunei, which he entered at noon on the twentieth.
From there, he sent to Manila, according to his instructions,
the 16th Cruiser Division, composed of the heavy cruiser *Aoba,*
the light cruiser *Kinu,* and the destroyer *Uranami.*

Vice Admiral Ozawa was still commander of the 1st Mobile

Fleet, but the geographical dispersion of the various forces prevented him from exercising effective command, and in consequence Vice Admiral Kurita was put directly under the orders of Admiral Toyoda.

D-Day for the attack was fixed for October 25. The orders were:

"At dawn on the twenty-fifth the 1st Diversion Attack Force will open a passage in the direction of the zone of Tailoban. After destroying the surface forces, it will attack the landing forces."

Most of the cruisers' and battleships' aircraft were sent to Mindoro, to scout the route for the fleet to the east of the Philippines. After he had conferred with his chief of staff, Rear Admiral Koyanagi, Kurita ordered:

"The main body of the 1st Force will weigh anchor from Brunei at 0800 on the twenty-second, speed sixteen knots. Course north of Palawan to arrive south of Mindoro on the twenty-fourth, then speed between twenty and twenty-four knots. Arrival at the eastern entry to San Bernardino Strait at sunset the same day. At 0400 hours, arrival at Soulouan Island, from where a passage will be forced as far as the enemy anchorage. The 3rd section [Admiral Nishimura's unit] will weigh anchor from Brunei in the afternoon of the twenty-second. It will cross the Jolo Sea and arrive at the western extremity of Surigao Strait one hour before sunset on the day D-1. It will force a passage in the direction of the [enemy] anchorage in cooperation with the main body."

The 3rd section was in fact composed of the battleships *Yamashiro* and *Fuso,* whose speed was only some twenty-one knots. It had to operate separately for fear of preventing the other sections from profiting by their twenty-six knots. It can be imagined that, under these conditions, it would be very difficult to concert the two movements, and it seemed probable that, in any event, each force would have to give battle on its own.[2]

---

2. *This was a fatally weak and defective dispersal of force. It would have been much sounder to have had Nishimura's battleships steam in company with those of Kurita. If the tactical situ-*

In spite of everything, the training had given confidence to all. Full of faith, the staffs and crews got ready to repulse the enemy attacks and, after a favorable struggle, to penetrate as far as the enemy transport anchorage.

It should be noted that the date fixed for the battle was much more than two days after the landing, the maximum delay stipulated by the High Command. Even before the action, it could be foreseen that the principal objective, the destruction of the transports, would be without any particular effect, since these would certainly be about empty.

Even in the fundamental conceptions of the operation, there were important contradictions. It was designed to repulse the American landings in the Philippines. The prime requisites for success in such an operation were timely information of the enemy and the positioning of one's own forces to react promptly. The Japanese plans disregarded both these essential factors. Consequently, the American invasion was in its sixth day when the Japanese were ready to attack. At most, they could then hope for nothing more than the spectacular massacre of empty transports and cargo ships. In return, they risked heavy losses from powerful concentrations of carrier task forces and submarines covering the approaches to the American an-

---

ation should later so demand, the latter could increase speed beyond the twenty-one knots of which the Fuso *and* Yamashiro *were capable, and those vessels could follow at best speed and would thus probably never be out of tactical supporting distance from the faster group. As it was, Nishimura was in a hopeless tactical situation in Surigao Strait, and the assured sacrifice of his two battleships and one heavy cruiser could in no way aid the accomplishment of the Japanese aims. His fate was sealed from the start, unless his move through Surigao Strait caught the enemy completely by surprise, and air observation was an almost perfect guarantee that that could not happen. And if he did get safely into the waters approaching Leyte Gulf, he was still faced with the most difficult of all tactical problems, to coordinate his actions with those of the Japanese major forces in the face of an active enemy. He never had a chance. (*R.A.T.*)*

chorage. And an unfortunate complication for them was the necessity of opposing the enemy carrier air forces with land-based
forces of their own, with the handicap which liaison with such
forces always imposes.

Vice Admiral Shima's force left Amamio Shima on the seventeenth. After some hesitation, he received the order to follow the
movements and to support the attack of the Third Night Combat Unit. His force was then designated as the Second Diversion
Attack Force. He entered Coron on the twenty-third to repro-
vision.

Sacrifice mission

The decision of Admiral Toyoda, during the battle of Formosa, to attach the air groups of the 3rd and 4th Carrier Divisions to the Second Air Fleet had completely upset Vice Admiral Ozawa's plans. Furthermore, Admiral Shima's force had
also been taken from him, and his carriers were very nearly disarmed. What would he be able to do?

Ozawa was an outstanding personality. A big man, dignified
and scrupulous, he had those rare qualities which make a leader
respected and loved. On the seventeenth he sent his chief of
staff, Captain Omae, to Kure, and the latter brought back the
following instructions from Tokyo: "The aircraft carriers will be
incorporated in a force charged with playing the role of bait.
They will embark all the aircraft of the 1st, 2nd, 3rd, and 4th
Divisions which have not been sent to Formosa."

But not 150 pilots remained.

On October 20, Ozawa received his final instructions: "Co-
ordinating its action with that of the 1st Diversion Attack Force,
the Mobile Fleet will maneuver east of Luzon to draw the
enemy northward. It will use every means to attack this enemy
and to destroy it."

The mission was one of sacrifice from the start.

On the seventeenth, the four carriers *Zuikaku, Zuiho, Chitose,*
and *Chiyoda,* of which only the first had been built as such,
and the two battleships *Ise* and *Hyuga,* which had been modified into hybrid carriers with flight decks aft, filled up with fuel

and proceeded to Oita to embark the aircraft. The pilots were
so poorly trained that it had been decided not to permit
them to fly their aircraft onto carriers.

On the news that the big American carriers were steaming
southward, east of the Philippines, Ozawa weighed anchor on
the twentieth. His squadron comprised the four incompletely
armed carriers, the two battleships with their stern turrets removed but without a single aircraft aboard, two light cruisers,
and only eight destroyers, the *Fuyutsuki* and the *Suzutsuki* having been torpedoed a few days before.

At 1700 the Decoy Carrier Striking Force cleared Bungo
Strait.

In this manner the forces of the Japanese navy converged on
Leyte Gulf. At the same time, every available submarine was
sent to the sector, together with army contingents. The 16th
Cruiser Division, detached for the purpose by Vice Admiral
Kurita, transported to Leyte troops from Formosa and Luzon.
The narrow channels of the Philippines were furrowed by
motor boats, sail boats, and barges, bringing the garrisons from
Mindanao, Cebu, and Panay.

The 2nd Air Fleet, which received an uninterrupted flow of
reinforcements, set out for the Philippines, and it was decided
that, on the twenty-fourth, it would deliver an all-out attack
on the American aircraft carriers.

Having issued these various orders, Admiral Toyoda realized
that his role had ended for the moment. There was nothing
more that he could then do. He had thrown into the balance
all the forces at his disposal and could only await the outcome,
without too many illusions. In principle, it was the navy's headquarters in Tokyo which should have conducted the battle, in
which were intermingled some military and air units, in addition to the far more numerous naval units; units attached to
various commands which extended from Manila to Saigon. In
fact, communications were too difficult for this exercise of command by the navy to be feasible. Four or five hours frequently
elapsed between the sending of a dispatch and the receipt of
the reply. Therefore, the fleet and force commanders had to
make the necessary high-command decisions, often without

knowing the action taken by their colleagues, with whom their operations should have been coordinated in the interest of unity of effort. These command difficulties should have been taken care of by chains of command in the operating forces. The failure to do this was solely Admiral Toyoda's.

It is not astonishing that, in these circumstances, the Imperial Navy failed to accomplish its mission. At least this immense outburst of energy, as the Japanese dashed to the rescue in one last supreme effort, had its touch of pathetic grandeur.

The difficulty of being seen

After October 21, Ozawa daily sent out nine reconnaissance aircraft. An average of three failed to return, because of the incompetence of the pilots and the difficulty of transmissions.

The admiral wanted to be within attacking range of the American aircraft carriers by the morning of the twenty-fourth, in order to draw them away from Kurita. On that date, the Decoy Carrier Striking Force should be 250 miles east of the northern part of Luzon.

On the twenty-third, the Carrier Force formed into two groups to facilitate anti-aircraft defense. The right column was composed of the *Zuikaku*, the *Zuiho*, and the battleship *Ise*; the left column, of the *Chitose*, the *Chiyoda*, and the *Hyuga*; the light cruisers *Tama* and *Oyodo* were in the lead, while the *Isuzu* brought up the rear.

In the evening of the twenty-third, the squadron still seemed not to have been sighted by the enemy. Nevertheless, it was absolutely necessary to prevent the American forces from concentrating east of San Bernardino Strait. Japanese forces had so often been sighted by the enemy when they did not want to be, but now that, on the contrary, their plan called for American attention to be drawn as quickly as possible to a naval formation, the latter could not manage to make its presence known. At 2000, the *Zuikaku* sent a long radio message to ensure that the bearing of this transmission would be obtained by the enemy.

The following day, from 0545, reconnaissance aircraft were sent out to attack the enemy, trying to draw him northward at the moment when the squadrons of Kurita and Nishimura would be gliding from the west between the islands.

If the adversary did not take the bait, Ozawa would continue as far as the neighborhood of Samar and attack on the morning of the twenty-fifth with every available aircraft. This daring action would certainly bring about the destruction of his vessels, but it was the only chance of saving the whole operation.

It was understood that the surviving carrier aircraft would, after their action, make for airfields ashore.

24 Days of Mirage

On October 22, at 0805, the main body of the 1st Diversion Attack Force left Brunei.

In the heavy cruiser *Atago*, Kurita was at the head of a first group which proceeded in two columns: to port, three heavy cruisers and the *Nagato;* to starboard, three heavy cruisers and the two giant battleships *Yamato* and *Musashi,* bristling with nine 17.9-inch guns.

Three and a half miles astern, steamed a second group, also in two columns: there were the battleship *Haruna,* preceded by two heavy cruisers, and to her starboard the *Kongo* with the heavy cruisers *Kumano* and *Suzuya.*

In the morning of October 23, Kurita's force followed the corridor which skirts the west coast of Palawan, whose wooded slopes stood out in the night. The vessels zigzagged at eighteen knots to throw off the submarines, known to be numerous in those waters.

At 0634 the leading group suddenly altered course to port, as yells showed that the look-outs had sighted the wakes of torpedoes coming toward the vessels.

Hurried orders followed to the man at the wheel and to the engine room, but it was too late. The *Atago* received the terrible shock of four torpedoes; her masts were broken away; from her gaping boilers rose clouds of steam; fire broke out in her magazines and water rose in her depths. The vessel was lost.

The *Takao* also was struck by two torpedoes but, although

her wounds were not so serious, she was sent back as soon as
it was possible to get her going again. She was accompanied
as far as Brunei by the destroyers *Naganami* and *Asashimo*.

Kurita transferred to the *Kishinami*. A few minutes later, the
Atago disappeared under a black sheet of oil.

To get away from the attack, the squadron made a sudden
alteration of course to starboard, then returned to its original
course. At 0656 the *Maya* was shattered in her turn by four
torpedoes, and quickly sank. The *Chokai* moved to replace the
Maya in the 5th Division.

The catastrophe had a deep effect on the spirits of the crews.
Now the look-outs saw submarines everywhere. Evasive action
followed evasive action. It was not until 1550 that Kurita was
able to board the *Yamato* and hoist his flag on that ship.

On the morning of October 24, the fleet doubled the southern point of Mindoro. Now aerial attacks had to be watched
for. The admiral ordered the fleet into the formation recognized as the best to meet that eventuality—battleships and
cruisers in a circle, interspersed with destroyers.

At 0810 three aircraft appeared in the north and remained
in sight for a quarter of an hour before turning back.

The squadron had been discovered by the enemy, and it
would certainly not be long before it would be attacked by aircraft.

"We will do our best."

Admiral Nishimura, with the 3rd Night Combat Unit, also
called the "3rd Section," left Brunei on the twenty-second at
0015, with the *Yamashiro*, the *Fuso*, the *Mogami*, and four destroyers.

A gruff and eccentric old sailor, Nishimura did not even
know the commanders of the ships he was leading into action.
His reaction to orders and to advice that one tried to give him
was: "Bah! We'll do our best."

He entered Jolo Sea on the morning of the twenty-third by
Balabac Strait. The dawn of the twenty-fourth saw him with
the cape to the southeast, at the entry to the Mindanao Sea.

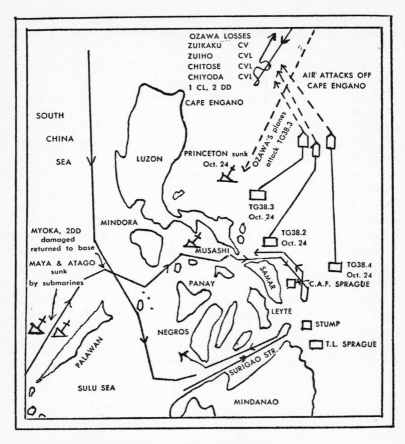

BATTLES FOR LEYTE GULF, OCTOBER 24–25, 1944

The admiral ordered the launching of a reconnaissance aircraft, which set course for Leyte. About 0700 its pilots discovered the panorama of the gulf, the contours of which stood out clearly in the freshness of the day. Before the beaches which bordered the dark-green banks with a white belt, an immense flock of a hundred or so transports was assembled. Farther to the south, were four battleships, two cruisers, and two destroyers. In Surigao Strait small vessels were maneuvering.

The pilot advanced to the southeast, where he had made out some tall silhouettes. He counted twelve aircraft carriers, surrounded by destroyers.

Now Nishimura knew what he was up against. He transmitted the information to Kurita.

The 3rd Section was passing to the south of Negros at 0930 when a score of aircraft dived from the skies. The *Fuso* was struck; her two seaplanes caught fire on their catapults, the gasoline also caught fire, and the blaze raged for more than an hour. When the fire was at last checked, the deck of the ship was devastated, but her power was intact.

The *Shigure* received a bomb which exploded in the forward turret, and all the destroyer's armament was put out of action.

To the great astonishment of everyone, the attack was not repeated. The Sea of Mindanao was crossed without hindrance.

Shima left Coron on the twenty-fourth at 0200. He crossed the Jolo Sea and took up station, well astern of Nishimura and without joining him.

It so happened that the two admirals did not get on with each other. An incident during their careers had put them at loggerheads, and this misunderstanding now acted to prevent the close contact which should have been established between them, on the naval level, in these grave circumstances.[1]

---

1. The silence maintained by the two admirals with respect to each other and the consequent lack of cooperation between their forces could well have been for the reason stated. However, there is another possible cause. It is almost a certainty that the Japanese High Naval Command intended that Vice Admiral Nishimura should command the Surigao Strait forces—it was a serious weakness of the operation order that these command arrangements were not made explicitly clear. Nevertheless, it seems a fair assumption that Nishimura should have taken both forces under his command—his force was far superior to that of Shima and was to lead into the strait. But a second possible defect in the operation order, if that was what was intended, was the title assigned Shima's force. That title placed Shima in the echelon of command with Kurita, or one step in the chain of command

Land-based aircraft, so greatly needed . . .

At the time of the landing at Leyte, the First Air Fleet had been reduced to fewer than a hundred aircraft, of which scarcely half were operational.

Admiral Fukudome, commanding the Second Air Fleet, moved his command post to Manila on the twenty-second. He was followed by 850 aircraft. About 200 others were put at the disposal of the naval commander by the Fourth Army Air Force, which also had its base at Manila.

Such were the air forces on which Tokyo relied to counterbalance the embarked aircraft of the Americans.

But the weather was bad. On the twenty-third, no Japanese aircraft from the Philippines managed to sight the enemy's forces. On the twenty-fourth, meteorological conditions remained unfavorable. Nevertheless, early in the morning a reconnaissance plane sighted a group of American aircraft carriers. Fukudome ordered his forces to attack. During the three hundred or so sorties of the day, a light enemy carrier, the *Princeton,* was struck and set on fire, and was later sunk by the Americans.

Such was the reduced aid brought by the land-based aircraft to the squadrons which converged boldly on Leyte Gulf to meet all the naval forces of the leading World Power.

Almost all the Japanese airmen were inexperienced. They knew neither how to locate the enemy at a specified position nor how to attack him effectively when they did contact him. Wind, rain, poor visibility were insurmountable obstacles for

---

above Nishimura. Both Kurita and Shima commanded diversion attack forces. Nishimura only commanded a night combat unit. By title, Shima should command the Surigao forces. If the two admirals refused to speak to each other, even in the conduct of their Emperor's business, any confusion over the command setup could never be straightened out, and the straightening out could have made no difference if neither would signal the other. At best, it is difficult to imagine fighting an enemy under any such handicap as this. (R.A.T.)

them. The American pilots, on the contrary, flew under poor conditions as easily as when on exercise in good weather.

The Japanese engaged practically without air support in this terrible battle, the last in which they could still hope to save their country.

"Since they ignore us, attack them."

Off the northern extremity of Luzon, was Vice Admiral Ozawa's Decoy Carrier Force. All during the morning of the twenty-fourth, the admiral launched unfruitful reconnaissances, but at last, at 1115, the enemy was reported at 180 miles' distance, bearing 210 degrees.

The feverish activity preceding the departure of air raids immediately began in the carriers. The elevators spilled the aircraft on deck, and mechanics busied themselves with the final preparations.

Violent squalls were reported from the zone where the enemy vessels were said to be. It was still understood that, if pilots found it difficult to return on board, they should land on Nichols Field near Manila.

At 1145 Admiral Ozawa, his heart in his mouth, watched the departure of forty fighters, twenty-eight dive bombers, two scouting aircraft, and two torpedo aircraft. That was all that remained of the seaborne aviation, whose domination of the eastern seas, two and a half years earlier, had been uncontested.

The Japanese radio communications were defective. Kurita did not receive notification of the attack; Ozawa himself remained without news from his reconnaissance aircraft.

After a long time had elapsed, only three aircraft returned, and they had not found the enemy. Most of their companions had steered toward landing fields ashore.

Signals arrived: Kurita was being heavily attacked in the Shibuyan Sea.

"Something definite must be done," Ozawa declared, "to draw the enemy toward us. Since they ignore us, let us attack them."

"At last we are engaged."

At 1500 the commander of the vanguard, Rear Admiral Matsuda on board the *Hyuga,* was steaming south at full speed, followed by the *Ise.* Four destroyers surrounded the battleships.

The four aircraft carriers were making their way slowly westward, while waiting for the return of the aircraft. But no information came from the reconnaissance missions, and no planes returned from the airfields ashore.

At 1635 a black dot rose over the horizon. It was an American plane. Ozawa's force was spotted at last! The maneuver had some hopes of succeeding.

The Musashi

At 0810 that morning, Kurita saw the enemy aircraft arrive and at once increased the speed of his group—the 1st Division of the First Diversion Attack Force—to twenty-four knots. Then, as nothing happened, speed was dropped again to twenty knots. For two hours the radars were busy; they recorded contact with aircraft, but these did not approach. Only at about 1000, did the luminous specks converge rapidly toward the centers of the screens. Fire opened against some thirty machines, attacking from starboard.

For twenty-five minutes, American bombers and torpedo planes attacked without cessation. No air defense hindered them; they circled at their ease around their prey and chose the more favorable moments.

When the enemy flew away, the *Musashi* had been torpedoed but was not very seriously damaged. The big cruiser *Myoko* had been struck under the starboard counter; unable to follow the formation, she had to return to Brunei.

Four heavy cruisers were already out of action.

At 1203, a new swarm of some thirty aircraft arrived and concentrated its efforts on the *Musashi*. Several of the attackers were shot down; but the attack was pressed home violently.

Eight minutes after fire had been opened, the enormous vessel, struck by two torpedoes and two bombs, settled bows down; she could no longer maintain her speed.

A third wave appeared at 1331. For twenty minutes the infernal merry-go-round went on. The *Yamato* was struck twice forward without suffering much damage. The *Musashi*, already paralyzed by her wounds, was hit by three new torpedoes and four bombs which flattened out the anti-aircraft batteries. The foredeck of the battleship sank to sea level and the sea broke around the two enormous turret structures.

The *Musashi* stayed astern, convoyed by the *Tone*.

The respite that followed this third attack did not last long. Between 1426 and 1450, a new American formation dropped a bomb on the *Yamato* and two on the *Nagato*, whose transmission gear was damaged.

About 1500, the most vigorous attack of the day concentrated on the *Musashi*. Struck by six bombs and four torpedoes, the big battleship listed to port and her forepart disappeared under water. At 1935 she turned over slowly, taking 1100 men with her.

"With God's help . . ."

Admiral Kurita had lost a battleship, four heavy cruisers, and four destroyers; his squadron could make no more than twenty-two knots, and from the violence of the attacks he had suffered, it was clear that the Japanese land-based aircraft had not succeeded in neutralizing the American carriers. Kurita was without news of Ozawa, and it seemed that he was alone in the battle, which made his efforts appear wholly unsuccessful.

The planned itinerary was along closed-in narrows, where new air attacks could be parried only with difficulty. If air raids continued at the same frequency, the whole force would be wiped out by the enemy carrier aircraft, which seemed to be concentrated off Lamon Bay.

For these reasons the admiral turned half circle at 1530 and remained in the Shibuyan Sea, where the squadron could maneuver while it waited for the situation to be made clear. A signal from Kurita warned the commander in chief:

"If we had continued to advance in order to force the passage according to plan, we would have offered ourselves to the enemy with very little chance of success. We decided that the best thing to do was to withdraw temporarily out of reach of the enemy aircraft, until our air force could gain a decisive advantage over the adversary."

At the same time Kurita called on the land-based air forces to attack as agreed.

This unexpected withdrawal of the principal Japanese naval force had some peculiar consequences. From this moment until the following day, the Americans had eyes only for the Japanese squadron in the north, toward which they directed their attention. And so, unexpectedly, there arose exactly the situation aimed at by all the strategic maneuvers conceived by the Japanese staff, especially as the 1st Division of the First Diversion Attack Force, after having drawn breath for a moment, was about to return to the charge.

About 1715 this force dressed its wounds, and without receiving a reply from the commander in chief of the Combined Fleet, Kurita, who kept his own mission well in mind, resumed his progress toward San Bernardino Strait. While on his course, he was confirmed in his resolution by a signal from Admiral Toyoda:

"With God's help, every force will attack."

A few minutes later, a second signal arrived:

"Since the start of the operation, all groups have maneuvered together in remarkable harmony. A change in the program of the 1st Attack Force would cause the failure of our offensive. Let this Force go on according to plan."

The march to the sacrifice

Warned of Kurita's turning back, Ozawa was at first afraid that he would find himself alone, and to no purpose, in front of the American concentration. He recalled the vanguard and set course north.

Then, about midnight, supplied with later information, he returned to a southerly course and steamed to the sacrifice. He had in his carriers only nineteen fighters, five fighter bombers, one dive bomber, and four torpedo aircraft. How could the Americans, who were advancing to meet him, guess that this Japanese admiral, coming from the north, was to confront their enormous forces with four empty aircraft carriers?

Nothing happens!

Kurita passed through San Bernardino Strait at twenty knots, believing that, in these confined waters, he would have to force his passage. In spite of their weariness, the crews were at action stations.

The night was clear; officers and look-outs swept the horizon with their glasses; radar swept the sky. The destroyers were ready to leap on any submarines, betrayed by the tips of their periscopes or the wakes from their torpedoes.

But nothing happened.

Quite taken aback, the 1st Diversion Attack Force entered the Philippine Sea at 0037 on October 25.

"Continue the advance."

We had left Admiral Nishimura's 3rd Section in the Mindanao Sea on the afternoon of the twenty-fourth. This Force was six hours ahead of the 1st Attack Force, which at that moment was temporizing in the Shibuyan Sea. Nishimura neglected the cooperation arranged with Kurita's Force and risked finding himself alone, at any moment faced by an overwhelming enemy concentration.

At 2100, the 3rd Section passed to the south of Bohol Island. The *Mogami* went ahead with three destroyers to explore the approaches to Panaon. Soon afterward, an attack by American destroyers was easily repelled by the battleships.

Then a signal arrived from Kurita fixing the rendezvous for 0900 on the twenty-fifth at Soulouan.

According to the schedule thus set, the 3rd Section was still an hour and a half in advance, and it was too late to fall back into the channels of the eastern Mindanao Sea. Nevertheless,

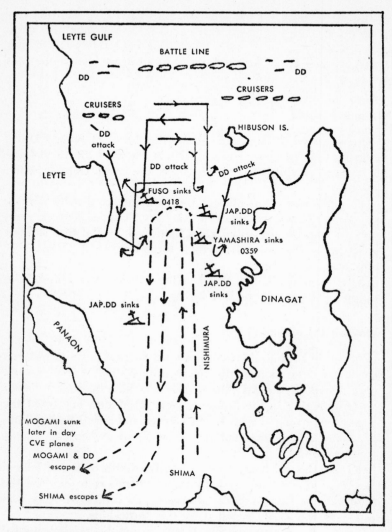

ACTION IN SURIGAO STRAIT, OCTOBER 25, 1944

the whole operation depended on an exactly calculated meeting of all the Japanese forces coming from the west. But Nishimura took things lightly.[2]

At 0200 the 3rd Section passed through the strait separating Panaon from Mindanao and set course north.

After he had repelled two destroyer attacks, about 0320 Nishimura ordered his vessels to take up position for battle. At the head were the four destroyers, followed by the *Yamashiro* and the *Fuso*, with the *Mogami* bringing up the rear. During the maneuver, two groups of enemy motor torpedo boats came from port and starboard, out of the scattered squalls, and immediately launched their torpedoes and escaped. The *Yamagumo*, which was in the lead, disappeared in an explosion, the *Mishishio* and the *Asagumo* were reduced to wreckage. The admiral's vessel was also struck, but her fighting strength was not greatly impaired.

Calmly, Nishimura signaled the surviving vessels:

"Continue the advance, and attack everything you meet."

Those were his last words. At 0340 the *Yamashiro* blew up, broke, and disappeared.

Almost immediately the *Fuso* and the *Mogami* were taken under fire from American battleships at the entrance to Leyte Gulf, the last goal of the Japanese advance. At 0400, the blazing *Mogami* steamed slowly south, under a hail of shells. The *Fuso* replied energetically to the enemy, but a series of explosions tore her apart, and the Japanese battleship stopped, waiting for death.

The *Shigure*, damaged by near misses and taking water through her torn plates, escaped at thirty knots.

Nishimura had wanted to fight alone, and at once. His squadron was almost wiped out.

---

2. *There seems little to worry about in this. With the strong probability of having to fight his way through opposition, he might easily expect to use all this time margin and more, before the night was over.* (R.A.T.)

Tragic rendezvous

At 0235 Admiral Shima also penetrated into Surigao Strait. After meeting some violent squalls, which sent him temporarily astray, the 2nd Diversion Attack Force arrived in a good weather zone, and speed was increased to twenty-six knots.

An American motor torpedo boat, invisible in the darkness, launched a torpedo which struck the cruiser *Abukuma,* third in the line. The vessel fell off while the rest of the Force altered course north at twenty-eight knots.

The *Nachi* was ahead, followed by the *Ashigara,* with the destroyers closing the rear.

Suddenly, like a hallucination, there appeared over the sea a trail of heavy smoke, lit by flashes and streaked through by tracer shells. To starboard drifted two blazing ships. One of them was the *Mogami,* which the new arrivals recognized just as the radar indicated enemy vessels near. To launch their torpedoes at their target, Shima's cruisers altered course to starboard.

The attention of everyone on the bridge was so concentrated on this attack that the *Nachi* steamed straight for the *Mogami,* which was almost out of control.

In spite of frenzied efforts, the two ships collided violently, and amid showers of sparks the plates buckled like paper. The *Nachi* got clear with a hole in her port plating and her speed reduced to twenty knots.

What could now be done with two cruisers, one of them damaged, and four destroyers against a formidable American force? Nishimura's squadron was destroyed; that of Kurita could not arrive, at best, for several hours. Going ahead without support, Shima would merely be heading straight for sure destruction. The 2nd Diversion Attack Force reversed course and fell back behind a smoke screen.

The *Mogami* was still ablaze. Attacked from the air and seriously damaged, she had to be abandoned and left to sink.

The diversion succeeds

On October 25, at 0700, Ozawa's two battleships rejoined his main formation. He was still to the eastward of Cape Engano, the northern extremity of Luzon.

At 0740, radar contacts made out the arrival, planned for and hoped for, of numerous formations of enemy planes. The anti-aircraft guns were fully manned; the last fighters were hurriedly made ready for their take-offs.

At 0813, the attackers arrived. Sixty aircraft headed for Carrier Division 4, eighty others toward Carrier Division 3. Soon the *Chitose* was stopped; the light cruiser *Tama*, torpedoed, dropped astern of the formation; the *Zuikaku* was reduced to hand steering; the destroyer *Akitsuki* blew up. The *Chitose* sank at 0937.

Ozawa headed north at full speed. He signaled Kurita that the diversion had succeeded. Once again, the signal did not reach its destination.

About 1000, some thirty aircraft attacked the damaged *Chiyoda,* which was following with difficulty. The carrier, bombed once again, slowed and then stopped. With admirable tenacity, Rear Admiral Matsuda fought to save her. But about 1920, as fresh groups of attacking aircraft renewed the attack, he had to give up.

The destroyers *Isuzu* and *Maki* took her crew on board and then sank the vessel.

The *Hyuga* which, throughout the day, had stood by, supported by three destroyers, then set course to join Ozawa, screened by the *Shimotsuki.*

In the meantime, the *Zuikaku* had had her speed reduced to eighteen knots, and her damaged condition prevented the admiral from exercising his command. He would have to shift his flag to another ship of the formation.

"What is the good?" Ozawa protested. "All my vessels are destined to be sunk. Our task is accomplished. I want to die in my *Zuikaku.*"

At last he yielded to the pleas of his staff, and his flag was broken on the light cruiser *Oyoda*.

The dreamed-of occasion

Where, at this moment, was the principal Japanese force, whose lightninglike action was expected to justify these enormous sacrifices?

Kurita had passed through San Bernardino Strait and into the Philippine Sea. At 0550 he had put his squadron in the circular formation which was standard for the resistance of air attacks. He had just been informed of the annihilation of Nishimura, whom he should have joined at dawn.

An eighteen-knot wind blew from the northeast; a light swell furrowed the sea; the ceiling was low and the sun was unable to pierce the clouds.

The look-outs reported at 0640, "Masts southeast at varying distances." Almost at the same moment, the vessels opened fire on some enemy aircraft.

Speed was increased, and the alarm klaxons sounded. As the vessels approached, numerous silhouettes showed up on the horizon. These high, flat hulls were undoubtedly aircraft carriers. Six were counted. Around them circulated cruisers and destroyers.

Japanese hearts fluttered. In spite of so many deceptions and reverses, this seemed to be the occasion dreamed of for three years. This crowd of dispersed vessels, with which the 1st Attack Division had made contact by surprise, must surely be the heart of American naval power, and if Ozawa's diversion had drawn off their embarked air forces, the operation was culminating as the Japanese had planned.

At 0659 the *Yamato* opened fire at 34,000 yards. The admiral, who saw that the operation's success depended on his promptness of action, simply signaled: "Everyone attack!"

Two minutes later, all the battleships had opened fire on the enemy who, visibly surprised, withdrew to the eastward.

The Japanese formation was irregular, since the pursuit had begun at the moment when the 1st Division was changing

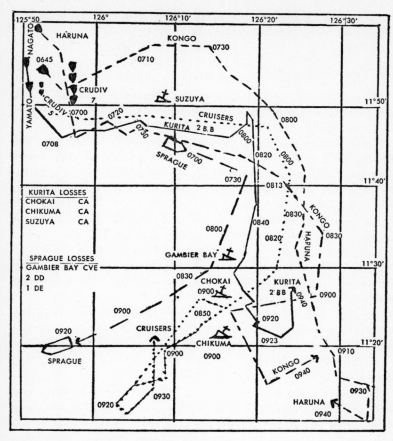

ACTION OFF SAMAR, OCTOBER 25, 1944

from its night to its day station. Nevertheless, little by little, order was reestablished as the cruisers gave way forward to the *Yamato* and the destroyers took up their stations. From the opening of fire, the *Kongo* had independently set an easterly course, and she continued ahead of the main formation.

Over the water spread a smoke screen laid by the retreating carriers. Rain squalls interrupted visibility, and fire was suspended due to temporary lack of targets.

From 0710 onward, the Japanese force suffered the repeated assaults of small groups of aircraft which attacked with spirit and skill but, in each instance, were easily driven off. Clearly, the main body of the American forces was occupied elsewhere. This must be the result of Ozawa's maneuver—but what Kurita did not know was that this maneuver had also drawn away to the northward the big American carriers.

Curtains of smoke and artificial fog trailed over the sea. From time to time, groups of small vessels emerged from them followed by long white wakes, firing every gun as they proceeded toward their torpedo-firing positions. At 0730 Kurita released his cruisers to the attack. A few minutes later, the *Kumano* was struck by a torpedo and forced out of formation. By 0750 the 1st Attack Force had scattered over some fifteen miles.

The American carriers[3] hurried southward, then southwest, headed by the cruisers which pushed ahead furiously. The Japanese battleships were now less obstructed by the smoke. The American force was hemmed in closely for half an hour. The *Kongo* sank a carrier. The *Yamato* saw a ship blow up which she believed was a cruiser (actually a destroyer).

The aircraft attacks began again, favored by the squalls which facilitated surprise. At 0900, the heavy cruisers *Chikuma* and *Chokai* were put out of action. The *Tone*, which was leading this cruiser column, did not slacken speed. Supported by the *Haguro*, she opened rapid salvo fire on the carriers, and dull red flashes, growing in number, indicated that the fleeing ves-

---

3. *By this time, the Japanese must have recognized them for what they were,* escort carriers. (R.A.T.)

sels were being frequently hit. The fire was intensified. Hunted and hunter were separated by less than 10,000 yards.

The Japanese crews were overjoyed, but on board the *Yamato* the situation did not seem so advantageous. The battleships were steaming at full speed, but they did not appear to be appreciably closing their targets. The illusion that the pursued carriers were vessels capable of making thirty knots was reinforced. It seemed they would escape from the Japanese fleet, since the premature action of Nishimura and Shima had led to the destruction of their own forces—the second arm of the pincer which was to have closed from the south on the American fleet off Leyte. Again the curtains of smoke veiled the horizon. There was no news of the cruisers, and the two reconnaissance aircraft sent off by the *Yamato* had not returned.

Also, the continuous steaming at full speed was rapidly reducing the level of the fuel in the tanks of all the vessels.

The prey gets away

Kurita rapidly reviewed the situation with his chief of staff. It seemed to them that the American carriers, which they had surprised east of San Bernardino Strait, must be supported by several other groups whose intentions doubtless were to encircle the attackers. The American formation then under pursuit must be merely the southern group.

Uncoded signals, intercepted by the Japanese, proved that an American airfield had been hurriedly constructed at Leyte and that it was ready to launch an attacking squadron. Indeed, Admiral Kinkaid was urgently demanding, by radio, rapid aid from such a force. The same signals indicated that the American Seventh Fleet was in those waters. Finally, Japanese Southwestern Headquarters signaled that an American fast carrier force was 130 miles distant and bearing five degrees from Soulouan.

Under these conditions, it seemed that if Kurita pushed on as far as Leyte Gulf, as planned, he would probably discover that the transports, the objective marked out for him, had departed under the protection of the Seventh Fleet. In any case, five days after the landing, they must have discharged the bulk of their cargoes. By entering the narrow gulf, the 1st Attack Force would risk becoming an easy prey for the enemy aircraft, both carrier and land-based. In such a case, the end would be inevitable and humiliating.

On the contrary, since, according to the latest information, the 1st Attack Force appeared to be surrounded by several groups of aircraft carriers, it would be better to turn back against the northern group. This would locate the prospective actions with enemy air forces farther from the Leyte airfield and nearer to the Japanese aircraft based at Manila. If those at last should intervene, a combined attack could be envisaged as a possibility, and that would be the moment for the navy to strike a heavy blow.[4] If the force should remain east of the Philippines for any considerable length of time, that would be its sublime ending.

At 0911 Kurita ordered every ship to rally on a northerly course. A few minutes later the *Tone* and the *Haguro* altered course to port, abandoning their prey. The naval battle had, in fact, ended for the 1st Attack Force. Kurita had begun his withdrawal, when at last the Japanese land-based aircraft appeared and swooped on the American carriers which had been the targets of the Japanese cruisers.

This time the Japanese pilots, instead of maneuvering to launch their bombs by using their bomb sights, dashed their machines on the enemy vessels.

Some missed the target and, hit by projectiles, sank like stones into the ocean.

Others struck the decks at frightening speed, piercing them

---

4. *This reasoning is a perfect example of Japanese sophistry to cloak a clear-cut decision to retreat. Kurita merely confuses the issue in holding thoughts of a later offensive in the front of his mind, as he decides to retreat out of the Philippine Sea and back through San Bernardino Strait. He was a good naval officer and a determined fighter. But he was getting out because, if he did not, his force would certainly be destroyed. And he could accomplish nothing by staying. All excellent reasons for a warrior to do what he then did, and no apologies are needed.* (R.A.T.)

like shells while the wings flew to splinters; the bombs burst between decks and the gasoline in the tanks caught fire and spread the blaze.

In this way, no blow failed from clumsiness or bad luck; every attacker not brought down by gunfire was a projectile which went to the target.

It had happened several times in the course of the war that, in the exasperation of the struggle, pilots had thrown themselves on the adversary, to sell dearly the lives which they knew to be lost. But this maneuver of desperation was to become a systematic tactic, especially in the Okinawa campaign. The Japanese airmen, conscious of their mediocrity, had noted that their attacks were often in vain, and their bombs badly aimed.

Some young officers, in impassioned discussion, had already advanced the opinion that, while training could not be improved, it was necessary to make the most of what existed. In the present circumstances, it was essential to employ a simple and brutal method of attack within the capabilities of all. It was unfortunate that it carried with it the obligatory sacrifice of pilots. The Empire was assured of finding thousands of young men willing to give their lives for her welfare.

The present operations crystallized these ideas. As the fleet had undertaken a desperate action, as every sailor in the vessels which converged on Leyte Gulf had accepted the strong possibility of the supreme sacrifice, the airmen must not lag behind but must share in the holocaust. It was their opportunity to give for Japan lives that would have little meaning if she should cease to exist.

The crews of the remaining five American aircraft carriers saw falling upon them like a whirlwind the dark machines in which, tensed at the controls, a man with set face closed his eyes at the instant when he was about to crash.

Under this furious assault one of the vessels, the *Saint Lo*, was sunk and four others were damaged.

The *Kamikaze* were born.

These tactics were systematically applied in the course of the coming months and soon, in the approaches to the mother country, they were completed in a funereal apotheosis.

The Zuikaku, *the* Zuiho, *the* Tama . . .

In the north, the remaining ships of Ozawa's group were scattered over some sixty miles, and the swarms of American aircraft attacked them violently. These attacks were aimed particularly at the vessels with most chance of escaping. The blows rained down, the explosions were almost uninterrupted.

The *Zuikaku* sank at 1414; the *Zuiho* at 1527.

Matsuda despaired of bringing back the heavily damaged *Chiyoda,* and sank her himself. Then he moved on with the *Hyuga* and the *Shimotsuki.*

The *Hyuga* and the *Ise* then became the principal objective of the indefatigable bombers. Although riddled by splinters and badly shaken, the two battleships escaped major damage.

Ozawa had drawn the enemy air forces upon his decoy force and had fully carried out his task. But at what a cost! He had lost four aircraft carriers, as he had foreseen. The *Tama,* damaged, sank with all hands on her way back to Japan. Two destroyers had also been sunk.

Ghost squadron

Kurita retired northward, to the east of Samar. He still had four battleships, two heavy cruisers, two light cruisers, and seven destroyers. He attempted to locate the carrier group which had been reported in that vicinity. The retreat was made under repeated aerial attacks, which, however, did not cause any major damage to the vessels.

But he did not make contact with the enemy. All the reconnaissances made by the squadron's seaplanes and by land-based aircraft were unfruitful.

Without information, the admiral hesitated. He had turned away from his first objective, he had abandoned the pursuit of the first American group which he had thought too fast for him, and now he could not find the second! The destroyers were short of fuel. Reluctantly, Kurita set course for San Bernardino Strait, which he cleared at 2130.

Of all his ships, only the destroyer *Yukikaze* was intact . . .
What was left of the 1st Division of the Diversion Attack
Force got away. The *Kumano* and the *Hayashimo,* delayed by
damage, sailed on a separate course through the channels of the
Visayas, escorted by the *Fujinami* and the *Okinami.*

In every ship the anti-aircraft crews manned their guns before dawn on the twenty-sixth. The men's faces were drawn by
extreme weariness and the nervous tension imposed on them by
the last two days of fighting. Eyes blinked; ears buzzed. These
excellent sailors needed all their respect for duty to keep them
from falling limply into a corner and abandoning themselves to
whatever might befall.

The expected attack began. Between 0834 and 0900, eighty
American aircraft swooped on the Japanese vessels. The *Yamato*
received two more bombs. The light cruiser *Noshiro* sank at
1100.

At 1041, it again became necessary to repel an assault from
twenty-seven Flying Fortresses. Twelve of their bombs exploded
very near the admiral's vessel, riddling the superstructure with
splinters and mowing down the crew. Rear Admiral Koyanagi
was seriously wounded.

It was the last convulsion of the battle.

On the 28th, at 2130, a shadow of the former squadron returned to Brunei.

Death sentence

The battle of Leyte can be regarded as the death sentence on
the Imperial Navy. It could be said that only debris remained,
and the surviving vessels one by one fell an easy prey to the
enemy.

What had happened? In reality, Kurita had not encountered
the enemy's principal force, but only a part of the supports for
his landing force. He had not been faced by the big, fast carriers, accompanied by heavy cruisers, but by six of the small
escort carriers, capable at most of a speed of eighteen knots,
and seven destroyers. The fast large carriers had set out to the
north to attack Ozawa's Force, whose maneuver had thus suc-

ceeded beyond all hopes, although at great cost. The poor visibility, the adroit handling of the American escort carriers and destroyers, whose torpedo attacks frequently obliged the Japanese battleships to take evasive action, the delays caused by the threats from the air, faulty communications—all these circumstances had united to give Kurita the impression that he was facing the big carriers. The high freeboard of the destroyers had also caused them to be mistaken for cruisers. Kurita may well have thought that, without aircraft, he could not overtake such ships, and he knew that Nishimura and Shima were not there to attack them from behind.

If Kurita had understood the situation better, if he had received accurate information from his reconnaissance planes, he would certainly have continued toward Leyte and would have wiped out most of the transports.

The affair would surely have ended in disaster. The entire Japanese fleet would have perished in an apotheosis of destruction. As things now stood, the remnants of the fleet were to undergo a long agony, engaging in a few more confused battles which would be nothing more than dying convulsions.

Conclusions *

Despite the interest which it will long command, only limited strategic and tactical conclusions can be drawn from this complicated and eventful battle. This is so because the comparative strengths of the opposing air forces were so greatly out of balance. It did emphasize, once again, the primacy of air power in the naval warfare of World War II, and the fact that carriers will still have their necessary functions in the sea fighting of the have supplanted battleships as the shock forces of the present-day navy. It also demonstrated that, while other naval types future, they can always expect heavy casualties unless they have adequate air support at hand or within call.

The future of naval tactics is highly unpredictable. Who can

---

* This section was written by Admiral Theobald.

say how long the carrier task force, supreme today, will maintain itself in that position in naval warfare? What a transition has taken place since the days of Nelson: steel, steam, and the breech-loading gun, instead of wood, sail, and the muzzle-loader; the gun turret and the anchored mine of the American Civil War; radio at the turn of the century, to end the communication isolation of ships out of sight of others or of land; the automobile torpedo in the Russo-Japanese War; the submarine in World War I; the aircraft, carrier-based, in World War II. With such modern developments as guided missiles, what form will the challenge take, when it arrives to terminate the present preeminent position of the air force in sea warfare?

In October 1944, the Japanese navy could not meet its enemy in decisive battle with any real prospect of success, because it was so woefully weak in all the essential elements of air strength.

That the Japanese High Naval Command fully appreciated these facts was made amply evident by the plans it devised to combat the American return to the Philippines. Here was an immediate challenge to Japan to make an all-out fight for command of the sea in her own front yard. The strongest action that her leaders could conceive—and not much else could have been done—was to send their navy into desperate jeopardy to destroy a few empty transports and possibly to damage a few enemy naval vessels in the process. (R.A.T.)

JAPANESE FORCES IN BATTLE OF LEYTE, OCTOBER 25, 1944

Combined Fleet, Admiral Toyoda

First Mobile Fleet, Vice Admiral Ozawa
Main Body,[1] Vice Admiral Ozawa
   Carrier Division 3: Zuikaku, Zuiho, Chitose, Chiyoda (1 CV, 3 CVL)*

Abbreviations: CV, aircraft carrier; CVL, light carrier; BB, modern battleship; OBB, old battleship; CA, heavy cruiser; CVE, escort carrier; CL-AA, anti-aircraft light cruiser; CL, light cruiser; DD, destroyer.
[1] Main Body fought Cape Engano battle.

Carrier Division 4: Hyuga, Ise, Junyo, Ryujo   (2 OBB converted to CV, 2 CVL)

Screens: 3 light cruisers, 10 destroyers

First Diversion Attack Force, Vice Admiral Kurita

First and Second Night Combat Units,[2] Vice Admiral Kurita

Battleship Division 1: Yamato, Musashi, Nagato   (2 BB, 1 OBB)

Battleship Division 3: Kongo, Haruna   (2 OBB)

Cruiser Division 4: Atago, Takao, Chokai, Maya   (4 CA)

Cruiser Division 5: Myoko, Haguro   (2 CA)

Cruiser Division 7: Kumano, Suzuya, Tone, Chikuma   (4 CA)

Screens: 2 light cruisers, 17 destroyers

Third Night Combat Unit,[3] Vice Admiral Nishimura

Battleship Division 2: Yamashiro, Fuso, Mogami   (2 OBB, 1 CA)

Screen: 4 destroyers

Second Diversion Attack Force,[4] Vice Admiral Shima

Cruiser Division 21: Nachi, Ashigara   (2 CA)

Screen: 1 light cruiser, 4 destroyers

UNITED STATES FORCES IN BATTLE OF LEYTE, OCTOBER 25, 1944

Third Fleet, Admiral W. F. Halsey

Task Force 38, Vice Admiral M. A. Mitcher

    Task Group 38.1, Vice Admiral J. S. McCain

    Wasp, Hornet, Hancock, Monterey, Cowpens (3 CV, 2 CVL)

    Chester, Pensacola, Salt Lake City, Boston (4 CA)

    San Diego, Oakland (2 CL-AA)

    Screens: 14 destroyers

---

[2] First and Second Night Combat Units were San Bernardino Strait forces, which fought Samar Battle.

[3] Third Night Combat Unit fought the Surigao Strait battle.

[4] Shima's force followed that of Nishimura into Surigao Strait, but 40 miles behind, and Admiral Shima, sensing Nishimura's fate, retired without becoming engaged. There was no communication between the two admirals. The strength of Nishimura's force seems to suggest that he should have exercised the supreme command in the Strait, although the title of Shima's force appears to place him one step above Nishimura in the echelons of the fleet commands.

Task Group 38.2, Rear Admiral G. F. Bogan
Intrepid, Cabot, Independence   (1 CV, 2 CVL)
Iowa, New Jersey   (2 BB)
Biloxi, Vincennes, Miami   (3 CL)
Screens: 16 destroyers

Task Group 38.3, Rear Admiral F. C. Sherman
Lexington, Essex, Princeton, Langley   (2 CV, 2 CVL)
Massachusetts, South Dakota   (2 BB)
Santa Fe, Birmingham, Mobile, Reno   (4 CL)
Screens: 13 destroyers

Task Group 38.4, Rear Admiral R. E. Davison
Enterprise, Franklin, San Jacinto, Belleau Wood   (2 CV, 2 CVL)
Washington, Alabama   (2 BB)
Wichita, New Orleans   (2 CA)
Screens: 15 destroyers

Central Philippine Attack Force, Task Force 77, Vice Admiral T. C. Kinkaid

Bombardment and Fire Support Group, Task Group 77.2,
Rear Admiral J. B. Oldendorf
(Surigao Strait Force)
Battleship Division 2: Pennsylvania, California, Tennessee   (3 OBB)
Battleship Division 3: Mississippi   (OBB)
Battleship Division 4: Maryland, West Virginia   (2 OBB)
Screen: 6 destroyers
Cruiser Division 4: Louisville, Portland, Minneapolis   (3 CA)
Cruiser Division 12: Denver, Columbia   (2 CL)
Cruiser Division 15: Phoenix, Boise, H.M.A.S. Shropshire   (2 CL, 1 CA)
Destroyer Squadrons 24, 54, 56 [5]   (20 DD)

Escort Carrier Group 77.4, Rear Admiral T. L. Sprague
Panaon Carrier Group 77.4.1, Rear Admiral Sprague
Carrier Division 22: Sangamon, Suwanee, Chenango, Santee   (4 CVE)
Carrier Division 28: Petrof Bay, Saginaw Bay   (2 CVE)
Screens: 3 destroyers, 5 destroyer escorts

Southern Carrier Group 77.4.2, Rear Admiral Stump
Carrier Division 24: Natoma Bay, Manila Bay   (2 CVE)
Carrier Division 27: Marcus Island, Kadashan Bay, Savo Island, Ommaney
   Bay (4 CVE)
Screens: 3 destroyers, 5 destroyer escorts

[5] These destroyers delivered important torpedo attacks during battle of
Surigao Strait.

Northern Carrier Group [6] 77.4.3, Rear Admiral C. A. F. Sprague
Carrier Division 25: Fanshaw Bay, Saint Lo, White Plains, Kalinin Bay   (4 CVE)
Carrier Division 26: Kitkun Bay, Gambier Bay   (2 CVE)
Screens: 3 destroyers, 5 destroyer escorts

SHIP LOSSES IN BATTLE OF LEYTE, OCTOBER 25, 1944

JAPANESE LOSSES [7]

Musashi, Yamashiro, Fuso   (1 BB, 2 OBB)
Zuikaku, Chitose, Choyoda, Zuiho   (1 CV, 3 CVL)
Atago, Maya, Chokai, Suzuya, Mogami, Chikuma   (6 CA)
Abukuma, Tama, Noshiro, Kinu   (4 CL)
11 destroyers

UNITED STATES LOSSES

Princeton (CVL)
Gambier Bay, St. Lo   (2 CVE)
2 destroyers, 2 destroyer escorts

[6] This Carrier Group bore the brunt of the Japanese attack off Samar.
[7] The Japanese navy suffered the following large-ship losses in addition to those sustained in the battles and engagements mentioned above:
   Mutsu (OBB) total loss from accidental explosion in Hiroshima Bay, June 8, 1943;
   Kongo (OBB) sunk by submarine off Foochow, China, November 21, 1944;
   Haruna (OBB), *Hyuga, Ise* (2 OBB converted to CV) sunk in Kure Navy Yard, July 28, 1945, by air attacks.
The following large vessels of the Japanese Fleet survived the war:
   Nagato (OBB) badly damaged and out of action at Yokosuka Navy Yard;
   Amagi (CV) heavily damaged and out of action at Kure Navy Yard;
   Junyo, Hiyo (2 CVL) laid up at home yards badly damaged;
   Myoko, Takao (2 CA) out of action at Singapore.

25 Suicide War

As a result of the Philippines operations, the Japanese were to lose a further battleship, two aircraft carriers, one escort carrier, four cruisers, twenty-three destroyers, and ten submarines.

These operations resembled those which were so greatly prolonged at Guadalcanal. The Japanese sought to reinforce their air force and army in the Philippines; but this time their efforts were contested by the fast Carrier Task Force.

Between October 23 and December 11, nine echelons of troops were disembarked in the archipelago—around 30,000 men. The price was high—one cruiser, eight destroyers, one minesweeper, five patrol boats, and eight transports. In the month of November alone, more than 700 aircraft and 134,000 tons of merchant shipping were destroyed.

But these Japanese sacrifices were in vain. At the beginning of December, the Americans landed on the west coast of Leyte, in spite of *Kamikaze* attacks.

On the thirteenth Mindoro was occupied. A small Japanese squadron stood in to bombard the landing beach and withdrew after receiving much damage. It was to be the last naval intervention in the south.

December 20 marked the end of organized resistance on Leyte. In January, after a brief but devastating preparation, Luzon was invaded without difficulty.

Fuel oil cut off

From then on, communications were cut between Japan and the empire to the south, which she had conquered. In three days the fast aircraft carriers operating between Luzon and Formosa swept the sea as far as Cam-Ranh Bay, in Indo-China, and Hongkong. They sank 150,000 tons of shipping, including seven big oil tankers.

The supply of fuel oil and gasoline was cut off and, in consequence, the training flights of Japanese pilots were reduced to a hundred flying hours. The Americans received five times as much. In the Inland Sea, the few surviving warships had enough fuel to steam as far as a meeting with the enemy, with no hope of return.

Iwo Jima, Okinawa

From then on, events moved rapidly. On February 16, 1945, the Americans landed on Iwo Jima, while their carrier aircraft bombed Tokyo. On March 16, after a frightful struggle, organized resistance on Iwo Jima was at an end. The Americans had lost 21,000 men, one escort carrier, and 168 aircraft; thirty vessels had been damaged.

But Japan was henceforth within bombing range.

It was the approach for the kill.

Okinawa was directly threatened, and the attacker did not spare his means. He put into play 1213 vessels, 564 seaplanes and 451,866 men, supported by 919 carrier aircraft, to which were added 244 planes from British aircraft carriers. This did not include the long-distance bombers of the Strategic Air Command.

The Japanese had decided to make a gigantic effort, at least to inflict maximum losses on the enemy. To revive the lost air strength, all the forces assigned to the defense of Okinawa were put under the orders of the commander in chief of the Combined Fleet.

The assault on Okinawa began on March 1 at 0850.

The moment had arrived to initiate the full force of the *Kamikaze* attacks, named for the divine wind of Ise which, by a celebrated miracle, destroyed a wave of Mongol invaders in 1281.

For the young airmen who were thus massed against the American ships, it was not a question of conquer or die but, if that were possible, of dying in order to conquer.

The suicide aircraft were flown from Kyushu. The pilots, almost all young, if not adolescent, saluted their chiefs and the comrades whom they would not see again. They took their places alone in their sparsely fitted aircraft and without hesitation set out to accomplish their pathetic mission.

Soon another engine of death appeared—a wooden aircraft, in the nose of which rode the pilot, seated on a one-ton bomb. The machine was towed by a bomber as far as the battleground, and then released to continue its course propelled by three rockets. When the airman had found his prey, he swooped on it in a nose dive.

From April 6 on, the Japanese air power spent itself in unprecedented fury. From then to June 22, ten big attacks were made by the *Kamikaze* (Operation Kikusui). The nearness of Kyushu and Formosa allowed every type of aircraft to be employed, even the most ancient, and any pilots, even the most inexperienced.

During this period, about 4000 Japanese aircraft were destroyed in action, of which 1900 were *Kamikaze*.

The results were impressive. Of twenty-eight American vessels sunk from the air, twenty-six were the victims of suicide aircraft, which also damaged 164 other ships.

It is impossible to describe the feelings of the Anglo-Saxons, people of so rational a turn of mind, when they saw in the skies above their ships these clouds of desperate assailants, often mounted in unbelievable "chariots"; attackers whom it was impossible to scare or turn aside by a barrage of fire or by the attacks of fighters. It was absolutely essential to kill them in flight, before they reached the hulls and decks toward which their mad course was directed. Before this infernal onslaught, which went beyond anything one could expect in the Western

World, how could the conquerors of the Pacific remain free from horror and surprise, as if they were watching the unleashing of some evil and mysterious force?

When, on June 21, resistance was broken on Okinawa, the Americans had lost thirty-six ships and 763 aircraft in the battle. The number of damaged ships rose to 368.

As to the total losses of the Japanese, at this startling turn of the "suicide war," they rose to 7800 aircraft.

The last *Kamikaze* had died in a crowning explosion of superhuman patriotism.

26 Twilight of the Gods

Yamato is the country of the Gods. The celestial ancestor founded its principle, and the Goddess of the Sun deigned to transmit it to his long line.

JINNO SHOTOKI

April 1, 1945. A breath of anguish blew through Japan. The Americans had landed on Okinawa!

The big battleship *Yamato,* not long repaired, left the arsenal at 1000, and in the evening moored at Mitajuri.

As soon as she arrived, the three thousand men of her crew filled the immense fore deck. Her commanding officer, Captain Ariga, appeared on top of the forward turret, from which jutted the barrels of three enormous 17.9-inch guns.

"My friends," he said, "the enemy is at our doors. Already he is trampling the sacred soil of Okinawa. There our gallant troops are fighting to repel the invader. Our special attack aircraft, the *Kamikaze,* are causing him terrible losses. The pilots are gladly giving their lives for the motherland. We have the honor to be chosen to help them. We are going to draw on us part of the forces opposing them and our guns are going to sow destruction among our adversaries. Remember the words of our ancestors:

"*Shikishima no Yamatogokoro o hito towaba Asahi ni niou Yamazakura bana.*" ("If you are asked what is the heart of Yamato, reply that it is the scent of the wild cherry tree in the Rising Sun.")

An immense cheer went up. These men were as full of ardor as on the first day of the war, which had already cost so many sacrifices, so much weariness and deception.

On April 3 and 4, the *Yamato* weighed anchor to escape being surprised at her moorings by the enemy, whose scouts appeared above the bay.

On the evening of the fourth, the crew were given *sake* with the salty biscuits called *sembes*.

The good hot liquor livened the sailors and put color in their cheeks. They joked, drank to victory, to a glorious death. The assembly was sounded at 2300. The voice of the second in command echoed through the loud-speaker:

"My friends, we have been cheered by seeing you enjoy yourselves so well. Now our hour has come. To your posts."

That night the crew jettisoned everything not of use in action. Everything wooden, paints, canvas, hemp, even the boats went over the side. The covers were screwed down on the supply holes to the fuel lines.

Fuel was so scarce that, when refueling was ended, it was plain that the *Yamato* could steam as far as Okinawa to fight but that she did not have enough fuel for a return trip.

The eternal Japan of the islands

At 1600 on April 6, Admiral Ito Seichi climbed to his bridge. The anchor chain came aboard link by link, and the *Yamato* weighed anchor majestically for her last voyage. Ahead of her steamed the light cruiser *Yahagi*. Seven destroyers escorted her.

The little squadron navigated between the islets of the Inland Sea, and the charming pictures of their country unrolled before the Japanese sailors, as if prepared for them. In the depths of gracious bays, surrounded by tall crags, nestled fishing villages, the little wooden houses, with their panes of paper, in ordered ranks along the beach. On the sand, boats were drawn up, and women with their heads swathed in white scarves waved encouragement to the warships. The pines spread their branches like parasols over the cliffs, home of the sacred heron.

The eternal Japan of the islands unrolled before those who

were going to their deaths to save her. For some of these sailors, it was their place of birth. They meditated upon it, and many eyes grew moist at the sight of these countrysides which had fashioned their souls, their past, their way of life, and which they would see no more.

Night fell. The vessels passed into Bungo Strait between Kyushu and Shikoku.

In the ward room, after dining, those officers not on watch exchanged their impressions.

"What's the state of our aviation now? I suppose there is almost nothing left of it."

"Have you seen the reports on the American forces at Okinawa? Ours seem very weak in comparison."

"In any case, we have no air cover. We are like a man straying in the country on an inky night with a paper lantern!"

"That's without reckoning that tonight we could be victims of a submarine attack."

That, at least, did not happen. At sunrise on the seventh, the *Yamato* arrived to the south of Kagoshima, the homeland of the most rugged of Nippon's warriors. The battleship altered course to the east, and at 0800 to the southwest.

The Yamato

At 1000 an aircraft appeared, a single machine which followed the squadron from afar and then withdrew. The significance was plain to everybody.

The gunners were put on the alert, the radar was searching, and every eye looked ahead and to port. Over there lay Okinawa.

At noon, when the *Yamato* and her companions had covered half the distance, the drama began.

The sky, cloudy in the morning, had cleared. Soon, very far off in the blue, forty to fifty little moving specks surged into view and grew larger. They were American planes. The formation circled the little squadron, calmly gaining height. Why should they worry themselves or hurry? The air was theirs.

The admiral increased speed to twenty-five knots and altered course to the westward, into the wind, to help the evasive maneuvers.

At 1220 the attack came in. In spite of rapid fire from all the light guns, the bombers dived and straightened out with a prolonged rumble. Immediately afterward, a new assault by bombers and torpedo aircraft began. Now even the big guns thundered, lifting enormous fountains of water before the attackers.

When an ephemeral calm returned, the admiral looked at his vessels. The *Hamakaze* was already far astern, with only her forepart still in view. The *Yahagi* spat steam and seemed to have stopped.

Half an hour later came a third attack. The guns began again, deafeningly; the fire from the 17.9-inch battery shook the whole ship. The sky was dotted with bursts. Around and on the ships, explosions multiplied. The gunners shot down a goodly number of American aircraft, but for each of those ablaze, exploding in the air, or swallowed up by the waves, came one, three, ten others. It seemed that the enemy had understood the symbolic meaning of this last battle. This target, already broken and disjointed, was more than a powerful warship, the most wonderful of her kind that had ever existed; it was the Imperial Navy, it was Japan herself! The attackers felt it, and this idea inspired them to unequaled violence.

One after another, the turrets in the *Yamato* fell silent. The big guns stopped as the electric current was interrupted. In the enormous blocks of steel, from which jutted the formidable muzzles, the gun crews looked at each other, trembling.

Finally, at 1345, spray ceased to fall on the deck. The battleship had been hit already by two bombs and six torpedoes, all to port. She began to list in a disturbing manner, and must be righted at all costs.

But the safety squads were almost wiped out, and the central command post was damaged. Over the loud-speaker the captain repeated: "All hands right ship."

The only remedy was to flood the starboard engine room, but there was insufficient time to evacuate the men below. Suddenly, with frightful force, water rushed into the compartment, where several hundred men were still busy. It had become necessary to sacrifice them in this manner.

The battleship righted herself a little, but too late, and the speed diminished still further.

The admiral had altered course to the northwest, when the fourth attack wave arrived at 1400.

Fire became sporadic, and a number of guns were silent. And the martyrdom began again, even more painful, more poignant. Three fresh bombs made the vessel shudder; enormous bursts of water whipped the bridge and crashed on deck. The aircraft, weaving back and forth, machine-gunned the superstructures, on which the red splashes grew larger.

Ensign Yoshida ran toward the radio cabin to have a signal sent. He drew back; the compartment, although specially built to make it watertight, was full of water on which bodies floated.

Transmission had been cut completely. Fire broke out on all sides. An ensign was sent to the operations room to give the admiral an account of the losses. The young officer had to move between fires, clamber round sheets of ripped plating, and squeeze through breaches. He arrived only to start back with horror. The hospital room, almost obliterated, was no more than a heap of blood-spattered iron debris. The doctors and wounded had been wiped out together.

At 1412, over a telephone which had remained intact, came a communication: "Flooding of the steering compartment imminent."

A torpedo had struck the stern.

The ship began to circle to port like a drunken man.

The list steadily increased; speed was reduced to seven knots. New waves of planes attacked, not so numerous as their predecessors. Clinging to the bridge, the captain cried: "Stand fast! Stand fast!" But his voice was not heard. The loud-speakers were mute.

Imperial Navy

At last the attacks ceased; there was no further reason for them.

The list of the *Yamato* reached forty degrees and there was no means of correcting it.

Calmly, the admiral said farewell to the officers of his staff, shook hands, and returned to his cabin, carefully closing the door.

The navigator and his assistant lashed themselves to the binnacle to be sure of sinking with their ship. In the meantime the captain ordered: "Everyone on the upper deck."

Captain Ariga signaled the only two remaining destroyers, the *Fuyuzuki* and the *Yukikaze,* to come alongside; but the little vessels feared to be embroiled in the capsizing of the battleship. Ships must not be risked in order to save men.

An officer of the *Yamato* had gone to the admiral's saloon to look for the portrait of the Emperor, which he carried away in a silken wrapping. He tied this precious burden to his chest.

Now the mast was in the water. The starboard keel emerged. Some men slid there and crawled accordingly as the vessel inclined. A young seaman gained the stern and, clinging to the flagstaff, mounted guard until the end near the flag bearing the rays of the Rising Sun.

Finally a spontaneous cry burst forth and was repeated three times: "Long live the Emperor!"

In the sea, a cone formed 160 feet deep and boiled round the battleship as she settled heavily. The big shells, escaping from their racks, fell into the magazines with a dull rolling sound. Bulkheads burst in, and explosions sounded in the depths of the vessel like the last beatings of an injured heart. Suddenly came a convulsive swirl, and a tongue of flame licked high into the sky announcing to Kagoshima that the *Yamato* was no more. With her died the Imperial Navy.

Miyo Tokai

The Imperial Navy had committed grave fundamental errors in disdaining to protect its own shipping, and in neglecting to attack the enemy's lines of communication. Those of Japan should have been maintained at any cost, as both the existence of the

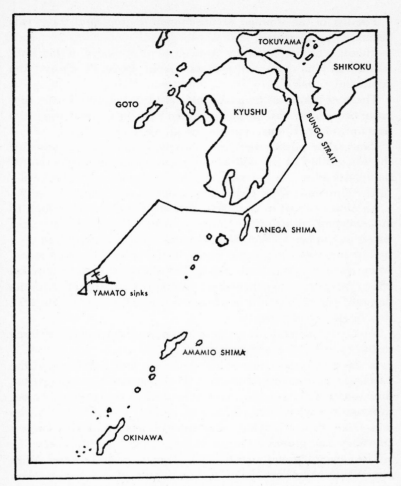

THE FINAL ACT OF JAPAN'S NAVY IN PACIFIC WAR

Japanese homeland and the prosecution of the war depended almost entirely on imports from overseas.

Similarly, the exceptional length of the enemy's lines of communication should have induced those responsible for the naval building programs to include large numbers of submarines.

Finally, in the conduct of the operations as practiced by the Japanese, it is impossible to overlook such defects of execution as these: a strong tendency to dispersion; an excess of individualism, at times, on the part of officers exercising important commands; their disregard for human life—their own included.

These errors of commission and omission are the direct consequence of the national temperament of Japan and flow from her warrior traditions. Some of them were also caused by the obvious disproportion between the industrial potential, which is the foundation of all military effort, and the ambitions of the national leaders.

The Imperial Navy could not have had too much of the industrial power of the country obligated to it in its fight against an adversary with such unlimited resources. Yet, throughout the war, the Japanese fleet was always held within the meager portion allotted by a blind government. It had to choose between such possibilities of action as were open to it, and it too often chose those beyond its capabilities, inclined thereto by its natural bent instead of sound reason—the offensive at any cost, the big spectacular battles.

When the Japanese lines of communication had been stretched to their utmost and when, in addition, they were threatened by ever more effective depredations on their commerce by the American submarines, imports had decreased, production had dropped, and the means of supply had grown continually scarcer in proportion. Each day, and in increasing progression, the gap separating the industrial capacity of Japan from that of her adversary had grown wider.

The eleven big and medium aircraft carriers, put on the stocks after 1941, had allowed the Americans two years later to form the magnificent Task Force 58, whose pilots, with their superior training, became from then on the uncontested masters of the Pacific.

Not until some months after Midway, at the beginning of 1943, did the Japanese decide on the construction of twenty aircraft carriers and the conversion of the *Shinano*.

The *Shinano* was sunk on November 28, 1944, during her trials in Tokyo Bay by the submarine *Acherfish*—a striking condemnation of the glaringly ineffective character of the Japanese coastal defenses. The other projected carriers, with the exception of the *Taiho*, were unable to enter service before the end of the war. Had they been made ready in time, they could only have been manned by poorly trained pilots, because the lack of reserves of gasoline greatly restricted the hours of flight training.

The tremendous industrial failure of Japan in the Pacific war was paid for by the lives of the heroic Japanese sailors. Foreseeing this, the great Yamamoto had strongly opposed war, up to the moment when the die was cast.

Then the Imperial Navy entered the struggle wholeheartedly, without complaint, and spurred on by an intense love for the country of its ancestors. During more than three years, it had fought without respite, showing in victory and defeat the same indomitable courage, the same warrior virtues, the same extraordinary disregard for death.

Victims of the misfortunes their leaders had foreseen but could not forestall, the sailors of Nippon had held the flag of the Rising Sun high aloft until the end.

> *Behold in the east the sky lightening the sea.*
> *When the Rising Sun gleams in the firmament*
> *It exalts the soul of the universe*
> *And hope hovers over the Great Island.*
> *Oh, when in the clear mists of morning*
> *The outline of Mount Fuji rises*
> *Like a symbol of absolute fidelity to our Emperor,*
> *We feel full of pride, we the Japanese.*
> — *Miyo Tokai*, popular Japanese song.

Bibliography

JAPANESE SOURCES

Admiral Takagi: *The Pacific War*
Commandant Mitsuo Fuchida: *The Pearl Harbor Attack*
Commandants Mitsuo Fuchida and Masatake Okumiya: *Midway*
Commandant Toshikaze Omae: *Guadalcanal*
Commandant Hajime Fukaya: *Shokaku and Zuikaku*
Commandant Atsuki Aoi: *Japanese Struggle against American Submarines*
Ensign Mitsuru Yoshida: *The End of the Yamato*

AMERICAN SOURCES

Admiral Samuel Eliot Morison: *History of United States Naval Operations in World War II* (thirteen volumes)
Commandant Pineau: Articles in *U. S. Naval Institute Proceedings*
James A. Field: *The Battle of Leyte*
Walter Karig: *Battle Report* (six volumes)

Index